# The Life and Diary of David Brainerd

# The Life and Diary of David Brainerd

*Edited by*

Jonathan Edwards

# With a Biographical Sketch of the Life and Work of Jonathan Edwards

*by*

Philip E. Howard, Jr.

**BAKER BOOK HOUSE**
Grand Rapids, Michigan 49516

Copyright © 1949 by
Moody Bible Institute of Chicago

First reprinted 1989 by Baker Books
a division of Baker Book House Company
P.O. Box 6287, Grand Rapids, MI 49516-6287

ISBN: 0-8010-0976-6

Ninth printing, October 1997

*Printed in the United States of America*

For current information about all releases from Baker Book House,
visit our web site:
http://www.bakerbooks.com/

# PREFATORY NOTE

THE FOLLOWING ACCOUNT of David Brainerd's life and work among the American Indians has been taken from Volume III of *The Works of President Edwards, in Eight Volumes* (James Black & Son, London, 1817). The section covering the period from April 20, 1718, through May 7, 1745, is quoted from "The Life and Diary of the Reverend David Brainerd" (pp. 81–224, Edwards, Vol. III). It has been thought well to take the next large section from "Brainerd's Journal,"—"kept by order of the Honorable Society (in Scotland) for Propagating Christian Knowledge," which directed and supported Brainerd's work among the Indians (pp. 319–411, Edwards, Vol. III). The same period is also covered in "Brainerd's Life and Diary" (pp. 225–256, Edwards, Vol. III), but the record has in this case been taken from the "Journal" rather than the "Diary," as it is more extensive, not so subjective, and probably gives a more complete picture of the conditions of the Indians and the effect of the gospel among them.

The record of the last fifteen months of David Brainerd's life, from June 29, 1746, to October 9, 1747, is again taken from the "Life and Diary" (pp. 257–311, Edwards, Vol. III).

Brief portions of the "Life and Diary" and "Journal" have been omitted here and there for brevity's sake. In many cases these included summaries of Brainerd's activities during the days which either he or Edwards omitted from the record. There is additional material in Edwards' original volume (Volume III of his *Works*) which are not included here, such as Brainerd's "General Remarks on the Doctrines Preached

7

to the Indians"; his "Method of Learning the Indian Language, and of Instructing the Indians"; "A Short Account of Missions"; several of Brainerd's letters to his friends, and the sermon of the Rev. E. Pemberton, M.A., pastor of a Presbyterian Church in New York City, preached June 12, 1744, at Brainerd's ordination as a missionary to the Indians; and Edwards' "Reflections and Observations on Brainerd's Memoirs." But these are not properly parts of the "Diary" and "Journal."

Some changes have been made in the original punctuation and spelling. Brainerd's writing is full of Scripture, and he would often place within quotation marks phrases or sentences that followed the text very closely, but which may not have been direct and exact quotations. This punctuation has not been changed, nor has an attempt been made to conform all of these passages to the exact words of the King James Version in the present volume.

Since President Edwards knew Brainerd personally, and carefully edited the young missionary's Diary and Journal himself, it is believed that, apart from the few omissions and additional material mentioned above, this volume now makes available again a fairly complete record of the self-denying life and strenuous labors of David Brainerd as he preached the gospel to the American Indians.

PHILIP E. HOWARD, JR.

OCTOBER, 1948

# CONTENTS

## BRAINERD'S JOURNAL

## BRAINERD'S LIFE AND DIARY

# A BIOGRAPHICAL SKETCH
# OF THE LIFE AND WORK
# OF JONATHAN EDWARDS

IT WAS AN UNUSUAL and divinely ordained combination of extraordinary intellectual power and utterly selfless devotion that gave to the world a little over two hundred years ago *The Life and Diary of the Reverend David Brainerd*. For Jonathan Edwards, who edited this moving narrative, was looked upon throughout the English-speaking world as one of the greatest philosophers since the days of the apostle Paul and Augustine; while the personal records of the strenuous labors of the young missionary to the Indians has been an inspiration to hundreds, perhaps thousands of other Christian workers ever since his day. It seems fitting, therefore, that in the same volume which makes available a new edition of the Journal there should be some record of the life and work of its brilliant editor.

JONATHAN EDWARDS was born at East Windsor, Connecticut, on October 5, 1703. His parents were the Rev. Timothy Edwards, for sixty-four years pastor of the Congregational Church of East Windsor; and Esther Stoddard, daughter of the Rev. Solomon Stoddard, who was for more than fifty years pastor of the church of Northampton, Massachusetts. Jonathan was the only son in a family of eleven children. As great credit is always due the mother of any large and well-trained family, it is interesting to have a glimpse of the talented Mrs. Edwards. Dr. Samuel Miller, Professor of Ecclesiastical History and Church Government in Princeton Theological Seminary, in 1856 wrote: "The character of Esther Stoddard . . . was no less eminent than that of her husband. She is represented, by tradition, as a woman of distinguished strength of mind, of superior education, peculiarly fond of reading, and of ardent piety; and, of course, as well adapted to adorn and to bless the large domestic circle committed to her care."

Timothy Edwards was well known as a Latin, Greek, and Hebrew scholar, and he and his capable wife gave their ten daughters and one son their early education at home. Jonathan began the study of Latin at six years of age. "He was early taught, by his excellent father, to use the pen abundantly," says Dr. Miller; "to study with it habitually in his hand; to make a record of his doubts, his difficulties, and his comments on every subject, and to bring all his knowledge to the test of expressing it on paper for himself. In a word, it seems to have been a leading principle of his father, in regard to his son, and indeed all his children, to encourage them, from their tenderest years, to engage frequently in letter-writing, and every other kind of composition, as one of the best means of intellectual discipline. That this early habit exerted much influence on his subsequent studies and investigations, and contributed, in no small degree, to give a character to his after-life, cannot be doubted." When he was ten years old he wrote a reply to a fellow student, who held that the soul is material, which was marked by humor and sarcasm and showed an unusual depth of thought. At twelve he wrote an essay on the Wood Spider, with many detailed notes and observations concerning its habits.

Jonathan entered Yale College at New Haven in 1716, just before his thirteenth birthday. The college in those days was in an unsettled condition, for it had been founded at Saybrook, in 1701, but the president lived at Killingworth, eight or ten miles away, where he was the pastor of a church. The students had to live at Killingworth and the commencements were held at Saybrook. When young Edwards entered the college, thirteen students lived at New Haven, fourteen at Wethersfield, and four at Saybrook. But Edwards had already formed habits of self-discipline and concentration and

was therefore not turned aside from his studies by such difficulties in the college life.

"Though his fellow students became disorderly, and, at
length, mutinous, yet he took no part in the mutiny and in-
subordination which surrounded him, but studied with diligence and success; and such were his dignity and scholar-
ship that he maintained, by the acknowledgment of all, the
highest standing in his class, and the entire respect and confidence of his fellow-students, notwithstanding his refusal to
unite with them in their disorderly proceedings." In his
second year in college he read thoroughly Locke's *Essay on
the Human Understanding*, and said that he had more pleasure in it "than the most greedy miser finds, when gathering
up handfuls of silver and gold from some newly discovered
treasure." He was then only fourteen years old.

Jonathan had been deeply affected by an awakening in his
father's church when he was seven or eight years old. He
used to pray five times a day privately, spent much time in
religious conversation and prayer with other boys, and enjoyed his religious exercises. But these impressions wore off,
and he declared later that they were not deep or genuine,
though some of his devout friends disagreed with him. He
himself considered that his life as a true Christian began toward the latter part of his college course. Here is his own account of that experience:

"I was brought to seek salvation in a manner that I never
was before. I felt a spirit to part with all things in the world
for an interest in Christ. My concern continued and prevailed,
with many exercising thoughts and inward struggles; but
yet it never seemed to be proper to express that concern by
the name of terror. From my childhood up, my mind had been
full of objections against the doctrine of God's sovereignty in
choosing whom He would to eternal life, and rejecting whom
He pleased. It used to appear like a horrible doctrine to me.
But I remember the time very well when I seemed to be convinced and fully satisfied as to this sovereignty of God, and
His justice in thus eternally disposing of men according to

His sovereign pleasure. But I never could give an account how, or by what means, I was thus convinced; not in the least imagining at the time nor for a long time after, that there was any extraordinary influence of God's Spirit in it; but only that now I saw further, and my reason apprehended the justice and reasonableness of it. However, my mind rested in it; and it put an end to all those cavils and objections.

"And there has been a wonderful alteration in my mind with respect to the doctrine of God's sovereignty, from that day to this; so that I scarce ever have found so much as the rising of an objection against it, in the most absolute sense, in God's showing mercy to whom He will show mercy and hardening whom He will. But I have often, since that first conviction, had quite another kind of sense of God's sovereignty than I had then. I have often, since, had not only a conviction, but a *delightful* conviction. The doctrine has very often appeared exceedingly pleasant, bright, and sweet. Absolute sovereignty is what I love to ascribe to God. But my first conviction was not so. The first instance that I remember of that sort of inward, sweet delight in God and divine things, that I have lived much in since, was on reading these words, I Timothy 1:17: 'Now unto the King eternal, immortal, invisible, the only wise God, be honor and glory for ever and ever. Amen.'

"As I read the words, there came into my soul, and was as it were diffused through it, a sense of the glory of the Divine Being; a new sense, quite different from anything I ever experienced before. Never any words of Scripture seemed to me as these words did. I thought with myself, how excellent a Being that was, and how happy I should be, if I might enjoy that God, and be rapt up to Him in Heaven, and be, as it were, swallowed up in Him forever. I kept saying, and as it were singing, over these words of Scripture to myself, and went to pray to God that I might enjoy Him; and prayed in a manner quite different from what I used to do, with a new sort of affection.

"From about that time, I began to have a new kind of apprehensions and ideas of Christ, and the work of redemption, and the glorious way of salvation by Him. An inward, sweet sense of these things, at times, came into my heart, and my soul was led away in pleasant views and contemplations of them. My mind was greatly engaged to spend my time in reading and meditating on Christ, on the beauty and excellency of His person, and the lovely way of salvation by free grace in Him. I found no books so delightful to me, as those which treated of these subjects.

"Those words, Canticles 2:1, used to be abundantly with me. They seemed to me sweetly to represent the loveliness and beauty of Jesus Christ. The whole book of Canticles used to be pleasant to me, and I used to be much in reading it about that time, and found, from time to time, an inward sweetness, that would carry me away in my contemplations. This I know not how to express otherwise, than by a calm, sweet abstraction of soul from all the concerns of this world; and sometimes a kind of vision, or fixed ideas and imaginations of being alone in the mountains, or some solitary wilderness, far from all mankind, sweetly conversing with Christ, and wrapped and swallowed up in God. The sense I had of divine things would often, of a sudden, kindle up, as it were, a sweet burning in my heart; an ardor of soul that I know not how to express.

"Not long after I first began to experience these things, I gave an account to my father of some things that had passed in my mind. I was pretty much affected by the discourse which we had together; and, when the discourse was ended, I walked abroad alone in a solitary place in my father's pasture, for contemplation. And as I was walking there, and looking upon the sky and clouds, there came into my mind so sweet a sense of the glorious majesty and grace of God, as I know not how to express. I seemed to see them both in a sweet conjunction; majesty and meekness joined together. It was a sweet and gentle, and holy majesty; and also a majestic meekness; an awful sweetness; a high, and great, and holy gentleness.

"After this, my sense of divine things gradually increased, and became more and more lively, and had more of that inward sweetness. The appearance of everything was altered. There seemed to be, as it were, a calm, sweet cast, or appearance of divine glory, in almost everything. God's excellency, His wisdom, His purity, and love seemed to appear in everything; in the sun, moon, and stars; in the clouds and sky; in the grass, flowers, and trees; in the water and all nature; which used greatly to fix my mind. I often used to sit and view the moon for a long time; and, in the day, spent much time in viewing the clouds and sky, to behold the sweet glory of God in these things; in the meantime, singing forth, with a low voice, my contemplations of the Creator and Redeemer.

"And scarce anything, among all the works of nature, was so sweet to me as thunder and lightning; although formerly nothing had been so terrible to me. Before, I used to be uncommonly terrified with thunder, and to be struck with terror when I saw a thunderstorm rising; but now, on the contrary, it rejoiced me. I felt God, if I may so speak, at the first appearance of a thunderstorm, and used to take the opportunity at such times, to fix myself in order to view the clouds, and see the lightnings play, and hear the majestic and awful voice of God's thunder, which oftentimes was exceedingly entertaining, leading me to sweet contemplations of my great and glorious God.

"While thus engaged, it always seemed natural for me to sing or chant forth my meditations, or to speak my thoughts in soliloquies, with a singing voice. I had vehement longings of soul after God and Christ, and after more holiness, wherewith my heart seemed to be full, and ready to break; which often brought to my mind the words of the Psalmist, Psalm 119:20: 'My soul breaketh for the longing that it hath.' I often felt a mourning and lamenting in my heart, that I had not turned unto God sooner, that I might have had more time to grow in grace. My mind was greatly fixed on divine things; indeed almost perpetually in the contemplation of them.

"I spent most of my time in thinking of divine things, year after year; often walking alone in the woods and solitary places for meditation, soliloquy, and prayer, and converse with God. It was always my manner, at such times, to sing forth my contemplation. I was almost constantly in ejaculatory prayer, wherever I was. Prayer seemed to be natural to me, as the breath by which the inward burnings of my heart had vent. The delights, which I now felt in the things of religion, were of an exceedingly different kind from those before mentioned, that I had when a boy; and what then I had no more notion of, than one born blind has of pleasant and beautiful colors. They were of a more inward, pure, soul-animating and refreshing nature. Those former delights never reached my heart, and did not arise from any sight of the divine excellency of the things of God; or any taste of the soul-satisfying and life-giving good there is in them."

In September, 1720, just before his seventeenth birthday, Jonathan Edwards graduated from Yale College with the highest honors. He continued on in graduate study for nearly two years, and in June or July, 1722, was licensed to preach the gospel. In September, 1723, he received the degree of master of arts from Yale, and was elected as a tutor. Though he supplied the pulpit of a small church in New York City for several months, he could not agree to accept a permanent charge *until he had spent six years in study* after his graduation from college. Remarking that in this Jonathan Edwards was like John Calvin, who, even after he had published his *Institutes of the Christian Religion*, "did not consider himself as sufficiently mature in knowledge to undertake the pastoral office," Dr. Samuel Miller cannot resist the following observation: "When will young men, unspeakably inferior to these master-minds, both in capacity and attainment, learn to resist that spirit of superficial, presumptuous haste, which is hurrying them prematurely into the pulpit, and burdening the church, to a lamentable extent, with 'blind leaders of the blind'?"

During this preparatory period, while he was living for

some months at his father's house in East Windsor, Edwards drew up a set of seventy resolutions as standards for his own life. In order that these "Resolutions" may be preserved, and since they give an insight into Edwards' methodical mind, habits of self-discipline, and his consuming desire to glorify God in all things, they are here given in full:

"Being sensible that I am unable to do anything without God's help, I do humbly entreat Him by His grace, to enable me to keep these resolutions, so far as they are agreeable to His will, for Christ's sake.

"Remember to read over these resolutions once a week.

"1. *Resolved*, That I will do whatsoever I think to be most to the glory of God and my own good, profit, and pleasure, in the whole of my duration, without any consideration of the time, whether now, or never so many myriads of ages hence. *Resolved*, to do whatever I think to be my duty, and most for the good of mankind in general. *Resolved* so to do, whatever difficulties I meet with, how many soever, and how great soever.

"2. *Resolved*, To be continually endeavoring to find out some new contrivance and invention to promote the fore-mentioned things.

"3. *Resolved*, If ever I shall fall and grow dull, so as to neglect to keep any part of these resolutions, to repent of all I can remember, when I come to myself again.

"4. *Resolved*, Never to *do* any manner of thing, whether in soul or body, less or more, but what tends to the glory of God; nor *be*, nor *suffer* it, if I can possibly avoid it.

"5. *Resolved*, Never to lose one moment of time, but to improve it in the most profitable way I possibly can.

"6. *Resolved*, To live with all my might while I do live.

"7. *Resolved*, Never to do anything which I should be afraid to do, if it were the last hour of my life.

"8. *Resolved*, To act, in all respects, both speaking and doing, as if nobody had been so vile as I, and as if I had committed the same sins, or had the same infirmities or failings as others; and that I will let the knowledge of their failings promote nothing but shame in myself, and prove only an occasion of my confessing my own sins and misery to God.

"9. *Resolved*, To think much, on all occasions, of my own dying, and of the common circumstances which attend death.

"10. *Resolved*, When I feel pain, to think of the pains of martyrdom and of hell.

"11. *Resolved*, When I think of any theorem in divinity to be solved, immediately to do what I can towards solving it, if circumstances do not hinder.

"12. *Resolved*, If I take delight in it as a gratification of pride or vanity, or on any such account, immediately to throw it by.

"13. *Resolved*, To be endeavoring to find out fit objects of charity and liberality.

"14. *Resolved*, Never to do anything out of revenge.

"15. *Resolved*, Never to suffer the least motions of anger towards irrational beings.

"16. *Resolved*, Never to speak evil of anyone so that it shall tend to his dishonor, more or less, upon no account, except for some real good.

"17. *Resolved*, That I will live so, as I shall wish I had done when I come to die.

"18. *Resolved*, To live so at all times, as I think it best, in my most devout frames, and when I have the clearest notion of the things of the gospel and another world.

"19. *Resolved*, Never to do anything which I should be afraid to do, if I expected it would not be above an hour before I should hear the last trump.

"20. *Resolved*, To maintain the strictest temperance in eating and drinking.

"21. *Resolved*, Never to do anything, which, if I should see in another, I should account a just occasion to despise him for, or to think any way the more meanly of him.

"22. *Resolved*, To endeavor to obtain for myself as much happiness in the other world, as I possibly can, with all the might, power, vigor, and vehemence, yea, violence, I am capable of, or can bring myself to exert, in any way. . . .

"23. *Resolved*, Frequently to take some deliberate action, which seems most unlikely to be done for the glory of God, and trace it back to the original intention, designs, and ends of it; and, if I find it not to be for God's glory, to repute it as a breach of the fourth resolution.

"24. *Resolved*, Whenever I do any conspicuously evil action, to trace it back till I come to the original cause; and then, both carefully to endeavor to do so no more, and to fight and pray with all my might against the original of it.

"25. *Resolved*, To examine carefully and constantly what that one thing in me is, which causes me in the least to doubt of the love of God; and to direct all my forces against it.

"26. *Resolved*, To cast away such things as I find do abate my assurance.

"27. *Resolved*, Never willfully to omit anything, except the omission be for the glory of God; and frequently to examine my omissions.

"28. *Resolved*, To study the Scriptures so steadily, constantly, and frequently, as that I may find, and plainly perceive myself to grow in the knowledge of the same.

"29. *Resolved*, Never to count that a prayer, nor to let that pass as a prayer, nor that as a petition of a prayer, which is so made, that I cannot hope that God will answer it; nor that as a confession, which I cannot hope God will accept.

"30. *Resolved*, To strive every week to be brought higher in religion, and to a higher exercise of grace than I was the week before.

"31. *Resolved*, Never to say anything at all against anybody, but when it is perfectly agreeable to the highest degree of Christian honor, and of love to mankind; agreeable to the lowest humility and sense of my own faults and failings; and agreeable to the Golden Rule; often when I have said anything against anyone, to bring it to, and try it strictly by, the test of this resolution.

"32. *Resolved*, To be strictly and firmly faithful to my trust, that that in Proverbs 20:6, 'A faithful man, who can find?' may not be partly fulfilled in me

"33. *Resolved*, To do always towards making, maintaining, and preserving peace, when it can be done without an overbalancing detriment in other respects.

"34. *Resolved*, In narrations, never to speak anything but the pure and simple verity.

"35. *Resolved*, Whenever I so much question whether I have done my duty, as that my quiet and calm is thereby disturbed, to set it down, and also how the question was resolved.

"36. *Resolved*, Never to speak evil of any, except I have some particular good call to it.

"37. *Resolved*, To inquire every night, as I am going to bed, wherein I have been negligent; what sin I have committed; and, wherein I have denied myself. Also at the end of every week, month, and year.

"38. *Resolved*, Never to utter anything that is sportive, or matter of laughter, on a Lord's Day.

"39. *Resolved*, Never to do anything of which I so much question the lawfulness, as that I intend at the same time to consider and examine afterwards whether it be lawful or not, unless I as much question the lawfulness of the omission.

"40. *Resolved*, To inquire every night before I go to bed, whether I have acted in the best way I possibly could with respect to eating and drinking.

"41. *Resolved*, To ask myself, at the end of every day, week, month, and year, wherein I could possibly, in any respect, have done better.

"42. *Resolved*, Frequently to renew the dedication of myself to God, which was made at my baptism; which I solemnly renewed when I was received into the communion of the church; and which I have solemnly remade this twelfth day of January, 1723.

"43. *Resolved*, Never, henceforward, till I die, to act as if I were any way my own, but entirely and altogether God's; agreeably to what is to be found in Saturday, January 12, 1723.

"44. *Resolved*, That no other end but religion shall have

any influence at all on any of my actions; and that no action shall be, in the least circumstance, any otherwise than the religious end will carry it.

"45. *Resolved*, Never to allow any pleasure or grief, joy or sorrow, nor any affection at all; nor any degree of affection, nor any circumstance relating to it, but what helps religion.

"46. *Resolved*, Never to allow the least measure of fretting or uneasiness at my father or mother. *Resolved*, to suffer no effects of it, so much as in the least alteration of speech, or motion of my eye; and to be especially careful of it with respect to any of our family.

"47. *Resolved*, To endeavor, to my utmost, to deny whatever is not most agreeable to a good and universally sweet and benevolent, quiet, peaceable, contented and easy, compassionate and generous, humble and meek, submissive and obliging, diligent and industrious, charitable and even, patient, moderate, forgiving, and sincere temper; and to do, at all times, what such a temper would lead me to, and to examine, strictly, at the end of every week, whether I have so done.

"48. *Resolved*, Constantly, with the utmost niceness and diligence, and the strictest scrutiny, to be looking into the state of my soul, that I may know whether I have truly an interest in Christ or not; that, when I come to die, I may not have any negligence respecting this, to repent of.

"49. *Resolved*, That this shall never be, if I can help it.

"50. *Resolved*, That I will act so, as I think I shall judge would have been best and most prudent, when I come into the future world.

"51. *Resolved*, That I will act so, in every respect, as I think I shall wish I had done, if I should at last be damned.

"52. I frequently hear persons in old age say how they would live, if they were to live their lives over again. *Resolved*, that I will live just so as I can think I shall wish I had done, supposing I live to old age.

"53. *Resolved*, To improve every opportunity, when I am in the best and happiest frame of mind, to cast and venture my soul on the Lord Jesus Christ, to trust and confide in Him, and consecrate myself wholly to Him; that from this I may have assurance of my safety, knowing that I confide in my Redeemer.

"54. *Resolved*, Whenever I hear anything spoken in commendation of any person, if I think it would be praiseworthy in me, that I will endeavor to imitate it.

"55. *Resolved*, To endeavor, to my utmost, so to act as I can think I should do, if I had already seen the happiness of heaven, and hell torments.

"56. *Resolved*, Never to give over, nor in the least to slacken, my fight with my corruptions, however unsuccessful I may be.

"57. *Resolved*, When I fear misfortunes and adversity, to examine whether I have done my duty, and resolve to do it, and let the event be just as Providence orders it. I will, as far as I can, be concerned about nothing but my duty and my sin.

"58. *Resolved*, Not only to refrain from an air of dislike, fretfulness, and anger in conversation; but to exhibit an air of love, cheerfulness, and benignity.

"59. *Resolved*, When I am most conscious of provocations to ill-nature and anger, that I will strive most to feel and act good-naturedly; yea, at such times to manifest good nature, though I think that in other respects it would be disadvantageous, and so as would be imprudent at other times.

"60. *Resolved*, Whenever my feelings begin to appear in the least out of order, when I am conscious of the least uneasiness within, or the least irregularity without, I will then subject myself to the strictest examination.

"61. *Resolved*, That I will not give way to that listlessness which I find unbends and relaxes my mind from being fully and fixedly set on religion, whatever excuse I may have for it.

"62. *Resolved*, Never to do anything but my duty, and then, according to Ephesians 6:6–8, to do it willingly and cheerfully as unto the Lord and not to man; knowing that whatever good any man doth, the same shall he receive of the Lord.

"63. On the supposition that there never was to be but one individual in the world at any one time who was properly a complete Christian, in all respects of a right stamp, having Christianity always shining in its true luster, and appearing excellent and lovely, from whatever part, and under whatever character viewed;—Resolved, to act just as I would do, if I strove with all my might to be that one, who should live in my time.

"64. Resolved, When I find those 'groanings which cannot be uttered,' of which the apostle speaks, and those 'breakings of soul for the longing it hath,' of which the Psalmist speaks (Ps. 119:20), that I will promote them to the utmost of my power, and that I will not be weary of earnestly endeavoring to vent my desires, nor of the repetitions of such earnestness.

"65. Resolved, Very much to exercise myself in this, all my life long, namely, with the greatest openness of which I am capable, to declare my ways to God, and lay open my soul to Him, all my sins, temptations, difficulties, sorrows, fears, hopes, desires, and everything, and every circumstance, according to Dr. Manton's sermon on the One Hundred Nineteenth Psalm.

"66. Resolved, That I will endeavor always to keep a benign aspect, and air of acting and speaking, in all places and in all companies, except it should so happen that duty requires otherwise.

"67. Resolved, After afflictions, to inquire, What am I the better for them? What good I have got by them, and what I might have got by them?

"68. Resolved, To confess frankly to myself all that which I find in myself, either infirmity or sin; and, if it be what concerns religion, also to confess the whole case to God, and implore needed help.

"69. Resolved, Always to do that which I shall wish I had done, when I see others do it.

"70. Let there be something of benevolence in all that I speak."

Mr. Edwards was in the habit of setting apart special days for prayer, self-examination, and fasting. His fasting at such times was not spiritual but literal, and he "considered literal abstinence from food, either entire or partial, according to the state of his health and other circumstances, as essentially included in this duty." He kept a diary, and from it the following extracts are taken. These entries show a conscientiousness, seriousness, ethical sense, and practical application of Christian doctrine that are greatly needed today.

"Friday night, October 7, 1723. I see there are some things quite contrary to the soundness and perfection of Christianity, in which almost all good men do allow themselves, and where innate corruption has an unrestrained, secret vent, which they never take notice of, or think to be no hurt, or cloak under the name of virtue; which things exceedingly darken the brightness and hide the loveliness of Christianity. Who can understand his errors? Oh, that I might be kept from secret faults!

"Thursday, October 18. To follow the example of Mr. B., who, though he meets with great difficulties, yet undertakes them with a smiling countenance, as though he thought them but little, and speaks of them as if they were very small.

"Tuesday night, December 31. Concluded never to suffer, nor express, any angry emotions of mind, more or less, except the honor of God calls for it in zeal to Him, or to preserve myself from being trampled on.

"Monday, February 3, 1724. Let everything have the value now which it will have on a sick bed; and frequently, in my pursuits, of whatever kind, let this question come into my mind, How much shall I value this on my deathbed?

"Wednesday, February 5. I have not, in times past, in my prayers, enough insisted on the glorifying of God in the world; on the advancement of the kingdom of Christ, the prosperity of the Church, and the good of man. Determined that the following objection is without weight, namely, that it is not likely that God will make great alterations in the whole world and overturnings in kingdoms and nations only for the prayers of one obscure person, seeing such things used to be done in answer to the united prayers of the whole Church; and that, if my prayers should have some influence, it would be but imperceptible and small.

"Thursday, February 6. More convinced than ever of the usefulness of free religious conversation. I find by conversing on natural philosophy that I gain knowledge abundantly faster and see the reason of things much more clearly, than in private study; wherefore, earnestly to seek at all times for religious conversation, and for those with whom I can at all times with profit and delight and with freedom, so converse.

"Saturday, February 22. I observe, that there are some evil habits which do increase and grow stronger, even in some good people, as they grow older; habits that much obscure the beauty of Christianity; some things which are according to their natural temper, which, in some measure, prevails when they are young in Christ, and, the evil disposition having an unobserved control, the habit at last grows very strong, and commonly regulates the practice until death. By this means, old Christians are very commonly, in some respects, more unreasonable than those who are young. I am afraid of contracting such habits, particularly of grudging to give, and to do, and of procrastinating.

"Tuesday, July 7. When I am giving the relation of a thing, remember to abstain from altering, either in the matter or manner of speaking, so much as that, if every one, afterwards, should alter as much, it would at last come to be properly false.

"Tuesday, February 10, 1725. A virtue which I need in a higher degree, to give luster and beauty to my behavior, is gentleness. If I had more of an air of gentleness, I should be much mended.

"June 11. To set apart days of meditation on particular subjects; as, sometimes, to set apart a day for the consideration of the greatness of my sins; at another, to consider the dreadfulness and certainty of the future misery of ungodly men; at another, the truth and certainty of religion; and so of the great future things promised and threatened in the Scriptures.''

In the summer of 1726 Mr. Edwards was invited to become the assistant to his grandfather, the Rev. Solomon Stoddard, pastor of the Congregational Church at Northampton, Massachusetts. He accepted the call, and on February 15, 1727, when he was twenty-four years old, he was ordained to the ministry and installed as co-pastor of the church. Six months later, on July 28, Jonathan Edwards married Sarah Pierrepont, daughter of the Rev. James Pierrepont, pastor of a church in New Haven, and one of the founders of Yale College. How blest he was in his life partner may be seen from Dr. Samuel Miller's description of her:

''Miss Pierrepont was a lady, who, to much personal attraction, added an unusual amount of those intellectual and moral qualities, which fit their possessor to adorn the most important stations. She had an understanding much above the ordinary grade; an education the best that the country afforded; fervent, enlightened piety; and an uncommon share of that prudence, dignity, and polish, which are so peculiarly valuable in the wife of a pastor. From a very early period after their union, she seems to have taken on herself the whole management of her family, and thus to have relieved her husband from all the anxieties and interruptions of domestic care, and left him at liberty to pursue his studies without remission. In short, he appears to have been completely relieved by her from all secular concerns. Her wisdom, energy, economy, and persevering industry enabled her to preside over a large family, and manage her children with singular felicity, fidelity, and acceptance.''

Jonathan and Sarah Edwards had an unusually happy married life of a little more than thirty years, and, as in his father's family, there were eleven children—three sons and eight daughters. His second son, Jonathan, became a minister, and both his talents and his experience paralleled his father's in many respects.

It was Mr. Edwards' habit when in good health to spend thirteen hours every day in his study. His wife would come in at least once a day for a time of prayer with him. And although it is hard to understand how he could find the time to do it, yet, when he was at home, he would usually spend an hour with his family after supper. "In this conversation," wrote Dr. Miller, "the great subject of religion never failed, in a greater or less degree, to occupy a place. And, although he was accustomed to leave the entire management of all his temporal concerns to his wife, who was admirably fitted to conduct them in the wisest and happiest manner, yet, in the government and discipline of their children, he did not, as many studious men have too often done, leave his wife to toil and struggle alone; but, when attention to this subject became necessary, he entered into it with all the zeal of a tender, sympathizing husband and an anxious father; manifesting a readiness to share the burden, and a desire to discharge the duty, of a faithful parent."

Mr. Edwards could never have done such a prodigious amount of work as a minister and author if he had not been exceedingly careful in all his habits. He was abstemious in eating and drinking, and took physical exercise whenever he could. He liked to ride horseback out into the pleasant country surrounding Northampton, but even then he would meditate and make notes. If in the night thoughts occurred to him which he considered worth recording, he would get up, light a candle, and put them down in writing.

"So exact was the distribution of his time," says an early, unnamed biographer, "and so perfect the command of his mental powers, that, in addition to his preparation of two discourses in each week, his stated and occasional lectures and his customary pastoral duties, he continued regularly his *Notes on the Scriptures*, his *Miscellanies*, his *Types of the Messiah*, and his *Prophecies of the Messiah in the Old Testament, and their Fulfilment*. In February, 1729, Mr. Stoddard died, and the whole care of a large congregation came upon the young pastor.

As the result of the unceasing prayer and labor of the pastor, and under the blessing of God, revival came to the church in Northampton and continued through the years 1734 and 1735. It extended to every part of the town, and someone in nearly every household was touched. There were more than 300 conversions in a few months, and the whole atmosphere of the town was changed. In answer to an inquiry from Dr. Coleman of Boston, Mr. Edwards wrote an account of the work of grace in Northampton, and this was forwarded to Dr. Isaac Watts and Dr. John Guyse of London. This aroused so much interest that Edwards enlarged the account and his *Narrative of Surprising Conversions* was published in London in 1736. In 1739 Edwards preached a series of sermons, which later grew into his celebrated work, *The History of the Work of Redemption.*

Northampton was the scene of a second revival in the spring of 1740. In the autumn George Whitefield, the great British evangelist, made a second visit to the American colonies and went to Northampton to see Mr. Edwards. They spent four days together, and Whitefield preached five sermons from the pulpit. As a result of the powerful preaching of Whitefield and Edwards, Gilbert and William Tennent of New Jersey, Mr. Buell of Long Island, and Mr. Wheelock of Connecticut, the revival spread, and more than one hundred and fifty congregations in New England, New York, New Jersey, Pennsylvania, Maryland, Virginia, South Carolina, and Georgia were greatly blessed. There were thousands of conversions and cold, dead churches were quickened into new life.

But when the Spirit of God works in special power, the Devil also rallies his forces. Jonathan Edwards and his colleagues were not exempt from the attacks of the Adversary. Much trouble and confusion were produced by untrained and ignorant lay preachers, public confession of sin, and particularly one fanatical young preacher, James Davenport. Mr. Edwards felt constrained to preach and write against these abuses, and accordingly produced his *Thoughts Concerning the Present Revival of Religion in New England,* and his famous *Treatise on Religious Affections.* A good example of the style of the latter may be seen in the following passage on the methods of the Spirit:

"The manner in which the Holy Spirit operates in those who are born of God is very often exceedingly mysterious: the effects only of those operations are discernible. It is to be feared that some have gone too far in attempting to direct the Spirit of the Lord, and to mark out His footsteps for Him. Experience clearly shows that we cannot trace the operations of the Holy Spirit in the conversion of some who afterward prove the best of Christians. He does not proceed discernibly in the steps of any particular, established scheme, by any means so often as is imagined.

"A rule received and established by common consent, has very great, though to many persons an insensible influence in forming their notions of the process of their own experience. I know very well how they proceed as to this matter, for I have had frequent opportunities of observing their conduct. Very often their experience at first appears like a confused chaos, but then those parts are selected which bear the nearest resemblance to such particular steps as are insisted on; and these are dwelt upon in their thoughts, and spoken of from time to time, till they grow more and more conspicuous in their view, and other parts which are neglected grow more and more obscure. Thus what they have experienced is insensibly strained, so as to bring it to an exact conformity to the scheme already established in their minds.

"And it becomes natural also for ministers, who have to deal with those who insist upon distinctness and clearness of method, to do so too. But yet so much has been seen of the operations of the Spirit of God of late, that those who have had much to do with souls and are not blinded by prejudice, must know that the Holy Spirit is so exceedingly various in the manner of His operations, that, in many cases, it is impossible to trace Him."

Jonathan Edwards was now becoming well known not only throughout the colonies but also in England, and his writings were highly valued by eminent British theologians. This brought about an extensive correspondence between Edwards and such men as John McLaurin of Glasgow, William McCulloch of Cambuslang, John Robe of Kilsyth, Thomas Gillespie of Carnoch, John Willison of Dundee, and Dr. John Erskine, then minister of Kirkintilloch, afterwards of Edinburgh.

A group of Scottish ministers invited Mr. Edwards in 1744 to join them in a call for united and special prayer to God, "that He would deliver the nations from their miseries, and fill the earth with His glory." The plan was to set apart a time for prayer every Saturday evening and Sabbath morning, and a stated day every quarter to be spent in private, social, or public prayer, "for the effusion of the Holy Spirit on the Church and the world." Mr. Edwards gladly accepted the plan and persuaded a number of other ministers in New England to adopt it. It was followed for two years, and in 1746 was extended for an indefinite period. It was then that Edwards wrote another of his famous works, *An Humble Attempt to Promote Explicit Agreement and Visible Union among God's People, in Extraordinary Prayer for the Revival of Religion, and the Advancement of Christ's Kingdom on Earth, Pursuant to Scripture Promises and Prophecies Concerning the Last Time.*

Jonathan Edwards' close friendship with David Brainerd began in September, 1743. Mr. Edwards was at New Haven, attending the Yale College commencement, and there he met the young missionary to the Indians. But it was a sad and trying time for Brainerd, for he had been dismissed from the college for reasons which to any fair-minded person, who knows all the facts, were clearly insufficient and unjust. (Edwards' own explanation of the circumstances is given in Appendix I in this volume.)

Four years later, in May, 1747, because of ill health, David Brainerd came to live in Mr. Edwards' home at Northampton, at his invitation. It was there that he died on October 9, in

the thirtieth year of his age. Mr. Edwards preached his
funeral sermon from II Corinthians 5:8: "We are confident,
I say, and willing rather to be absent from the body, and to be
present with the Lord"; and this was later published under
the title *True Saints, When Absent from the Body, Are Present
with the Lord.*

Trouble came to Jonathan Edwards and his church in 1744.
He publicly took a stand against some licentious books found
in the possession of some of his young people. His people
agreed that the matter should be investigated, but Edwards
unfortunately read from the pulpit the names of those pos-
sessing the books and the committee appointed to investigate
them, without discriminating between them, and thus alienated many of his members.

To this was added another difficulty. Mr. Stoddard, grandfather and colleague of Mr. Edwards, had "adopted and
preached the opinion that the Lord's Supper was designed to
be a converting ordinance; that genuine piety was not necessary in order to a proper and acceptable approach to it; and
consequently that persons who knew themselves to be entirely destitute of faith and repentance, if they were sober
and moral, might, with propriety, unite themselves with the
visible professing people of God." Mr. Stoddard's own church
and some others accepted this view; but Edwards seriously
doubted the correctness of it, and in 1749 published his *Humble Inquiry into the Rules of the Word of God, Concerning the Qualifications, Requisite to a Complete Standing and Full Communion
in the Visible Christian Church.*

A bitter controversy arose, extending beyond the limits of
Northampton, and it finally led to Edwards' dismissal from
the Northampton church. His biographer, Dr. Miller, said
of him: "In all the proceedings, however, of the people and
of the council, he was enabled 'in patience to possess his
soul.' All his communications were marked with a degree of
dignity, mildness, self-respect, and Christian equity, which,
although they failed of making any favorable impression on
the minds of an excited congregation at the time, have been

ever since admired by the religious community as a noble monument of Christian forbearance and submission." Dr. Erskine invited Mr. Edwards to Scotland, and urged him to take charge of a church there. But while he expressed his gratitude for the invitation, yet he did not feel that it was God's call for him to cross the Atlantic.

Six months after his dismissal from his church, Mr. Edwards received an invitation from a church in Stockbridge to be their pastor, and also to take charge of a mission to the Indians. This work was under the immediate direction of commissioners in Boston who represented "The Society in London, for Propagating the Gospel in New England, and the Parts Adjacent." He went alone in January, 1751, to Stockbridge, to begin his ministry, and the following August brought his large family from Northampton. But his years in Stockbridge were not peaceful, for there were divisions and quarrels among the white population which hindered the work among the Indians. Mr. Edwards became involved in some of these difficulties, always standing for the right, and taking the part of the Indians against unscrupulous whites. In June, 1754, he was taken with a severe fever which lasted until the following January and greatly weakened his constitution.

One of Mr. Edwards' daughters, in the summer of 1752, married the Rev. Aaron Burr, president of the College of New Jersey, which was then at Newark, but afterwards removed to Princeton. In September Mr. Edwards visited his daughter and son-in-law. The college commencement and the annual meeting of the Synod of New York were held at the same time. Mr. Edwards preached before the Synod a sermon on James 2:19, entitled, *True Grace Distinguished from the Experience of Devils*, which was soon after printed at the request of the Synod. This visit and sermon were doubtless very significant, in view of the important invitation that came later to Jonathan Edwards.

Before leaving Northampton Mr. Edwards had planned a "Treatise on the Freedom of the Will, and Moral Agency,

in Opposition to the Arminian System." Toward the end
of 1752 he was able to give his attention to it again, and the
next spring he announced to Dr. Erskine of Scotland that he
had almost finished the first draft of his famous work on
*The Freedom of the Will.* It was published a year later, in the
spring of 1754, in Boston.

In the providence of God, the close of Jonathan Edwards'
very full and useful life was not far off. The news reached
him in Stockbridge of the death of his son-in-law, Aaron
Burr, president of Princeton, just before the annual commencement in the autumn of 1757. This was followed shortly by
word that Mr. Edwards himself had been elected to the pres-
idency on September 27, 1757. He was greatly perplexed as
to whether he should give up his church and mission work
in Stockbridge, where he had been for six years, and he wrote
a long letter on October 19 to the trustees, telling of his perplexity, setting forth with remarkable candor some of his own
defects, and saying that he would ask the advice of some of
his friends and learn whether the Boston commissioners
would give him liberty to go to Princeton.

On the fourth of January, 1758, a small council met in
Stockbridge and heard Mr. Edwards' objections, and the
earnest pleas of the Rev. Caleb Smith and the Rev. John
Brainerd made on behalf of the college. The group of friends
finally decided that it was Mr. Edwards' duty to go. "When
the council publicly announced their judgment and advice
to Mr. Edwards, and to the people of his church, he appeared
much moved, and burst into tears, a thing very unusual with
him in the presence of others; and soon afterwards remarked
to the members of the council, that it was a matter of wonder
to him, that they could so easily, as they appeared to have
done, obviate the objections which he had urged against his
removal. But, as he thought it his duty to be governed by
their advice, he determined cheerfully to acquiesce in their
decision, and repair to the scene of his future labor."

Mr. Edwards went alone to Princeton in January, 1758,
hoping to bring his family down in the spring. He had with

him two daughters, Mrs. Burr, the widow of the late president, and Lucy, his fifth daughter, who afterwards married Mr. Woodbridge. He spent several weeks in Princeton before the trustees could come together, preached every Sunday in the college chapel, gave out questions in theology to the senior class, and kept on with his own studies and writing. He was inaugurated as president on February 16, 1758. It seems rather remarkable that, although he held this office for only five weeks, he has ever since been known as "President Edwards."

Cases of smallpox now began to appear in Princeton. President Edwards and his two daughters were inoculated on February 23 by a skillful physician who came from Philadelphia to attend them. At first he reacted favorably to the disease; but a secondary fever set in, his throat was obstructed, and he could not take the proper medicine or food. His strength failed steadily, and he died on March 22, 1758.

Jonathan Edwards' dying testimony, and the Christian fortitude of his wife and daughters as they faced their great loss, were entirely consistent with their buoyant faith in the goodness and sovereignty of God. When Mr. Edwards knew that the end was near, he called to him the daughter who had lovingly attended him during his illness, and said to her:

"Dear Lucy, it seems to me to be the will of God that I must shortly leave you; therefore give my kindest love to my dear wife, and tell her that the uncommon union which has so long subsisted between us, has been of such a nature as, I trust, is spiritual, and therefore will continue forever; and I hope she will be supported under so great a trial, and submit cheerfully to the will of God. And as to my children, you are now like to be left fatherless; which I hope will be an inducement to you all to seek a Father who will never fail you. And as to my funeral, I would have it to be like Mr. Burr's; and any additional sum of money that might be expected to be laid out in that way, I would have disposed of to charitable uses." (President Burr had especially requested an unpretentious and inexpensive funeral, and that the money which might have been spent on a fashionable funeral should be given to the poor.)

A few minutes before he died, as some who were near him were speaking with apprehension of the effect of his death on the college and the Christian church, thinking that he could not hear, Mr. Edwards said, "Trust in God, and ye need not fear."

Dr. William Shippen, the Philadelphia physician, wrote a remarkable letter to Mrs. Edwards at Stockbridge, giving her the sad news. After carefully and tactfully explaining the circumstances, he said:

"This afternoon, between two and three o'clock, it pleased God to let him sleep in that dear Lord Jesus, whose kingdom and interest he has been faithfully and painfully serving all his life. And never did any mortal man more fully and clearly evidence the sincerity of all his professions, by one continued, universal, calm, cheerful resignation, and patient submission to the divine will, through every stage of his disease, than he; not so much as one discontented expression, nor the least appearance of murmuring, through the whole. And never did any person expire with more perfect freedom from pain; not so much as one distorted hair; but, in the most proper sense of the words, he fell asleep. Death had certainly lost its sting as to him.

"Your daughter, Mrs. Burr, and her children, through the mercy of God, are safely over the disease, and she desires me to send her duty to you, the best of mothers. . . .

"I conclude with my hearty prayers, dear Madam, that you may be enabled to look to that God whose love and goodness you have experienced a thousand times, for direction and help, under this most afflictive dispensation of His providence, and under every other difficulty you may meet with here, in order to your being more perfectly fitted for the joys of heaven hereafter.

"I am, dear Madam, your most sympathizing and affectionate friend, and very humble servant,

William Shippen."

On April 3, Mrs. Edwards wrote as follows to her daughter, Mrs. Burr:

"My very dear Child, What shall I say? A holy and good God has covered us with a dark cloud! Oh, that we may kiss the rod, and lay our hands on our mouths! The Lord has done it. He has made me adore His goodness that we had him so long. But my God lives; and He has my heart. Oh, what a legacy my husband and your father has left us! We are all given to God; and there I am, and love to be. Your ever affectionate mother,

Sarah Edwards."

On the same sheet was the following letter from another of her daughters:

"My dear Sister, My mother wrote this with a great deal of pain in her neck, which disabled her from writing any more. She thought you would be glad of these few lines from her own hand.

"O dear sister, how many calls have we, one upon the back of another! Oh, I beg your prayers, that we, who are young in the family, may be awakened and excited to call more earnestly on God, that He would be our Father and friend forever.

"My father took leave of all his people and family, as affectionately as if he knew he should not come again. On the Sabbath afternoon he preached from these words: 'We have here no continuing city; therefore let us seek one to come.' The chapter that he read was Acts the twentieth. Oh, how proper! What could he have done more? When he had got out of doors, he turned about and said, 'I commit you to God.' I doubt not but God will take a fatherly care of us, if we do not forget Him. I am your ever affectionate sister,

Susannah Edwards."

How rare it is today to find physicians, and mothers, and daughters, who could, on the occasion of the death of a loved one, write such letters as these, in a flowing and dignified style, and so filled with humble trust in God and complete submission to His will!

It is remarkable that Mrs. Burr died on April 7 and Mrs. Edwards on October 2 of that same year. Both passed away suddenly, after very short illnesses.

A more complete estimate of the outstanding Christian character and great talents of Jonathan Edwards may be gained from the following opinions expressed by famous Scottish and English theologians.

Dr. Thomas Chalmers—"We cannot take leave of Edwards without testifying the whole extent of the reverence that we bear him. On the arena of metaphysics, he stood the highest of all his contemporaries, and that, too, at a time when Hume was aiming his deadliest thrusts at the foundations of morality, and had thrown over the infidel cause the whole éclat of his reputation. The American divine affords, perhaps, the most wondrous example, in modern times, of one who stood richly gifted both in natural and in spiritual discernment; and we know not what most to admire in him, whether the deep philosophy that issued from his pen, or the humble and child-like piety that issued from his pulpit; whether when, as an author, he deals forth upon his readers the subtilties of profoundest argument, or when, as a Christian minister, he deals forth upon his hearers the simplicities of the gospel; whether it is, when we witness the impression that he made, by his writings, on the schools and high seats of literature, or the impression that he made, by his unlabored addresses, on the plain consciences of a plain congregation."

Professor Taylor, author of the *Natural History of Enthusiasm*.—"This eminent man, whose intellectual superiority might have enabled him to shine in European colleges of learning, displayed a meek greatness of soul, which belongs only to those who derive their principles from the gospel. How refreshing is the contrast of sentiments, which strikes us in turning from the private correspondence of men who

thought of nothing beyond their personal fame as philosophers or writers, to the correspondence and diary of a man
like Edwards! In the one case, the single, paramount motive,
—literary or philosophic vanity,—lurks in every sentence;
unblushingly shows itself on many a page, and, when most
concealed, is concealed by an affectation as loathsome as the
fault it hides. But how much of this deformed self-love could
the most diligent detractor cull from the private papers or
works of the President of the College of New Jersey? We
question if a single sentence, which could be fairly construed
to betray the vanity or ambition of superior intelligence, is
anywhere to be found in them. Edwards daily contemplated a
glory,—an absolute excellence, which at once checked the
swellings of pride, and sickened him of the praise, which his
powers might have won from the world."

Dr. John Erskine.—"The loss sustained by his death, not
only by the College of New Jersey, but by the church in
general, is irreparable. I do not think our age has produced a
divine of equal genius or judgment."

Sir James Mackintosh.—"He [Robert Hall] led me to the
perusal of Jonathan Edwards' book on Free Will, which Dr.
Priestley had pointed out before. I am sorry that I never yet
read the other works of that most extraordinary man, who,
in a metaphysical age or country, would certainly have been
deemed as much the boast of America, as his great country-
man, Franklin." In another work he speaks of Edwards as
"the metaphysician of America," and declares that, "in the
power of subtile argument, he was, perhaps, unmatched, certainly unsurpassed among men."

Philip E. Howard, Jr.
October, 1948.

# THE WORKS OF PRESIDENT EDWARDS

## 1. Published by Himself

1. *God Glorified in Man's Dependence;* a Sermon on I Corinthians 1:29-31. Boston, 1731.
2. *A Divine and Supernatural Light Imparted to the Soul by the Spirit of God;* a Sermon on Matthew 16:17. Boston, 1734.
3. *Curse Ye Meroz;* a Sermon on Judges 5:23. Boston, 1735.
4. *A Faithful Narrative of the Surprising Work of God in the Conversion of Many Hundred Souls in Northampton, etc.* London, 1736. Boston, 1738.
5. *Five Discourses,* prefixed to the first American edition of the preceding work.
6. *Sinners in the Hands of an Angry God;* a Sermon on Deuteronomy 32:35. Boston, 1741.
7. *Sorrows of the Bereaved Spread Before Jesus;* a Sermon at the Funeral of the Rev. William Williams, on Matthew 14:12. Boston, 1741.
8. *Distinguishing Marks of a Work of the True Spirit;* a Sermon on I John 4:1, preached at New Haven, September 10th, 1741. Boston, 1741.
9. *Thoughts on the Revival of Religion in New England, in 1740.* Boston, 1742.
10. *The Watchman's Duty and Account;* a Sermon on Hebrews 13:17, preached at the Ordination of the Rev. Jonathan Judd. Boston, 1743.
11. *The True Excellency of a Gospel Minister;* a Sermon on John 5:35, preached at the Ordination of the Rev. Robert Abercrombie. Boston, 1744.
12. *A Treatise Concerning Religious Affections.* Boston, 1746.
13. *An Humble Attempt to Promote Explicit Agreement and Visible Union among God's People, in Extraordinary Prayer, etc.* Boston, 1746.
14. *True Saints, When Absent from the Body, Present with the Lord;* a Sermon on II Corinthians, v. 8, preached at the Funeral of the Rev. David Brainerd. Boston, 1747.
15. *God's Awful Judgments in Breaking the Strong Rods of the Community;* a Sermon on the Death of Colonel John Stoddard. Boston, 1748.
16. *Life and Diary of the Rev. David Brainerd.* Boston, 1749.
17. *Christ the Example of Gospel Ministers;* a Sermon on John 13:15, preached at the Ordination of the Rev. Job Strong. Boston, 1749.
18. *Qualifications for Full Communion in the Visible Church.* Boston, 1749.
19. *Farewell Sermon to the People of Northampton.* Boston, 1750.
20. *Misrepresentation Corrected, and Truth Vindicated,* in a Reply to the Rev. Mr. Solomon Williams's Book on Qualifications for Communion. To which is added a Letter from Mr. Edwards to his late Flock at Northampton. Boston, 1752.

41

21. *True Faith Distinguished from the Experience of Devils;* a Sermon from James 2:19, preached before the Synod of New York, at Newark, September, 1752. New York, 1752.
22. *Inquiry into the Freedom of the Will.* Boston, 1754.
23. *The Great Christian Doctrine of Original Sin Defended.* Boston, 1758.

## 2. POSTHUMOUS

24. *Eighteen Sermons,* annexed to the Life of Edwards, by Dr. Hopkins, Boston, 1765.
25. *The History of Redemption.* Edinburgh, 1777.
26. *Nature of True Virtue.* Boston, 1788.
27. *God's Last End in the Creation.* Boston, 1788.
28. *Practical Sermons.* Edinburgh, 1788.
29. *Twenty Sermons.* Edinburgh, 1789.
30. *Miscellaneous Observations on Important Theological Subjects.* Edinburgh, 1793.
31. *Remarks on Important Theological Controversies.* Edinburgh, 1796.
32. *Types of the Messiah.* 1829.
33. *Notes on the Bible.* 1829.

## BIBLIOGRAPHY

*The Works of President Edwards,* Vol. III; London, James Black & Son, 1817.

*Life of Jonathan Edwards, President of the College of New Jersey;* by Samuel Miller, D.D., Professor of Ecclesiastical History and Church Government in the Theological Seminary at Princeton, N. J.; Vol. VIII of the Library of American Biography, conducted by Jared Sparks; New York, Harper & Bros., publishers, 1856.

*The Treatise on Religious Affections,* by the late Rev. Jonathan Edwards, A.M.; Vol. III, the Evangelical Family Library, the American Tract Society, New York, undated but very old.

# PREFACE

## By Jonathan Edwards

THERE ARE TWO WAYS of representing and recommending true religion and virtue to the world; the one, by doctrine and precept; the other, by instance and example; both are abundantly used in the Holy Scriptures. Not only are the grounds, nature, design, and importance of religion clearly exhibited in the doctrines of Scripture—its exercise and practice plainly delineated, and abundantly enforced, in its commands and counsels—but there we have many excellent examples of religion, in its power and practice, set before us in the histories both of the Old and New Testament.

Jesus Christ, the great Prophet of God, when He came to be "the light of the world," to teach and enforce true religion, in a greater degree than ever had been before, made use of both these methods. In His doctrine He not only declared the mind and will of God, the nature and properties of that virtue which becomes creatures of our make and in our circumstances, more clearly and fully than ever it had been before; and more powerfully enforced it by what He declared of the obligations and inducements to holiness; but He also in His own practice gave a most perfect example of the virtue He taught. He exhibited to the world such an illustrious pattern of humility, divine love, discreet zeal, self-denial, obedience, patience, resignation, fortitude, meekness, forgiveness, compassion, benevolence, and universal holiness, as neither men nor angels ever saw before.

God also in His providence has been wont to make use of both these methods to hold forth light to mankind, and inducements to their duty, in all ages. He has from time to

43

time raised up eminent teachers to exhibit and bear testimony
to the truth by their doctrine, and to oppose the errors,
darkness, and wickedness of the world; and He has also raised
up some eminent persons who have set bright examples of
that religion which is taught and prescribed in the Word of
God; whose examples have, in the course of divine providence, been set forth to public view.

These have a great tendency both to engage the attention
of men to the doctrines and rules taught, and also to confirm
and enforce them; especially when these bright examples have
been exhibited in the same persons who have been eminent
teachers. Hereby the world has had opportunity to see a
confirmation of the truth, efficacy, and amiableness of the religion taught, in the practice of the same persons who have
most clearly and forcibly taught it; and above all, when these
bright examples have been set by eminent teachers, in a variety of unusual circumstances of remarkable trial; and when
God has withal remarkably distinguished them with wonderful success of their instructions and labors.

Such an instance we have in the excellent person whose life
is published in the following pages. His example is attended
with a great variety of circumstances tending to engage the
attention of religious people, especially in these parts of the
world. He was one of distinguished natural abilities, as all
are sensible who had acquaintance with him. As a minister
of the gospel, he was called to unusual services in that work;
and his ministry was attended with very remarkable and
unusual events. His course of religion began before the late
times of extraordinary religious commotion; yet he was not
an idle spectator, but had a near concern in many things that
passed at that time. He had a very extensive acquaintance
with those who have been the subjects of the late religious
operations in places far distant, in people of different nations,
education, manners, and customs. He had a peculiar opportunity of acquaintance with the false appearances and counterfeits of religion; was the instrument of a most remarkable
awakening, a wonderful and abiding alteration and moral

transformation of subjects who peculiarly render the change rare and astonishing.

In the following account, the reader will have an opportunity to see not only what were the external circumstances and remarkable incidents of the life of this person, and how he spent his time from day to day, as to his external behavior; but also what passed in his own heart. Here he will see the wonderful change he experienced in his mind and disposition, the manner in which that change was brought to pass, how it continued, what were its consequences in his inward frames, thoughts, affections, and secret exercises, through many vicissitudes and trials, for more than eight years.

He will also see, how all ended at last, in his sentiments, frame, behavior, during a long season of the gradual and sensible approach of death, under a lingering illness; and what were the effects of his religion in dying circumstances, or in the last stages of his illness. The account being written, the reader may have the opportunity at his leisure to compare the various parts of the story, and deliberately to view and weigh the whole, and consider how far what is related is agreeable to the dictates of right reason and the holy Word of God.

I am far from supposing that Mr. Brainerd's inward exercises and experiences, or his external conduct, were free from all imperfections. The example of Jesus Christ is the only example that ever existed in human nature as altogether perfect; which therefore is a rule, to try all other examples by; and the dispositions, frames, and practices of others must be commended and followed no further than they were followers of Christ.

There is one thing in Mr. Brainerd, easily discernible by the following account of his life, which may be called an imperfection in him, which, though not properly an imperfection of a moral nature, yet, may possibly be made an objection against the extraordinary appearances of religion and devotion in him, by such as seek for objections against everything that can be produced in favor of true vital religion; and that is, *that he was, by his constitution and natural temper, so prone to melancholy and dejection of spirit.* There are some who think that all serious strict religion is a melancholy thing, and that what is called Christian experience, is little else besides melancholy vapors disturbing the brain, and exciting enthusiastic imaginations.

But that Mr. Brainerd's temper or constitution inclined him to despondency is no just ground to suspect his extraordinary devotion to be only the fruit of a warm imagination. I doubt not but that all who have well observed mankind will readily grant that not all who by their natural constitution or temper are most disposed to dejection are the most susceptive of lively and strong impressions on their imagination; or the most subject to those vehement affections which are the fruits of such impressions. But they must well know that many who are of a very gay and sanguine natural temper are vastly more so; and if their affections are turned into a religious channel, are much more exposed to enthusiasm than many of the former.

As to Mr. Brainerd in particular, notwithstanding his inclination to despondency, he was evidently one of those who usually are the furthest from a teeming imagination; being of a penetrating genius, of clear thought, of close reasoning, and a very exact judgment; as all know, who knew him. As he had a great insight into human nature, and was very discerning and judicious in general; so he excelled in his judgment and knowledge in divinity, but especially in things appertaining to inward experimental religion.

He most accurately distinguished between real, solid piety, and enthusiasm; between those affections that are rational and scriptural, having their foundation in light and judgment, and those that are founded in whimsical conceits, strong impressions on the imagination, and vehement emotions of the animal spirits. He was exceedingly sensible of men's exposedness to these things; how much they had prevailed, and what multitudes had been deceived by them; of their pernicious consequences, and the fearful mischief they had done in the

Christian world. He greatly abhorred such a religion and was abundant in bearing testimony against it, living and dying; and was quick to discern when anything of that nature arose, though in its first buddings and appearing under the most fair and plausible disguises. He had a talent for describing the various workings of this imaginary enthusiastic religion, evincing its falseness and vanity, and demonstrating the great difference between this and true spiritual devotion, which I scarcely ever knew equaled in any person.

His judiciousness did not only appear in distinguishing among the experiences of others, but also among the various exercises of his own mind; particularly in discerning what within himself was to be laid to the score of melancholy; in which he exceeded all melancholy persons that ever I was acquainted with. This was doubtless owing to a peculiar strength in his judgment; for it is a rare thing indeed that melancholy people are well sensible of their own disease, and fully convinced that such and such things are to be ascribed to it, as are its genuine operations and fruits.

Mr. Brainerd did not obtain that degree of skill at once, but gradually; as the reader may discern by the following account of his life. In the former part of his religious course, he imputed much of that kind of gloominess of mind and those dark thoughts, to spiritual desertion which in the latter part of his life, he was abundantly sensible, were owing to the disease of melancholy; accordingly he often expressly speaks of them in his diary as arising from this cause. He often in conversation spoke of the difference between melancholy and godly sorrow, true humiliation and spiritual desertion, and the great danger of mistaking the one for the other, and the very hurtful nature of melancholy, discoursing with great judgment upon it, and doubtless much more judiciously for what he knew by his own experience.

But besides what may be argued from Mr. Brainerd's strength of judgment, it is apparent in fact that he was not a person of a warm imagination. His inward experiences, whether in his convictions or his conversion, and his religious views and impressions through the course of his life, were not excited by strong and lively images formed in his imagination; nothing at all appears of it in his diary from beginning to end. He told me on his deathbed, that although once, when he was very young in years and experience, he was deceived into a high opinion of such things, looking on them as superior attainments in religion, beyond what he had ever arrived at, was ambitious of them, and earnestly sought them; yet he never could obtain them. He moreover declared that he never in his life had a strong impression on his imagination of any outward form, external glory, or anything of that nature; which kind of impressions abound among enthusiastic people.

As Mr. Brainerd's religious impressions, views, and affections in their nature were vastly different from enthusiasm, so were their effects in him as contrary to it as possible. Nothing like enthusiasm puffs men up with a high conceit of their own wisdom, holiness, eminence, and sufficiency; and makes them so bold, forward, assuming, and arrogant. But the reader will see that Mr. Brainerd's religion constantly disposed him to a most mean thought of himself, an abasing sense of his own exceeding sinfulness, deficiency, unprofitableness, and ignorance; looking on himself as worse than others; disposing him to universal benevolence and meekness; in honor to prefer others, and to treat all with kindness and respect.

And when melancholy prevailed, and though the effects of it were very prejudicial to him, yet it had not the effects of enthusiasm; but operated by dark and discouraging thoughts of himself, as ignorant, wicked, and wholly unfit for the work of the ministry, or even to be seen among mankind. Indeed, at the time forementioned, when he had not learned well to distinguish between enthusiasm and solid religion, he joined and kept company with some who were tinged with no small degree of the former. For a season he partook with them in a degree of their dispositions and behaviors; though, as was observed before, he could not obtain those things wherein

their enthusiasm itself consisted, and so could not become
like them in that respect, however he erroneously desired and
sought it.

But certainly it is not at all to be wondered at that a youth,
a young convert, one who had his heart so swallowed up in
religion, and who so earnestly desired its flourishing state,
and who had so little opportunity for reading, observation,
and experience, should for a while be dazzled and deceived
with the glaring appearances of mistaken devotion and zeal;
especially considering the extraordinary circumstances of that
day. He told me on his deathbed that while he was in these
circumstances he was out of his element and did violence to
himself, while complying in his conduct with persons of a
fierce and imprudent zeal, from his great veneration of some
whom he looked upon as better than himself.

So that it would be very unreasonable that his error at that
time should nevertheless be esteemed a just ground of prejudice against the whole of his religion, and his character in
general; especially considering how greatly his mind was
soon changed, and how exceedingly he afterwards lamented
his error and abhorred himself for his imprudent zeal and misconduct at that time, even to the breaking of his heart, and
almost to the overbearing of his natural strength; and how
much of a Christian spirit he showed in condemning himself
for that misconduct, as the readers will see.

What has been now mentioned of Mr. Brainerd, is so far
from being a just ground of prejudice against what is related
in the following account of his life that, if duly considered,
it will render the history the more serviceable. For by his thus
joining for a season with enthusiasts he had a more full and
intimate acquaintance with what belonged to that sort of
religion; and so was under better advantage to judge of the
difference between that and what he finally approved, and
strove to his utmost to promote, in opposition to it.

And hereby the reader has the more to convince him, that
Mr. Brainerd in his testimony against it, and the spirit and
behavior of those who are influenced by it, speaks from im-

partial conviction, and not from prejudice; because therein he openly condemns his own former opinion and conduct, on account of which he had greatly suffered from his opposers, and for which some continued to reproach him as long as he lived.

Another imperfection in Mr. Brainerd, which may be observed in the following account of his life, *was his being excessive in his labors; not taking due care to proportion his fatigues to his strength*. Indeed the case was very often such, by the seeming calls of Providence, as made it extremely difficult for him to avoid doing more than his strength would well admit of; yea, his circumstances and the business of his mission among the Indians were such that great fatigues and hardships were altogether inevitable.

However, he was finally convinced that he had erred in this matter, and that he ought to have taken more thorough care, and been more resolute to withstand temptations to such degrees of labor as injured his health. Accordingly he warned his brother, who succeeds him in his mission, to be careful to avoid this error.

Besides the imperfections already mentioned, it is readily allowed, that there were some imperfections which ran through his whole life, and were mixed with all his religious affections and exercises; some mixture of what was natural with that which was spiritual; as it evermore is in the best saints in this world. Doubtless, natural temper had some influence in the religious exercises and experiences of Mr. Brainerd, as there most apparently was in the exercises of devout David, and the apostles Peter, John, and Paul. There was undoubtedly very often some influence of his natural disposition to dejection, in his religious mourning; some mixture of melancholy with truly godly sorrow and real Christian humility; some mixture of the natural fire of youth with his holy zeal for God; and some influence of natural principles mixed with grace in various other respects, as it ever was and ever will be with saints while on this side heaven.

Perhaps none were more sensible of Mr. Brainerd's imperfections than he himself; or could distinguish more accurately than he, between what was natural and what was spiritual. It is easy for the judicious reader to observe that his graces ripened, the religious exercises of his heart became more and more pure, and he more and more distinguishing in his judgment, the longer he lived; he had much to teach and purify him, and he failed not to make his advantage.

But notwithstanding all these imperfections, I am persuaded, every pious and judicious reader will acknowledge that what is here set before him is indeed a remarkable instance of true and eminent Christian piety in heart and practice, tending greatly to confirm the reality of vital religion, and the power of godliness, that it is most worthy of imitation, and in many ways calculated to promote the spiritual benefit of the careful observer.

It is fit the reader should be aware, that what Mr. Brainerd wrote in his diary, out of which the following account of his life is chiefly taken, was written only for his own private use, and not to get honor and applause in the world, nor with any design that the world should ever see it, either while he lived or after his death; excepting some few things that he wrote in a dying state, after he had been persuaded, with difficulty, not entirely to suppress all his private writings. He showed himself almost invincibly averse to the publishing of any part of his diary after his death; and when he was thought to be dying at Boston, he gave the most strict, peremptory orders to the contrary. But being by some of his friends there prevailed upon to withdraw so strict and absolute a prohibition, he was pleased finally to yield so far as that his papers should be left in my hands, that I might dispose of them as I thought would be most for God's glory and the interest of religion.

But a few days before his death, he ordered some part of his diary to be destroyed, which renders the account of his life the less complete. And there are some parts of his diary here left out for brevity's sake, that would, I am sensible, have been a great advantage to the history, if they had been inserted; particularly the account of his wonderful successes among the Indians; which for substance is the same in his private diary with that which has already been made public, in the journal he kept by order of the society in Scotland, for their information. That account, I am of opinion, would be more entertaining and more profitable if it were published as it is written in his diary, in connection with his secret religion and the inward exercises of his mind, and also with the preceding and following parts of the story of his life. But because that account has been published already, I have therefore omitted that part. However, this defect may in a great measure be made up to the reader by the public journal. But it is time to end this preface, that the reader may be no longer detained from the history itself.

# INTRODUCTORY NOTE

## By President Edwards

M R. DAVID BRAINERD was born April 20, 1718, at Haddam, a town of Hartford [County], in Connecticut, New England. His father was the Worshipful Hezekiah Brainerd, Esq.; one of His Majesty's council for that colony; who was the son of Daniel Brainerd, Esq.; a justice of the peace, and a deacon of the Church of Christ in Haddam. His mother was Dorothy Hobart, daughter to the Reverend Mr. Jeremiah Hobart; who preached a while at Topsfield, then removed to Hempstead on Long Island, and afterwards, by reason of numbers turning Quakers, and many others being so irreligious that they would do nothing towards the support of the gospel, settled in the work of the ministry at Haddam; where he died in the eighty-fifth year of his age. He went to the public worship in the forenoon, and died in his chair between meetings.

This reverend gentleman was a son of the Reverend Peter Hobart; who was, first, minister of the gospel at Hingham, in the county of Norfolk in England; and, by reason of the persecution of the Puritans, removed with his family to New England, and was settled in the ministry at Hingham, in Massachusetts. He had five sons, namely, Joshua, Jeremiah, Gershom, Japheth, and Nehemiah. His son Joshua was minister at Southold on Long Island. Jeremiah was Mr. David Brainerd's grandfather, minister at Haddam, as before observed; Gershom was minister of Groton in Connecticut; Japheth was a physician; he went in the quality of a doctor of a ship to England (before the time of taking his second degree at college), and designed to go from thence to the East

53

Indies; but never was heard of more. Nehemiah was sometime fellow of Harvard College, and afterwards minister at Newton in Massachusetts.

The mother of Dorothy Hobart (who was afterwards Brainerd) was a daughter of the Reverend Samuel Whiting, minister of the gospel, first at Boston in Lincolnshire, and afterwards at Lynn in Massachusetts, New England. He had three sons who were ministers of the gospel.

David Brainerd was the third son of his parents. They had five sons, and four daughters. Their eldest son is Hezekiah Brainerd, Esq.; a justice of the peace, and for several years past a representative of the town of Haddam, in the general assembly of Connecticut colony; the second was the Reverend Nehemiah Brainerd, a worthy minister at Eastbury in Connecticut, who died of a consumption, Nov. 10, 1742; the fourth is Mr. John Brainerd, who succeeds his brother David as missionary to the Indians, and pastor of the same church of Christian Indians in New Jersey; and the fifth was Israel, lately student at Yale College in New Haven, who died since his brother David. Mrs. Dorothy Brainerd having lived about five years a widow, died, when her son, of whose life I am about to give an account, was about fourteen years of age: so that in his youth he was left both fatherless and motherless. What account he has given of himself, and his own life, may be seen in what follows.

---

In Mr. Brainerd's account of himself here, and continued in his Diary, the reader will find a growing interest and pleasure as he proceeds; in which is beautifully exemplified what the inspired penman declares, "The path of the just is as the morning light, that shineth more and more unto the perfect day." And indeed even his diction and style of writing assume a gradual improvement.—W. (Note in 1817 vol.)

# DAVID BRAINERD'S
# LIFE AND DIARY

## PART I – VI

# PART I

## FROM HIS BIRTH, TO THE TIME WHEN HE BEGAN TO STUDY FOR THE MINISTRY

### *1718–1742*

I WAS FROM MY YOUTH somewhat sober, and inclined rather to melancholy than the contrary extreme; but do not remember anything of conviction of sin worthy of remark till I was, I believe, about seven or eight years of age. Then I became concerned for my soul and terrified at the thoughts of death, and was driven to the performance of duties; but it appeared a melancholy business that destroyed my eagerness for play. And though, alas! this religious concern was but short-lived, I sometimes attended secret prayer; and thus lived at "ease in Zion, without God in the world" and without much concern, as I remember, till I was above thirteen years of age.

But sometime in the winter 1732, I was roused out of carnal security by I scarce know what means at first; but was much excited by the prevailing of a mortal sickness in Haddam. I was frequent, constant, and somewhat fervent in duties; and took delight in reading, especially Mr. Janeway's *Token for Children.* I felt sometimes much melted in duties and took great delight in the performance of them; and I sometimes hoped that I was converted, or at least in a good and hopeful way for heaven and happiness, not knowing what conversion was. The Spirit of God at this time proceeded far with me. I was remarkably dead to the world, and my thoughts were almost wholly employed about my soul's concerns. I may indeed say, "Almost I was persuaded to be a Christian." I was also exceedingly distressed and melancholy at the death of my mother, in March, 1732. But afterwards my religious concern began to decline, and by degrees I fell back into a considerable degree of security, though I still attended secret prayer.

About the fifteenth of April, 1733, I removed from my father's house to East Haddam, where I spent four years; but still "without God in the world," though, for the most part, I went a round of secret duty. I was not much addicted to young company, or frolicking, as it is called, but this I know, that when I did go into such company, I never returned with so good a conscience as when I went. It always added new guilt, made me afraid to come to the throne of grace, and spoiled those good frames I was wont sometimes to please myself with. But, alas! all my good frames were but self-righteousness, not founded on a desire for the glory of God.

About the latter end of April, 1737, being full nineteen years of age, I removed to Durham to work on my farm, and so continued about one year; frequently longing, from a natural inclination, after a liberal education. When about twenty years of age, I applied myself to study and was now engaged more than ever in the duties of religion. I became very strict and watchful over my thoughts, words, and actions; and thought I must be sober indeed, because I designed to devote myself to the ministry; and imagined I did dedicate myself to the Lord.

Sometime in April, 1738, I went to Mr. Fiske's [pastor of the church at Haddam], and lived with him during his life. I remember he advised me wholly to abandon young company and associate myself with grave elderly people, which counsel I followed. My manner of life was now exceeding regular and full of religion, such as it was; for I read my Bible more than twice through in less than a year, spent much time every day in prayer and other secret duties, gave great attention to the Word preached, and endeavored to my utmost to retain it. So much concerned was I about religion that I agreed with some young persons to meet privately on Sabbath evenings for religious exercises, and thought myself sincere in these duties. After our meeting was ended, I used to repeat the discourses of the day to myself; recollecting what I could, though sometimes very late at night. I used sometimes on Monday mornings to recollect the same sermons; had considerable movings of pleasurable affection in duties and had many thoughts of joining the church. In short, I had a very good outside, and rested entirely on my duties, though not sensible of it.

After Mr. Fiske's death, I proceeded in my learning with my brother; was still very constant in religious duties, and often wondered at the levity of professors. It was a trouble to me that they were so careless in religious matters. Thus I proceeded a considerable length on a self-righteous foundation; and should have been entirely lost and undone, had not the mere mercy of God prevented.

Some time in the beginning of winter, 1738, it pleased God, on one Sabbath day morning, as I was walking out for some secret duties, to give me on a sudden such a sense of my danger and the wrath of God that I stood amazed, and my former good frames, that I had pleased myself with, all presently vanished. From the view I had of my sin and vileness, I was much distressed all that day, fearing the vengeance of God would soon overtake me. I was much dejected, kept much alone, and sometimes envied the birds and beasts their happiness, because they were not exposed to eternal misery as I evidently saw I was. Thus I lived from day to day, being frequently in great distress. Sometimes there appeared mountains before me to obstruct my hopes of mercy; and the work of conversion appeared so great, that I thought I should never be the subject of it. I used, however, to pray and cry to God and perform other duties with great earnestness; and thus hoped by some means to make the case better.

Though hundreds of times I renounced all pretenses of any worth in my duties, as I thought, even while performing them, and often confessed to God that I deserved nothing for the very best of them but eternal condemnation; yet still I had a secret hope of recommending myself to God by my religious duties. When I prayed affectionately and my heart seemed in some measure to melt, I hoped God would be thereby moved to pity me; my prayers then looked with some appearance of goodness in them, and I seemed to mourn for sin. Then I could in some measure venture on the mercy of God in Christ, as I thought, though the preponderating thought, the foundation of my hope, was some imagination of goodness in my heart-meltings, flowing of affections in duty, extraordinary enlargements.

Though at times the gate appeared so very strait that it looked next to impossible to enter, yet, at other times, I flattered myself that it was not so very difficult, and hoped I should by diligence and watchfulness soon gain the point. Sometimes after enlargement in duty and considerable affection I hoped I had made a good step towards heaven; imagined that God was affected as I was and that He would hear such sincere cries, as I called them. And so sometimes, when I withdrew for secret duties in great distress, I returned comfortable; and thus healed myself with my duties.

Sometime in February, 1739, I set apart a day for secret fasting and prayer, and spent the day in almost incessant cries to God for mercy, that He would open my eyes to see the evil of sin and the way of life by Jesus Christ. And God was pleased that day to make considerable discoveries of my heart to me. But still I trusted in all the duties I performed; though there was no manner of goodness in them, there being in them no respect to the glory of God, nor any such principle in my heart. Yet, God was pleased to make my endeavors that day a means to show me my helplessness in some measure.

Sometimes I was greatly encouraged and imagined that God loved me, and was pleased with me; and thought I should soon be fully reconciled to God. But the whole was founded on mere presumption, arising from enlargement in duty, or flowing of affections, or some good resolutions, and the like. When, at times, great distress began to arise on a sight of my vileness, nakedness, and inability to deliver myself from a sovereign God, I used to put off the discovery, as what I could not bear. Once, I remember, a terrible pang of distress seized me, and the thoughts of renouncing myself and standing naked before God, stripped of all goodness, were so dreadful to me, that I was ready to say to them as Felix to Paul, "Go thy way for this time."

Thus, though I daily longed for greater conviction of sin, supposing that I must see more of my dreadful state in order to a remedy; yet when the discoveries of my vile, hellish heart were made to me, the sight was so dreadful and showed me so plainly my exposedness to damnation that I could not endure it. I constantly strove after whatever qualifications I imagined others obtained before the reception of Christ, in order to recommend me to His favor. Sometimes I felt the power of a hard heart and supposed it must be softened before Christ would accept of me; and when I felt any meltings of heart, I hoped now the work was almost done. Hence, when my distress still remained, I was wont to murmur at God's dealings with me; and thought when others felt their hearts softened God showed them mercy; but my distress remained still.

Sometimes I grew remiss and sluggish, without any great convictions of sin, for a considerable time together; but after such a season, convictions seized me more violently. One night I remember in particular, when I was walking solitarily abroad, I had opened to me such a view of my sin that I feared the ground would cleave asunder under my feet and become my grave; and would send my soul quick [alive] into hell, before I could get home. Though I was forced to go to bed lest my distress should be discovered by others, which I much feared; yet I scarcely durst sleep at all, for I thought it would be a great wonder if I should be out of hell in the morning. And though my distress was sometimes thus great, yet I greatly dreaded the loss of convictions, and returning back to a state of carnal security, and to my former insensibility of impending wrath; which made me exceeding exact in my behavior lest I should stifle the motions of God's Holy Spirit.

When at any time I took a view of my convictions, and thought the degree of them to be considerable, I was wont to trust in them. But this confidence, and the hopes of soon making some notable advances towards deliverance, would ease my mind and I soon became more senseless and remiss. Then again, when I discerned my convictions to grow languid, and I thought them about to leave me, this immediately alarmed and distressed me. Sometimes I expected to take a large step, and get very far towards conversion, by some particular opportunity or means I had in view.

The many disappointments, great distresses and perplexity I met with, put me into a most horrible frame of contesting with the Almighty; with an inward vehemence and virulence finding fault with His ways of dealing with mankind. I found great fault with the imputation of Adam's sin to his posterity; and my wicked heart often wished for some other way of salvation than by Jesus Christ. Being like the troubled sea, my thoughts confused, I used to contrive to escape the wrath of God by some other means. I had strange projects, full of atheism, contriving to disappoint God's designs and decrees concerning me, or to escape His notice, and hide myself from Him.

But when, upon reflection, I saw these projects were vain and would not serve me, and that I could contrive nothing for my own relief; this would throw my mind into the most horrid frame, to wish there was no God, or to wish there were some other God that could control Him. These thoughts and desires were the secret inclinations of my heart, frequently acting before I was aware. But, alas! they were mine, although I was afrighted when I came to reflect on them. When I considered, it distressed me to think that my heart was so full of enmity against God; and it made me tremble, lest His vengeance should suddenly fall upon me.

I used before to imagine that my heart was not so bad as the Scriptures and some other books represented it. Sometimes I used to take much pains to work it up into a good frame, a humble submissive disposition; and hoped there was then some goodness in me. But, on a sudden, the thoughts of the strictness of the law, or the sovereignty of God, would so irritate the corruption of my heart, that I had so watched over and I hoped I had brought it to a good frame, that it would break over all bounds and burst forth on all sides, like floods of waters when they break down their dam.

Being sensible of the necessity of a deep humiliation in order to a saving close [saving faith] with Christ, I used to set myself to work in my own heart those convictions that were requisite in such a humiliation; as, a conviction that God would be just, if He cast me off forever; that if ever God should bestow mercy on me, it would be mere grace, though I should be in distress many years first and be never so much engaged in duty; that God was not in the least obliged to pity me the more for all past duties, cries, and tears.

I strove to my utmost to bring myself to a firm belief of these things and a hearty assent to them; and hoped that now I was brought off from myself, truly humbled, and that I bowed to the divine sovereignty. I was wont to tell God in my prayers that now I had those very dispositions of soul that He required, and on which He showed mercy to others, and thereupon to beg and plead for mercy to me. But when I found no relief and was still oppressed with guilt and fears of wrath, my soul was in a tumult, and my heart rose against God as dealing hardly with me.

Yet then my conscience flew in my face, putting me in mind of my late confession to God of His justice in my condemnation. And this giving me a sight of the badness of my heart, threw me again into distress, and I wished I had watched my heart more narrowly, to keep it from breaking out against God's dealings with me, and I even wished I had not pleaded for mercy on account of my humiliation, because thereby I had lost all my seeming goodness. Thus, scores of times, I vainly imagined myself humbled and prepared for saving mercy. And while I was in this distressed, bewildered, and tumultuous state of mind, the corruption of my heart was especially ir- ritated with the following things:

1. *The strictness of the divine law.* For I found it was impossible for me, after my utmost pains, to answer its demands. I often made new resolutions, and as often broke them. I imputed the whole to carelessness and the want of being more watchful, and used to call myself a fool for my negligence. But when, upon a stronger resolution, and greater endeavors, and close application to fasting and prayer, I found all attempts fail; then I quarreled with the law of God, as unreasonably rigid. I thought if it extended only to my outward actions and behaviors I could bear with it; but I found it condemned me for my evil thoughts and sins of my heart, which I could not possibly prevent.

I was extremely loth to own my utter helplessness in this matter: but after repeated disappointments, thought that, rather than perish, I could do a little more still; especially if such and such circumstances might but attend my endeavors and strivings. I hoped that I should strive more earnestly than ever if the matter came to extremity—though I never could find the time to do my utmost, in the manner I intended—and this hope of future more favorable circumstances, and of doing something great hereafter, kept me from utter despair in myself and from seeing myself fallen into the hands of a sovereign God, and dependent on nothing but free and boundless grace.

2. Another thing was, that *faith alone was the condition of salvation;* that God would not come down to lower terms and that He would not promise life and salvation upon my sincere and hearty prayers and endeavors. That word, Mark 16:16, "He that believeth not, shall be damned," cut off all hope there. I found faith was the sovereign gift of God, that I could not get it as of myself, and could not oblige God to bestow it upon me by any of my performances (Eph. 2:1–8). This, I was ready to say, is a hard saying, who can bear it? I could not bear that all I had done should stand for mere nothing, who had been very conscientious in duty, had been exceeding religious a great while, and had, as I thought, done much more than many others who had obtained mercy.

I confessed indeed the vileness of my duties; but then, what made them at that time seem vile was my wandering thoughts in them; not because I was all over defiled like a devil, and the principle corrupt from whence they flowed, so that I could not possibly do anything that was good. And therefore I called what I did, by the name of honest faithful endeavors; and could not bear it that God had made no promises of salvation to them.

3. Another thing was that *I could not find out what faith was;* or what it was to believe and come to Christ. I read the calls of Christ to the weary and heavy laden; but could find no way that He directed them to come in. I thought I would gladly come if I knew how, though the path of duty were never so difficult. I read Mr. Stoddard's *Guide to Christ*, (which I trust was, in the hand of God, the happy means of my conversion), and my heart rose against the author; for though he told me my very heart all along under convictions, and seemed to be very beneficial to me in his directions; yet here he failed, he did not tell me anything I could *do* that would bring me to Christ, but left me as it were with a great gulf between, without any direction to get through. For I was not yet effectually and experimentally taught that there could be no way prescribed whereby a natural man could, of his own strength, obtain that which is supernatural and which the highest angel cannot give.

4. Another thing to which I found a great inward opposition was *the sovereignty of God.* I could not bear that it should be wholly at God's pleasure, to save or damn me, just as He would. That passage, Romans 9:11-23, was a constant vexation to me, especially verse 21. Reading or meditating on this always destroyed my seeming good frames. For when I thought I was almost humbled and almost resigned, this passage would make my enmity against the sovereignty of God appear. When I came to reflect on my inward enmity and blasphemy, which arose on this occasion, I was the more afraid of God and driven further from any hopes of reconciliation with Him. It gave me such a dreadful view of myself

that I dreaded more than ever to see myself in God's hands, at His sovereign disposal, and it made me more opposite than ever to submit to His sovereignty; for I thought God designed my damnation.

All this time the Spirit of God was powerfully at work with me; and I was inwardly pressed to relinquish all self-confidence, all hopes of ever helping myself by any means whatsoever. The conviction of my lost estate was sometimes so clear and manifest before my eyes that it was as if it had been declared to me in so many words, "It is done, it is done; [it is] forever impossible to deliver yourself."

For about three or four days my soul was thus greatly distressed. At some turns, for a few moments, I seemed to myself lost and undone; but then would shrink back immediately from the sight, because I dared not venture myself into the hands of God as wholly helpless and at the disposal of His sovereign pleasure. I dared not see that important truth concerning myself, that I was "dead in trespasses and sins." But when I had as it were thrust away these views of myself at any time, I felt distressed to have the same discoveries of myself again; for I greatly feared being given over of God to final stupidity. When I thought of putting it off to a "more convenient season," the conviction was so close and powerful with regard to the present time that it was the best, and probably the only time, that I dared not put it off.

It was the sight of truth concerning myself, truth respecting my state as a creature fallen and alienated from God, and that consequently could make no demands on God for mercy but must subscribe to the absolute sovereignty of the Divine Being; the sight of the truth, I say, my soul shrank away from and trembled to think of beholding. Thus, he that doth evil, as all unregenerate men continually do, hates the light of truth, neither cares to come to it, because it will reprove his deeds and show him his just deserts (John 3:20).

And though, some time before, I had taken much pains, as I thought, to submit to the sovereignty of God, yet I mistook the thing; and did not once imagine that seeing and being made experimentally sensible of this truth, which my soul now so much dreaded and trembled at, was the frame of soul that I had been so earnest in pursuit of heretofore. For I had ever hoped that when I had attained to that humiliation, which I supposed necessary to go before faith, then it would not be fair for God to cast me off. But now I saw it was so far from any goodness in me to own myself spiritually dead and destitute of all goodness that, on the contrary, my mouth would be forever stopped by it; and it looked as dreadful to me to see myself and the relation I stood in to God—I a sinner and criminal, and He a great Judge and Sovereign—as it would be to a poor trembling creature to venture off some high precipice.

And hence I put it off for a minute or two, and tried for better circumstances to do it in; either I must read a passage or two, or pray first, or something of the like nature; or else put off my submission to God's sovereignty with an objection that I did not know how to submit. But the truth was I could see no safety in owning myself in the hands of a sovereign God, and that I could lay no claim to anything better than damnation.

But after a considerable time spent in such like exercises and distresses, one morning, while I was walking in a solitary place, as usual, I at once saw that all my contrivances and projects to effect or procure deliverance and salvation for myself were utterly in vain. I was brought quite to a stand as finding myself totally lost. I had thought many times before that the difficulties in my way were very great; but now I saw, in another and very different light, that it was forever impossible for me to do anything towards helping or delivering myself. I then thought of blaming myself that I had not done more, and been more engaged while I had opportunity, for it seemed now as if the season of doing was forever over and gone. But I instantly saw that, let me have done what I would, it would no more have tended to my helping myself than what I had done; that I had made all the pleas I ever could have made to all eternity; and that all my pleas were vain. The tumult that had been before in my mind was now quieted; and I was something eased of that distress which I felt while struggling against a sight of myself, and of the divine sovereignty. I had the greatest certainty that my state was forever miserable, for all that I could do; and wondered that I had never been sensible of it before.

While I remained in this state, my notions respecting my duties were quite different from what I had ever entertained in times past. Before this, the more I did in duty the more hard I thought it would be for God to cast me off; though at the same time I confessed, and thought I saw, that there was no goodness or merit in my duties. But now the more I did in prayer or any other duty, the more I saw I was indebted to God for allowing me to ask for mercy; for I saw it was self-interest had led me to pray, and that I had never once prayed from any respect to the glory of God. Now I saw there was no necessary connection between my prayers and the bestowment of divine mercy; that they laid not the least obligation upon God to bestow His grace upon me; and that there was no more virtue or goodness in them than there would be in my paddling with my hand in the water (which was the comparison I had then in my mind); and this because they were not performed from any love or regard to God. I saw that I had been heaping up my devotions before God, fasting, praying, pretending, and indeed really thinking sometimes that I was aiming at the glory of God; whereas I never once truly intended it, but only my own happiness.

I saw that as I had never done anything *for* God, I had no claim on anything *from* Him but perdition, on account of my hypocrisy and mockery. Oh, how different did my duties now appear from what they used to do! I used to charge them with sin and imperfection; but this was only on account of the wanderings and vain thoughts attending them, and not because I had no regard to God in them; for this I thought I had. But when I saw evidently that I had regard to nothing but self-interest, then they appeared a vile mockery of God, self-worship, and a continual course of lies. So that I now saw

that something worse had attended my duties than barely a
few wanderings; for the whole was nothing but self-worship,
and an horrid abuse of God.

I continued, as I remember, in this state of mind from Friday
morning till the Sabbath evening following (July 12, 1739),
when I was walking again in the same solitary place, where
I was brought to see myself lost and helpless, as beforementioned. Here, in a mournful, melancholy state, I was attempting to pray; but found no heart to engage in that or any
other duty. My former concern, exercise, and religious affections were now gone. I thought the Spirit of God had quite
left me, but still was not distressed; yet disconsolate, as if
there was nothing in heaven or earth could make me happy.

I had been thus endeavoring to pray, though as I thought,
very stupid and senseless, for near half an hour; then, as I was
walking in a dark thick grove, unspeakable glory seemed to
open to the view and apprehension of my soul. I do not mean
any external brightness, for I saw no such thing. Nor do I
intend any imagination of a body of light somewhere in the
third heavens, or anything of that nature; but it was a new
inward apprehension or view that I had of God, such as I
never had before, nor anything which had the least resemblance of it.

I stood still, wondered, and admired! I knew that I never
had seen before anything comparable to it for excellency and
beauty; it was widely different from all the conceptions that
ever I had of God, or things divine. I had no particular apprehension of any one Person in the Trinity, either the Father, the Son, or the Holy Ghost; but it appeared to be divine
glory. My soul rejoiced with joy unspeakable to see such a
God, such a glorious Divine Being; and I was inwardly
pleased and satisfied that He should be God over all for ever
and ever. My soul was so captivated and delighted with the
excellency, loveliness, greatness, and other perfections of God,
that I was even swallowed up in Him. At least to that degree
that I had no thought (as I remember) at first, about my own
salvation, and scarce reflected there was such a creature as I.

Thus God, I trust, brought me to a hearty disposition to exalt Him and set Him on the throne, and principally and ultimately to aim at His honor and glory, as King of the universe. I continued in this state of inward joy, peace, and astonishment, till near dark, without any sensible abatement; and then began to think and examine what I had seen; and felt sweetly composed in my mind all the evening following. I felt myself in a new world, and everything about me appeared with a different aspect from what it was wont to do.

At this time, the way of salvation opened to me with such infinite wisdom, suitableness, and excellency, that I wondered I should ever think of any other way of salvation; was amazed that I had not dropped my own contrivances, and complied with this lovely, blessed, and excellent way before. If I could have been saved by my own duties, or any other way that I had formerly contrived, my whole soul would now have refused it. I wondered that all the world did not see and comply with this way of salvation, entirely by the righteousness of Christ.

The sweet relish of what I then felt continued with me for several days, almost constantly, in a greater or less degree. I could not but sweetly rejoice in God, lying down and rising up. The next Lord's Day I felt something of the same kind, though not so powerful as before. But not long after I was again involved in thick darkness, and under great distress, yet not of the same kind with my distress under convictions. I was guilty, afraid, and ashamed to come before God; was exceedingly pressed with a sense of guilt. But it was not long before I felt, I trust, true repentance and joy in God. About the latter end of August, I again fell under great darkness; it seemed as if the presence of God was clean gone forever; though I was not so much distressed about my spiritual state, as I was at my being shut out from God's presence, as I then sensibly was. But it pleased the Lord to return graciously to me, not long after that.

In the beginning of September I went to college [Yale College in New Haven, now Yale University], and entered there; but with some degree of reluctancy, fearing lest I should not be able to lead a life of strict religion in the midst of so many temptations. After this, in the vacancy, before I went to tarry at college, it pleased God to visit my soul with clearer manifestations of Himself and His grace. I was spending some time in prayer and self-examination, when the Lord by His grace so shined into my heart that I enjoyed full assurance of His favor, for that time; and my soul was unspeakably refreshed with divine and heavenly enjoyments. At this time especially, as well as some others, sundry passages of God's Word opened to my soul with divine clearness, power, and sweetness, so as to appear exceeding precious, and with clear and certain evidence of its being the Word of God. I enjoyed considerable sweetness in religion all the winter following.

In January, 1740, the measles spread much in college; and I having taken the distemper, went home to Haddam. But some days before I was taken sick, I seemed to be greatly deserted, and my soul mourned the absence of the Comforter exceedingly. It seemed to me all comfort was forever gone; I prayed and cried to God for help, yet found no present comfort or relief. But through divine goodness, a night or two before I was taken ill, while I was walking alone in a very retired place and engaged in meditation and prayer, I enjoyed a sweet refreshing visit, as I trust, from above; so that my soul was raised far above the fears of death. Indeed I rather longed for death, than feared it. Oh, how much more refreshing this one season was than all the pleasures and delights that earth can afford!

After a day or two I was taken with the measles and was very ill indeed, so that I almost despaired of life; but had no distressing fears of death at all. However, through divine goodness I soon recovered: yet, by reason of hard and close studies and being much exposed on account of my freshmanship, I had but little time for spiritual duties. My soul often mourned for want of more time and opportunity to be alone with God. In the spring and summer following, I had better advantages for retirement and enjoyed more comfort in religion. Though indeed my ambition in my studies greatly wronged the activity and vigor of my spiritual life. Yet this was usually the case with me that "in the multitude of my thoughts within me, God's comforts principally delighted my soul"; these were my greatest consolations day by day.

One day I remember in particular (I think it was in June, 1740), I walked to a considerable distance from the college, in the fields alone at noon, and in prayer found such unspeakable sweetness and delight in God that I thought, if I must continue still in this evil world, I wanted always to be there, to behold God's glory. My soul dearly loved all mankind, and longed exceedingly that they should enjoy what I enjoyed. It seemed to be a little resemblance of heaven. On Lord's Day, July 6, being sacrament-day, I found some divine life and spiritual refreshment in that holy ordinance. When I came from the Lord's Table, I wondered how my fellow students could live as I was sensible most did. Next Lord's Day, July 13, I had some special sweetness in religion. Again, Lord's Day, July 20, my soul was in a sweet and precious frame.

Sometime in August following, I became so weakly and disordered, by too close application to my studies, that I was advised by my tutor to go home and disengage my mind from study, as much as I could; for I was grown so weak that I began to spit blood. I took his advice, and endeavored to lay aside my studies. But being brought very low, I looked death in the face more steadfastly; and the Lord was pleased to give me renewedly a sweet sense and relish of divine things. Particularly October 13, I found divine help and consolation in the precious duties of secret prayer and self-examination, and my soul took delight in the blessed God. . . .

Saturday, October 18, in my morning devotions, my soul was exceedingly melted, and bitterly mourned over my exceeding sinfulness and vileness. I never before had felt so pungent and deep a sense of the odious nature of sin as at this time. My soul was then unusually carried forth in love to God and had a lively sense of God's love to me. And this love and hope, at that time, cast out fear. Both morning and evening I spent some time in self-examination, to find the truth of grace, as also my fitness to approach to God at His Table the next day. Through infinite grace, found the Holy Spirit influencing my soul with love to God, as a witness within myself.

Lord's Day, October 19. In the morning I felt my soul hungering and thirsting after righteousness. In the forenoon, while I was looking on the sacramental elements and thinking that Jesus Christ would soon be "set forth crucified before me," my soul was filled with light and love, so that I was almost in an ecstasy. My body was so weak I could scarcely stand. I felt at the same time an exceeding tenderness and most fervent love towards all mankind, so that my soul and all the powers of it seemed, as it were, to melt into softness and sweetness. But during the communion there was some abatement of this life and fervor. This love and joy cast out fear; and my soul longed for perfect grace and glory. This frame continued till the evening, when my soul was sweetly spiritual in secret duties.

Monday, October 20. I again found the assistance of the Holy Spirit in secret duties, both morning and evening, and life and comfort in religion through the whole day.

Tuesday, October 21. I had likewise experience of the goodness of God in "shedding abroad his love in my heart," and giving me delight and consolation in religious duties. All the remaining part of the week, my soul seemed to be taken up with divine things. I now so longed after God and to be freed from sin that when I felt myself recovering and thought I must return to college again, which had proved so hurtful to my spiritual interest the year past, I could not but be grieved, and I thought I had much rather have died. For it distressed me, to think of getting away from God. But before I went, I enjoyed several other sweet and precious seasons of communion with God (particularly October 30 and November 4), wherein my soul enjoyed unspeakable comfort.

I returned to college about November 6 and, through the goodness of God, felt the power of religion almost daily for the space of six weeks.

November 28. In my evening devotion, I enjoyed precious discoveries of God and was unspeakably refreshed with that passage, Hebrews 12:22–24. My soul longed to wing away for the paradise of God; I longed to be conformed to God in all things. A day or two after, I enjoyed much of the light of God's countenance most of the day, and my soul rested in God.

Tuesday, December 9. I was in a comfortable frame of soul most of the day; but especially in evening devotions, when God was pleased wonderfully to assist and strengthen me; so that I thought nothing should ever move me from the love of God in Christ Jesus my Lord. Oh! one hour with God infinitely exceeds all the pleasures and delights of this lower world.

Some time towards the latter end of January, 1741, I grew more cold and dull in religion, by means of my old temptation, namely, ambition in my studies. But through divine goodness, a great and general awakening spread itself over the college, about the latter end of February, in which I was much quickened and more abundantly engaged in religion. [See Appendix I.]

# PART II

## April-July 1742

Mr. Brainerd, the spring after his expulsion, went to live with the Rev. Mr. Mills of Ripton, to pursue his studies with him, in order to his being fitted for the work of the ministry; where he spent the greater part of the time, till the Association licensed him to preach; but frequently rode to visit the neighboring ministers, particularly Mr. Cooke of Stratford, Mr. Graham of Southbury, and Mr. Bellamy of Bethlehem. While with Mr. Mills, he began the third book of his diary, in which the account he wrote of himself, is as follows.—J. Edwards.

THURSDAY, April 1, 1742. I seem to be declining with respect to my life and warmth in divine things; had not so free access to God in prayer as usual of late. Oh, that God would humble me deeply in the dust before Him! I deserve hell every day for not loving my Lord more, who has, I trust, loved me and given Himself for me. Every time I am enabled to exercise any grace renewedly, I am renewedly indebted to the God of all grace for special assistance. Where then is boasting? Surely it is excluded when we think how we are dependent on God for the being and every act of grace. Oh, if ever I get to heaven it will be because God wills, and nothing else; for I never did anything of myself but get away from God! My soul will be astonished at the unsearchable riches of divine grace when I arrive at the mansions, which the blessed Saviour is gone before to prepare.

Friday, April 2. In the afternoon I felt, in secret prayer, much resigned, calm, and serene. What are all the storms of this lower world, if Jesus by His Spirit does but come walking on the seas! Some time past, I had much pleasure in the prospect of the heathen being brought home to Christ, and desired that the Lord would employ me in that work. But now, my soul more frequently desires to die, to be with Christ. Oh. that my soul were rapt up in divine love, and my longing desires after God increased! In the evening, was refreshed in prayer, with the hopes of the advancement of Christ's kingdom in the world.

Saturday, April 3. Was very much amiss this morning and had a bad night. I thought, if God would take me to Himself now, my soul would exceedingly rejoice. Oh, that I may be always humble and resigned to God, and that He would cause my soul to be more fixed on Himself, that I may be more fitted both for doing and suffering!

Lord's Day, April 4. My heart was wandering and lifeless. In the evening God gave me faith in prayer, made my soul melt in some measure, and gave me to taste a divine sweetness. O my blessed God! Let me climb up near to Him, and love, and long, and plead, and wrestle, and stretch after Him, and for deliverance from the body of sin and death. Alas! my soul mourned to think I should ever lose sight of its Beloved again. "O come, Lord Jesus, amen."

> On the evening of the next day, he complains that he seemed to be void of all relish of divine things, felt much of the prevalence of corruption, and saw in himself a disposition to all manner of sin; which brought a very great gloom on his mind and cast him down into the depths of melancholy; so that he speaks of himself as amazed, having no comfort, but filled with horror, seeing no comfort in heaven or earth.—J. E.

Tuesday, April 6. I walked out this morning to the same place where I was last night, and felt as I did then; but was somewhat relieved by reading some passages in my diary, and seemed to feel as if I might pray to the great God again with freedom; but was suddenly struck with a damp [a sense of heaviness, making it hard to pray], from the sense I had of my own vileness. Then I cried to God to cleanse me from my exceeding filthiness, to give me repentance and pardon. I then began to find it sweet to pray; and could think of undergoing the greatest sufferings, in the cause of Christ, with pleasure. Found myself willing, if God should so order it, to suffer banishment from my native land, among the heathen, that I might do something for their salvation, in distresses and deaths of any kind.

Then God gave me to wrestle earnestly for others, for the kingdom of Christ in the world, and for dear Christian friends. I felt weaned from the world and from my own reputation amongst men, willing to be despised and to be a gazing stock for the world to behold. It is impossible for me to express how I then felt. I had not much joy, but some sense of the majesty of God, which made me as it were tremble. I saw myself mean and vile, which made me more willing that God should do what He would with me; it was all infinitely reasonable.

Wednesday, April 7. I had not so much fervency, but felt something as I did yesterday morning, in prayer. At noon I spent some time in secret, with some fervency, but scarce any sweetness; and felt very dull in the evening.

Thursday, April 8. Had raised hopes today respecting the heathen. Oh, that God would bring in great numbers of them to Jesus Christ! I cannot but hope I shall see that glorious day. Everything in this world seems exceeding vile and little to me: I look so on myself. I had some little dawn of comfort today in prayer; but especially tonight, I think I had some faith and power of intercession with God. I was enabled to plead with God for the growth of grace in myself; and many of the dear children of God then lay with weight upon my soul. Blessed be the Lord! It is good to wrestle for divine blessings.

Friday, April 9. Most of my time in morning devotion was

spent without sensible sweetness; yet I had one delightful prospect of arriving at the heavenly world. I am more amazed than ever at such thoughts, for I see myself infinitely vile and unworthy. I feel very heartless and dull; and though I long for the presence of God and seem constantly to reach towards God in desires, yet I cannot feel that divine and heavenly sweetness that I used to enjoy. No poor creature stands in need of divine grace more than I, and none abuse it more than I have done, and still do.

Saturday, April 10. Spent much time in secret prayer this morning and not without some comfort in divine things. And, I hope, had some faith in exercise; but am so low and feel so little of the sensible presence of God that I hardly know what to call faith, and am made to possess the sins of my youth, and the dreadful sin of my nature. I am all sin; I cannot think, nor act, but every motion is sin. I feel some faint hopes, that God will, of His infinite mercy, return again with showers of converting grace to poor gospel-abusing sinners. My hopes of being employed in the cause of God, which of late have been almost extinct, seem now a little revived. Oh, that all my late distresses and awful apprehensions might prove but Christ's school to make me fit for greater service, by teaching me the great lesson of humility!

Lord's Day, April 11. In the morning, I felt but little life, excepting that my heart was somewhat drawn out in thankfulness to God for His amazing grace and condescension to me, in past influences and assistances of His Spirit. Afterwards, I had some sweetness in the thoughts of arriving at the heavenly world. Oh, for the happy day! After public worship God gave me special assistance in prayer. I wrestled with my dear Lord with much sweetness, and intercession was made a delightful employment to me. In the evening, as I was viewing the light in the north, I was delighted in contemplation on the glorious morning of the resurrection.

Monday, April 12. This morning the Lord was pleased to lift up the light of His countenance upon me in secret prayer, and made the season very precious to my soul. Though I have been so depressed of late, respecting my hopes of future serviceableness in the cause of God, yet now I had much encouragement respecting that matter. I was especially assisted to intercede and plead for poor souls and for the enlargement of Christ's kingdom in the world, and for special grace for myself to fit me for special services. I felt exceedingly calm and quite resigned to God, respecting my future employment, when and where He pleased. My faith lifted me above the world and removed all those mountains that I could not look over of late.

I wanted not the favor of man to lean upon; for I knew Christ's favor was infinitely better, and that it was no matter when, nor where, nor how Christ should send me, nor what trials He should still exercise me with, if I might be prepared for His work and will. I now found revived, in my mind, the wonderful discovery of infinite wisdom in all the dispensations of God towards me, which I had a little before I met with my great trial at college; everything appeared full of divine wisdom.

Tuesday, April 13. I saw myself to be very mean and vile and wondered at those that showed me respect. Afterwards I was somewhat comforted in secret retirement and assisted to wrestle with God with some power, spirituality, and sweetness. Blessed be the Lord, He is never unmindful of me but always sends me needed supplies. From time to time when I am like one dead, He raises me to life. Oh, that I may never distrust infinite goodness!

Wednesday, April 14. My soul longed for communion with Christ and for the mortification of indwelling corruption, especially spiritual pride. Oh, there is a sweet day coming wherein the weary will be at rest! My soul has enjoyed much sweetness this day in the hopes of its speedy arrival.

Thursday, April 15. My desires apparently centered in God, and I found a sensible attraction of soul after Him sundry times today. I know I long for God and a conformity to His will, in inward purity and holiness, ten thousand times more than for anything here below.

Friday and Saturday, April 16, 17. I seldom prayed without some sensible joy in the Lord. Sometimes I longed much to be dissolved and to be with Christ. Oh, that God would enable me to grow in grace every day! Alas! my barrenness is such, that God might well say, Cut it down. I am afraid of a dead heart on the Sabbath now begun. [In America, they begin to keep the Lord's Day from six o'clock on Saturday evening.— Note in 1817 edition.] Oh, that God would quicken me by His grace!

Lord's Day, April 18. I retired early this morning into the woods for prayer; had the assistance of God's Spirit and faith in exercise. Was enabled to plead with fervency for the advancement of Christ's kingdom in the world and to intercede for dear absent friends. At noon, God enabled me to wrestle with Him and to feel, as I trust, the power of divine love in prayer. At night I saw myself infinitely indebted to God, and had a view of my shortcomings. It seemed to me that I had done as it were nothing for God, and that I never had lived to Him but a few hours of my life.

Monday, April 19. I set apart this day for fasting and prayer to God for His grace; especially to prepare me for the work of the ministry, to give me divine aid and direction in my preparations for that great work, and in His own time to send me into His harvest. Accordingly, in the morning, I endeavored to plead for the divine presence for the day, and not without some life. In the forenoon, I felt the power of intercession for precious, immortal souls; for the advancement of the kingdom of my dear Lord and Saviour in the world; and withal, a most sweet resignation and even consolation and joy in the thoughts of suffering hardships, distresses, and even death itself, in the promotion of it. Had special enlargement in pleading for the enlightening and conversion of the poor heathen.

In the afternoon, God was with me of a truth. Oh, it was blessed company indeed! God enabled me so to agonize in prayer that I was quite wet with perspiration, though in the shade and the cool wind. My soul was drawn out very much for the world, for multitudes of souls. I think I had more enlargement for sinners than for the children of God, though I felt as if I could spend my life in cries for both. I enjoyed great sweetness in communion with my dear Saviour. I think I never in my life felt such an entire weanedness from this world and so much resigned to God in everything. Oh, that I may always live to and upon my blessed God! Amen, amen.

Tuesday, April 20. This day I am twenty-four years of age. Oh, how much mercy have I received the year past! How often has God caused His goodness to pass before me! And how poorly have I answered the vows I made this time twelve month to be wholly the Lord's, to be forever devoted to His service! The Lord help me to live more to His glory for the time to come. This has been a sweet, a happy day to me; blessed be God. I think my soul was never so drawn out in intercession for others as it has been this night. Had a most fervent wrestle with the Lord tonight for my enemies. I hardly ever so longed to live to God and to be altogether devoted to Him. I wanted to wear out my life in His service, and for His glory.

Wednesday, April 21. Felt much calmness and resignation, and God again enabled me to wrestle for numbers of souls, and had much fervency in the sweet duty of intercession. I enjoyed of late more sweetness in intercession for others than in any other part of prayer. My blessed Lord really let me come near to Him and plead with Him.

Lord's Day, April 25. This morning I spent about two hours in secret duties and was enabled more than ordinarily to agonize for immortal souls. Though it was early in the morning and the sun scarcely shined at all, yet my body was quite wet with sweat. I felt much pressed now, as frequently of late, to plead for the meekness and calmness of the Lamb of God in my soul; and through divine goodness felt much of it this morning. Oh, it is a sweet disposition heartily to forgive all injuries done us; to wish our greatest enemies as well as we do our own souls! Blessed Jesus, may I daily be more and more conformed to Thee.

At night I was exceedingly melted with divine love and had some feeling sense of the blessedness of the upper world. Those words hung upon me with much divine sweetness, Psalm 84:7: "They go from strength to strength, every one of them in Zion appeareth before God." Oh, the near access that God sometimes gives us in our addresses to Him! This may well be termed appearing before God: it is so indeed, in the true spiritual sense, and in the sweetest sense. I think I have not had such power of intercession these many months, both for God's children and for dead sinners as I have had this evening. I wished and longed for the coming of my dear Lord: I longed to join the angelic hosts in praises, wholly free from imperfection. Oh, the blessed moment hastens! All I want is to be more holy, more like my dear Lord. Oh, for sanctification! My very soul pants for the complete restoration of the blessed image of my Saviour, that I may be fit for the blessed enjoyments and employments of the heavenly world.

> Farewell, vain world; my soul can bid Adieu:
> My Saviour's taught me to abandon you.
> Your charms may gratify a sensual mind;
> Not please a soul wholly for God design'd.
> Forbear to entice, cease then my soul to call:
> 'Tis fix'd through grace; my God shall be my ALL.
> While He thus lets me heavenly glories view,
> Your beauties fade, my heart's no room for you.

The Lord refreshed my soul with many sweet passages of His Word. Oh, the new Jerusalem! my soul longed for it. Oh, the song of Moses and the Lamb! And that blessed song that no man can learn but they who are redeemed from the earth! and the glorious white robes that were given to the souls under the altar!

> Lord, I'm a stranger here alone;
> Earth no true comforts can afford:
> Yet, absent from my dearest one,
> My soul delights to cry, My Lord!

Jesus, my Lord, my only love,
Possess my soul, nor thence depart:
Grant me kind visits, heavenly Dove;
My God shall then have all My heart.

Monday, April 26. Continued in a sweet frame of mind, but in the afternoon felt something of spiritual pride stirring. God was pleased to make it a humbling season at first, though afterwards He gave me sweetness. Oh, my soul exceedingly longs for that blessed state of perfect deliverance from all sin! At night, God enabled me to give my soul up to Him, to cast myself upon Him, to be ordered and disposed of according to His sovereign pleasure; and I enjoyed great peace and consolation in so doing. My soul took sweet delight in God; my thoughts freely and sweetly centered in Him. Oh, that I could spend every moment of my life to His glory!

Tuesday, April 27. I retired pretty early for secret devotions; and in prayer God was pleased to pour such ineffable comforts into my soul that I could do nothing for some time but say over and over, "O my sweet Saviour! O my sweet Saviour! whom have I in heaven but Thee? and there is none upon earth, that I desire beside Thee." If I had had a thousand lives my soul would gladly have laid them all down at once to have been with Christ. My soul never enjoyed so much of heaven before. It was the most refined and most spiritual season of communion with God I ever yet felt. I never felt so great a degree of resignation in my life.

In the afternoon I withdrew to meet with my God; but found myself much declined, and God made it a humbling season to my soul. I mourned over the body of death that is in me. It grieved me exceedingly that I could not pray to and praise God with my heart full of divine heavenly love. Oh, that my soul might never offer any dead, cold services to my God! In the evening had not so much divine love as in the morning; but had a sweet season of fervent intercession.

Wednesday, April 28. I withdrew to my usual place of retirement in great peace and tranquillity; spent about two hours in secret duties and felt much as I did yesterday morning, only weaker and more overcome. I seemed to depend wholly on my dear Lord, wholly weaned from all other dependences. I knew not what to say to my God, but only lean on His bosom, as it were, and breathe out my desires after a perfect conformity to Him in all things. Thirsting desires and insatiable longings possessed my soul after perfect holiness. God was so precious to my soul that the world with all its enjoyments was infinitely vile. I had no more value for the favor of men than for pebbles. The Lord was my ALL; and that He overruled all greatly delighted me. I think my faith and dependence on God scarce ever rose so high. I saw Him such a fountain of goodness that it seemed impossible I should distrust Him again, or be any way anxious about anything that should happen to me.

I now enjoyed great sweetness in praying for absent friends, and for the enlargement of Christ's kingdom in the world. Much of the power of these divine enjoyments remained with me through the day. In the evening my heart seemed to melt, and, I trust, was really humbled for indwelling corruption, and I mourned like a dove. I felt that all my unhappiness arose from my being a sinner. With resignation I could bid welcome to all other trials. But sin hung heavy upon me, for God discovered to me the corruption of my heart. I went to bed with a heavy heart because I was a sinner; though I did not in the least doubt of God's love. Oh, that God would purge away my dross, and take away my tin, and refine me seven times.

Thursday, April 29. I was kept off at a distance from God, but had some enlargement in intercession for precious souls.

Friday, April 30. I was somewhat dejected in spirit. Nothing grieves me so much as that I cannot live constantly to God's glory. I could bear any desertion or spiritual conflicts, if I could but have my heart all the while burning within me with love to God and desires of His glory. But this is impossible; for when I feel these, I cannot be dejected in my soul, but only rejoice in my Saviour who has delivered me from the reigning power, and will shortly deliver me from the indwelling of sin.

Saturday, May 1. I was enabled to cry to God with fervency for ministerial qualifications, that He would appear for the advancement of His own kingdom, and that He would bring in the heathen. Had much assistance in my studies. This has been a profitable week to me. I have enjoyed many communications of the blessed Spirit in my soul.

Lord's Day, May 2. God was pleased this morning to give me such a sight of myself as made me appear very vile in my own eyes. I felt corruption stirring in my heart, which I could by no means suppress. Felt more and more deserted; was exceeding weak, and almost sick with my inward trials.

Monday, May 3. Had a sense of vile ingratitude. In the morning I withdrew to my usual place of retirement and mourned for my abuse of my dear Lord; spent the day in fasting and prayer. God gave me much power of wrestling for His cause and kingdom, and it was a happy day to my soul. God was with me all the day and I was more above the world than ever in my life.

Lord's Day, May 9. I think I never felt so much of the cursed pride of my heart, as well as the stubbornness of my will before. Oh, dreadful! what a vile wretch I am! I could not submit to be nothing and to lie down in the dust. Oh, that God would humble me in the dust! I felt myself such a sinner all day that I had scarce any comfort. Oh, when shall I be delivered from the body of this death? I greatly feared lest through stupidity and carelessness I should lose the benefit of these trials. Oh, that they might be sanctified to my soul! Nothing seemed to touch me but only this, that I was a sinner. Had fervency and refreshment in social prayer in the evening.

Monday, May 10. I rode to New Haven and saw some Christian friends there. Had comfort in joining in prayer with them and hearing of the goodness of God to them since I last saw them.

Tuesday, May 11. I rode from New Haven to Weathersfield; was very dull most of the day; had little spirituality in this journey, though I often longed to be alone with God.

Was much perplexed with vile thoughts and was sometimes afraid of everything, but God was my helper. Caught a little time for retirement in the evening, to my comfort and rejoicing. Alas! I cannot live in the midst of a tumult. I long to enjoy God alone.

Wednesday, May 12. I had a distressing view of the pride, enmity, and vileness of my heart. Afterwards had sweet refreshment in conversing and worshiping God with friends.

Thursday, May 13. Saw so much of the wickedness of my heart that I longed to get away from myself. I never before thought there was so much spiritual pride in my soul. I felt almost pressed to death with my own vileness. Oh, what a body of death is there in me! Lord, deliver my soul. I could not find any convenient place for retirement, and was greatly exercised. Rode to Hartford in the afternoon. Had some refreshment and comfort in religious exercises with Christian friends, but longed for more retirement. Oh, the closest walk with God is the sweetest heaven that can be enjoyed on earth!

Friday, May 14. I waited on a council of ministers convened at Hartford, and spread before them the treatment I had met with from the rector and tutors of Yale College. They thought it advisable to intercede for me with the rector and trustees and to intreat them to restore me to my former privileges in college. [The application which was then made on his behalf, had not the desired success.—1817 edition.] After this, spent some time in religious exercises with Christian friends.

Saturday, May 15. I rode from Hartford to Hebron; was somewhat dejected on the road. Appeared exceeding vile in my own eyes, saw much pride and stubbornness in my heart. Indeed, I never saw such a week as this before; for I have been almost ready to die with the view of the wickedness of my heart. I could not have thought I had such a body of death in me. Oh, that God would deliver my soul!

Wednesday, May 19. (At Millington) I was so amazingly deserted this morning that I seemed to feel a sort of horror in my soul. Alas! when God withdraws, what is there that can afford any comfort to the soul!

Through the eight days next following, he expresses more calmness and comfort, and considerable life, fervency, and sweetness in religion.—J. E.

Friday, May 28. (At New Haven) I think I scarce ever felt so calm in my life; I rejoiced in resignation and giving myself up to God, to be wholly and entirely devoted to Him forever.

Tuesday, June 1. Had much of the presence of God in family prayer, and had some comfort in secret. I was greatly refreshed from the Word of God this morning, which appeared exceeding sweet to me. Some things that appeared mysterious were opened to me. Oh, that the kingdom of the dear Saviour might come with power, and the healing waters of the sanctuary spread far and wide for the healing of the nations! Came to Ripton but was very weak. However, being visited by a number of young people in the evening, I prayed with them.

Lord's Day, June 6. I feel much deserted; but all this teaches me my nothingness and vileness more than ever.

Monday, June 7. Felt still powerless in secret prayer. Afterwards I prayed and conversed with some little life. God feeds me with crumbs; blessed be His name for anything. I felt a great desire that all God's people might know how mean and little and vile I am; that they might see I am nothing that so they may pray for me aright, and not have the least dependence upon me.

Tuesday, June 8. I enjoyed one sweet and precious season this day. I never felt it so sweet to be nothing, and less than nothing, and to be accounted nothing.

Saturday, June 12. Spent much time in prayer this morning, and enjoyed much sweetness. Felt insatiable longings after God much of the day. I wondered how poor souls do to live that have no God. The world with all its enjoyments quite vanished. I see myself very helpless, but I have a blessed God to go to. I longed exceedingly to be dissolved and to be with Christ, to behold His glory. Oh, my weak, weary soul longs to arrive at my Father's house!

Lord's Day, June 13. Felt something calm and resigned in the public worship; at the sacrament saw myself very vile and worthless. Oh, that I may always lie low in the dust! My soul seemed steadily to go forth after God, in longing desires to live upon Him.

Monday, June 14. Felt something of the sweetness of communion with God and the constraining force of His love. How admirably it captivates the soul and makes all the desires and affections to center in God! I set apart this day for secret fasting and prayer, to intreat God to direct and bless me with regard to the great work I have in view, of preaching the gospel; and that the Lord would return to me, and show me the light of His countenance. Had little life and power in the forenoon. Near the middle of the afternoon, God enabled me to wrestle ardently in intercession for absent friends. But just at night, the Lord visited me marvelously in prayer; I think my soul never was in such an agony before. I felt no restraint, for the treasures of divine grace were opened to me. I wrestled for absent friends, for the ingathering of souls, for multitudes of poor souls, and for many that I thought were the children of God, personally, in many distant places. I was in such an agony, from sun half an hour high till near dark, that I was all over wet with sweat. Yet it seemed to me that I had wasted away the day and had done nothing. Oh, my dear Jesus did sweat blood for poor souls! I longed for more compassion towards them. Felt still in a sweet frame, under a sense of divine love and grace; and went to bed in such a frame, with my heart set on God.

Tuesday, June 15. Had the most ardent longings after God that ever I felt in my life. At noon in my secret retirement I could do nothing but tell my Lord, in a sweet calm, that He knew I longed for nothing but Himself, nothing but holiness; that He had given me these desires and He only could give me the thing desired. I never seemed to be so unhinged from myself and to be so wholly devoted to God. My heart was swallowed up in God most of the day.

In the evening I had such a view of the soul being as it were enlarged, to contain more holiness, that it seemed ready to separate from my body. I then wrestled in an agony for divine blessings; had my heart drawn out in prayer for some Christian friends, beyond what I ever had before. I feel differently now from whatever I did under any enjoyments before; more engaged to live to God forever, and less pleased with my own frames. I am not satisfied with my frames, nor feel at all more easy after such strugglings than before; for it seems far too little, if I could always be so. Oh, how short do I fall of my duty in my sweetest moments!

Friday, June 18. Considering my great unfitness for the work of the ministry, my present deadness, and total inability to do anything for the glory of God that way, feeling myself very helpless and at a great loss what the Lord would have me to do; I set apart this day for prayer to God and spent most of the day in that duty, but amazingly deserted most of the day. Yet I found God graciously near, once in particular. While I was pleading for more compassion for immortal souls, my heart seemed to be opened at once and I was enabled to cry with great ardency for a few minutes. Oh, I was distressed to think that I should offer such dead, cold services to the living God! My soul seemed to breathe after holiness, a life of constant devotedness to God. But I am almost lost sometimes in the pursuit of this blessedness, and ready to sink, because I continually fall short and miss of my desire. Oh, that the Lord would help me to hold out, yet a little while, till the happy hour of deliverance comes!

Saturday, June 19. Felt much disordered; my spirits were very low, but yet enjoyed some freedom and sweetness in the duties of religion. Blessed be God.

Lord's Day, June 20. Spent much time alone. My soul longed to be holy, and reached after God; but seemed not to obtain my desire. I hungered and thirsted, but was not refreshed and satisfied. My soul hung on God as my only portion. Oh, that I could grow in grace more every day!

Tuesday, June 22. In the morning, spent about two hours in prayer and meditation, with considerable delight. Towards night, felt my soul go out in longing desires after God, in secret retirement. In the evening, was sweetly composed and resigned to God's will; was enabled to leave myself and all my concerns with Him, and to have my whole dependence upon Him. My secret retirement was very refreshing to my soul. It appeared such a happiness to have God for my portion that I had rather be any other creature in this lower creation than not come to the enjoyment of God. I had rather be a beast, than a man, without God, if I were to live here to eternity. Lord, endear Thyself more to me!

Wednesday, June 30. Spent this day alone in the woods, in fasting and prayer; underwent the most dreadful conflicts in my soul that ever I felt, in some respects. I saw myself so vile that I was ready to say, "I shall now perish by the hand of Saul." I thought, and almost concluded, I had no power to stand for the cause of God, but was almost "afraid of the shaking of a leaf." Spent almost the whole day in prayer, incessantly. I could not bear to think of Christians showing me any respect. I almost despaired of doing any service in the world. I could not feel any hope or comfort respecting the heathen, which used to afford me refreshment in the darkest hours of this nature. I spent the day in bitterness of my soul. Near night, I felt a little better; and afterwards enjoyed some sweetness in secret prayer.

Thursday, July 1. Had some sweetness in prayer this morning. Felt exceeding sweetly in secret prayer tonight, and desired nothing so ardently as that God should do with me just as He pleased.

Friday, July 2. Felt composed in secret prayer in the morning. My desires ascended to God this day, as I was traveling, and was comfortable in the evening. Blessed be God for all my consolations.

Saturday, July 3. My heart seemed again to sink. The disgrace I was laid under at college seemed to damp me, as it opens the mouths of opposers. I had no refuge but in God. Blessed be His name that I may go to Him at all times and find Him a present help.

Lord's Day, July 4. Had considerable assistance. In the evening I withdrew and enjoyed a happy season in secret prayer. God was pleased to give me the exercise of faith, and thereby brought the invisible and eternal world near to my soul, which appeared sweetly to me. I hoped that my weary pilgrimage in the world would be short, and that it would not be long before I was brought to my heavenly home and Father's house. I was resigned to God's will, to tarry His time, to do His work, and suffer His pleasure. I felt thankfulness to God for all my pressing desertions of late; for I am persuaded they have been made a means of making me more humble and much more resigned. I felt pleased to be little, to be nothing, and to lie in the dust. I enjoyed life and consolation in pleading for the dear children of God, and the kingdom of Christ in the world; and my soul earnestly breathed after holiness, and the enjoyment of God. Oh, come, Lord Jesus, come quickly.

Lord's Day, July 11. Was deserted, and exceedingly dejected in the morning. In the afternoon, had some life and assistance, and felt resigned. I saw myself exceeding vile.

Wednesday, July 14. Felt a kind of humble resigned sweetness. Spent a considerable time in secret, giving myself up wholly to the Lord. Heard Mr. Bellamy preach towards night; felt very sweetly part of the time; longed for nearer access to God.

Monday, July 19. My desires seem especially to be carried out after weanedness from the world, perfect deadness to it, and to be even crucified to all its allurements. My soul longs to feel itself more of a pilgrim and stranger here below; that nothing may divert me from pressing through the lonely desert, till I arrive at my Father's house.

Tuesday, July 20. It was sweet to give away myself to God, to be disposed of at His pleasure; and had some feeling sense of the sweetness of being a pilgrim on earth.

Thursday, July 22. Journeying from Southbury to Ripton, I called at a house by the way; where being very kindly entertained and refreshed, I was filled with amazement and shame that God should stir up the hearts of any to show so much kindness to such a dead dog as I. Was made sensible, in some measure, how exceeding vile it is not to be wholly devoted to God. I wondered that God would suffer any of His creatures to feed and sustain me from time to time.

Thursday, July 29. I was examined by the Association [The Association of Ministers of the Eastern District of Fairfield County, Conn.] met at Danbury, as to my learning and also my experiences in religion, and received a license from them to preach the gospel of Christ. Afterwards felt much devoted to God; joined in prayer with one of the ministers, my peculiar friend, in a convenient place; went to bed resolving to live devoted to God all my days.

# PART III

FROM THE TIME OF HIS BEING LICENSED TO PREACH TILL HE
WAS APPOINTED AS MISSIONARY TO THE INDIANS

*July–November, 1742*

FRIDAY, July 30, 1742. Rode from Danbury to South-bury; preached there from I Peter 4:8, "And above all things have fervent charity." Had much of the comfortable presence of God in the exercise. I seemed to have power with God in prayer and power to get hold of the hearts of the people in preaching.

Saturday, July 31. Exceeding calm and composed, and was greatly refreshed and encouraged.

Lord's Day, August 8. In the morning I felt comfortably in secret prayer. My soul was refreshed with the hopes of the heathen coming home to Christ; was much resigned to God, and thought it was no matter what became of me. Preached both parts of the day at Bethlehem, from Job 14:14, "If a man die, shall he live again?" It was sweet to me to meditate on death. In the evening, felt very comfortably, and cried to God fervently in secret prayer.

Thursday, August 12. This morning and last night I was exercised with sore inward trials. I had no power to pray, but seemed shut out from God. I had in a great measure lost my hopes of God sending me among the heathen afar off, and of seeing them flock home to Christ. I saw so much of my hellish vileness that I appeared worse to myself than any devil. I wondered that God would let me live and wondered that people did not stone me, much more that they would ever hear me preach!

It seemed as though I never could nor should preach any more; yet about nine or ten o'clock the people came over, and I was forced to preach. And blessed be God, He gave me His presence and Spirit in prayer and preaching so that I was much assisted, and spake with power from Job 14:14. Some Indians cried out in great distress and all appeared greatly concerned. [It was in a place near Kent, in the western borders of Connecticut, where there are a number of Indians.—J. E.] After we had prayed and exhorted them to seek the Lord with constancy and hired an English woman to keep a kind of school among them, we came away about one o'clock and came to Judea, about fifteen or sixteen miles. There God was pleased to visit my soul with much comfort. Blessed be the Lord for all things I meet with.

Lord's Day, August 15. Felt much comfort and devotedness to God this day. At night, it was refreshing to get alone with God and pour out my soul. Oh, who can conceive of the sweetness of communion with the blessed God, but those who have experience of it! Glory to God forever, that I may taste heaven below.

Monday, August 16. Had some comfort in secret prayer in the morning. Felt sweetly sundry times in prayer this day, but was perplexed in the evening with vain conversation.

Tuesday, August 17. Exceedingly depressed in spirit; it cuts and wounds my heart to think how much self-exaltation, spiritual pride, and warmth of temper, I have formerly had intermingled with my endeavors to promote God's work. Sometimes I long to lie down at the feet of opposers and confess what a poor imperfect creature I have been, and still am. Oh, the Lord forgive me and make me for the future wise as a serpent, and harmless as a dove! Afterwards enjoyed considerable comfort and delight of soul.

Wednesday, August 18. Spent most of this day in prayer and reading. I see so much of my own extreme vileness that I feel ashamed and guilty before God and man; I look to myself like the vilest fellow in the land. I wonder that God stirs up His people to be so kind to me.

Thursday, August 19. This day, being about to go from Mr. Bellamy's at Bethlehem, where I had resided some time, I prayed with him and two or three other Christian friends. We gave ourselves to God with all our hearts, to be His forever; eternity looked very near to me while I was praying. If I never should see these Christians again in this world, it seemed but a few moments before I should meet them in another world.

Friday, August 20. I appeared so vile to myself that I hardly dared to think of being seen especially on account of spiritual pride. However, tonight I enjoyed a sweet hour alone with God (at Ripton); I was lifted above the frowns and flatteries of this lower world, had a sweet relish of heavenly joys, and my soul did as it were get into the eternal world and really taste of heaven. I had a sweet season of intercession for dear friends in Christ, and God helped me to cry fervently for Zion. Blessed be God for this season.

Saturday, August 21. Was much perplexed in the morning. Towards noon enjoyed more of God in secret and was enabled to see that it was best to throw myself into the hands of God, to be disposed of according to His pleasure, and rejoiced in such thoughts. In the afternoon, rode to New Haven; was much confused all the way. Just at night, underwent such a dreadful conflict as I have scarce ever felt. I saw myself exceeding vile and unworthy; so that I was guilty, and ashamed that anybody should bestow any favor on me or show me any respect.

Lord's Day, August 22. In the morning, continued still in perplexity. In the evening, enjoyed that comfort that seemed to me sufficient to overbalance all my late distresses. I saw that God is the only soul-satisfying portion, and I really found satisfaction in Him. My soul was much enlarged in sweet intercession for my fellow men everywhere, and for many Christian friends in particular, in distant places.

Monday, August 23. Had a sweet season in secret prayer; the Lord drew near to my soul and filled me with peace and divine consolation. Oh, my soul tasted the sweetness of the upper world and was drawn out in prayer for the world that it might come home to Christ! Had much comfort in the thoughts and hopes of the ingathering of the heathen; was greatly assisted in intercession for Christian friends.

Wednesday, August 25. In family prayer, God helped me to climb up near Him, so that I scarce ever got nearer.

Monday, August 30. Felt something comfortably in the morning; conversed sweetly with some friends; was in a serious composed frame and prayed at a certain house with some degree of sweetness. Afterwards, at another house, prayed privately with a dear Christian friend or two; and, I think, I scarce ever launched so far into the eternal world, as then. I got so far out on the broad ocean that my soul with joy triumphed over all the evils on the shores of mortality. I think, time and all its gay amusements and cruel disappointments never appeared so inconsiderable to me before. I was in a sweet frame; I saw myself nothing, and my soul reached after God with intense desire.

Oh, I saw what I owed to God in such a manner as I scarce ever did; I knew, I had never lived a moment to Him, as I should do. Indeed, it appeared to me I had never done anything in Christianity. My soul longed with a vehement desire to live to God. In the evening, sang and prayed with a number of Christians; felt the powers of the world to come in my soul, in prayer. Afterwards prayed again privately with a dear Christian or two, and found the presence of God; was something humbled in my secret retirement; felt my ingratitude because I was not wholly swallowed up in God.

Wednesday, September 1. Went to Judea to the ordination of Mr. Judd. Dear Mr. Bellamy preached from Matthew 24:46, "Blessed is that servant . . ." I felt very solemn most of the time; had my thoughts much on that time when our Lord will come. That time refreshed my soul much; only I was afraid I should not be found faithful, because I have so vile a heart. My thoughts were much in eternity, where I love to dwell. Blessed be God for this solemn season. Rode home tonight with Mr. Bellamy, conversed with some friends till it was very late, and then retired to rest in a comfortable frame.

Thursday, September 2. About two in the afternoon, I preached from John 6:67: "Then said Jesus unto the twelve, Will ye also go away?" and God assisted me in some comfortable degree but more especially in my first prayer. My soul seemed then to launch quite into the eternal world and to be as it were separated from this lower world. Afterwards preached again from Isaiah 5:4, "What could have been done more." God gave me some assistance, but I saw myself a poor worm.

Saturday, September 4. Much out of health, exceedingly depressed in my soul, and at an awful distance from God. Towards night, spent some time in profitable thoughts on Romans 8:2, "For the law of the spirit of life . . ." Near night, had a very sweet season in prayer. God enabled me to wrestle ardently for the advancement of the Redeemer's kingdom; pleaded earnestly for my own dear brother John, that God would make him more of a pilgrim and stranger on the earth, and fit him for singular serviceableness in the world. My heart sweetly exulted in the Lord, in the thoughts of any distresses that might alight on him or me, in the advancement of Christ's kingdom. It was a sweet and comfortable hour unto my soul, while I was indulged with freedom to plead, not only for myself, but also for many other souls.

Lord's Day, September 5. Preached all day; was somewhat strengthened and assisted in the afternoon, more especially in the evening. Had a sense of my unspeakable shortcomings in all my duties. I found, alas! that I had never lived to God in my life.

Monday, September 6. Was informed that they only waited for an opportunity to apprehend me for preaching at New Haven lately, that so they might imprison me. This made me more solemn and serious, and to quit all hopes of the world's friendship. It brought me to a further sense of my vileness and just desert of this, and much more, from the hand of God, though not from the hand of man. Retired into a convenient place in the woods and spread the matter before God.

Tuesday, September 7. Had some relish of divine things in the morning. Afterwards felt more barren and melancholy. Rode to New Haven to a friend's house at a distance from the town, that I might remain undiscovered and yet have opportunity to do business privately with friends which come to commencement.

Wednesday, September 8. Felt very sweetly when I first rose in the morning. In family prayer, had some enlargement but not much spirituality, till eternity came up before me and looked near. I found some sweetness in the thoughts of bidding a dying farewell to this tiresome world. Though some time ago I reckoned upon seeing my dear friends at commencement, yet being now denied the opportunity for fear of imprisonment, I felt totally resigned and as contented to spend this day alone in the woods, as I could have done if I had been allowed to go to town. Felt exceedingly weaned from the world today.

In the afternoon I discoursed on divine things with a dear Christian friend, whereby we were both refreshed. Then I prayed, with a sweet sense of the blessedness of communion with God. I think I scarce ever enjoyed more of God in any one prayer. Oh, it was a blessed season indeed to my soul! I knew not that ever I saw so much of my own nothingness in my life; never wondered so that God allowed me to preach His Word. This has been a sweet and comfortable day to my soul. Blessed be God. Prayed again with my dear friend, with something of the divine presence. I long to be wholly conformed to God and transformed into His image.

Thursday, September 9. Spent much of the day alone; enjoyed the presence of God in some comfortable degree; was visited by some dear friends, and prayed with them. Wrote sundry letters to friends; felt religion in my soul while writing; enjoyed sweet meditations on some scriptures. In the evening, went very privately into town, from the place of my residence at the farms, and conversed with some dear friends; felt sweetly in singing hymns with them. Made my escape to the farms again without being discovered by any enemies, as I knew of. Thus the Lord preserves me continually.

Friday, September 10. Longed with intense desire after God; my whole soul seemed impatient to be conformed to Him and to become "holy, as he is holy." In the afternoon, prayed with a dear friend privately, and had the presence of God with us. Our souls united together to reach after a blessed immortality, to be unclothed of the body of sin and death and to enter the blessed world where no unclean thing enters. Oh, with what intense desire did our souls long for that blessed day, that we might be freed from sin and forever live to and in our God! In the evening, took leave of that house, but first kneeled down and prayed. The Lord was of a truth in the midst of us; it was a sweet parting season. Felt in myself much sweetness and affection in the things of God. Blessed be God for every such divine gale of His Spirit, to speed me on in my way to the new Jerusalem! Felt some sweetness afterwards, and spent the evening in conversation with friends, and prayed with some life, and retired to rest very late.

Thursday, September 16. At night enjoyed much of God in secret prayer; felt an uncommon resignation to be and do what God pleased. Some days past, I felt great perplexity on account of my past conduct. My bitterness and want of Christian kindness and love has been very distressing to my soul. The Lord forgive me my unchristian warmth and want of a spirit of meekness!

Saturday, September 18. Felt some compassion for souls and mourned I had no more. I feel much more kindness, meekness, gentleness, and love towards all mankind, than ever. I long to be at the feet of my enemies and persecutors; enjoyed some sweetness in feeling my soul conformed to Christ Jesus, and given away to Him forever.

Thursday, September 30. Still very low in spirits; I did not know how to engage in any work or business, especially to correct some disorders among Christians; felt as though I had no power to be faithful in that regard. However, towards noon, I preached from Deuteronomy 8:2, "And thou shalt remember . . ." and was enabled with freedom to reprove some things in Christians' conduct, that I thought very unsuitable and irregular; insisted near two hours on this subject.

Lord's Day, October 17. Had a considerable sense of my helplessness and inability; saw that I must be dependent on God for all I want, and especially when I went to the place of public worship. I found I could not speak a word for God without His special help and assistance. I went into the assembly, trembling, as I frequently do, under a sense of my insufficiency to do anything in the cause of God as I ought to do. But it pleased God to afford me much assistance, and there seemed to be a considerable effect on the hearers. In the evening, I felt a disposition to praise God for His goodness to me, that He had enabled me in some measure to be faithful. My soul rejoiced to think that I had thus performed the work of one day more, and was one day nearer my eternal and, I trust, my heavenly home. Oh, that I might be "faithful to the death, fulfilling as an hireling my day," till the shades of the evening of life shall free my soul from the toils of the day!

This evening in secret prayer I felt exceeding solemn, and such longing desires after deliverance from sin and after conformity to God as melted my heart. Oh, I longed to be "delivered from this body of death"! I felt inward pleasing pain that I could not be conformed to God entirely, fully, and forever. I scarce ever preach without being first visited with inward conflicts and sore trials. Blessed be the Lord for these trials and distresses as they are blessed for my humbling.

Monday, October 18. In the morning, I felt some sweetness but still pressed through trials of soul. My life is a constant mixture of consolations and conflicts, and will be so till I arrive at the world of spirits.

Tuesday, October 19. This morning and last night, I felt

a sweet longing in my soul after holiness. My soul seemed so to reach and stretch towards the mark of perfect sanctity that it was ready to break with longings.

Wednesday, October 20. Exceeding infirm in body, exercised with much pain, and very lifeless in divine things. Felt a little sweetness in the evening.

Thursday, October 21. Had a very deep sense of the vanity of the world, most of the day. Had little more regard to it than if I had been to go into eternity the next hour. Through divine goodness, I felt very serious and solemn. Oh, I love to live on the brink of eternity, in my views and meditations! This gives me a sweet, awful, and reverential sense and apprehension of God and divine things, when I see myself as it were standing before the judgment seat of Christ.

Friday, October 22. Uncommonly weaned from the world today; my soul delighted to be a stranger and pilgrim on the earth; I felt a disposition in me never to have anything to do with this world. The character given of some of the ancient people of God, in Hebrews 11:13, was very pleasing to me: they "confessed that they were pilgrims and strangers on the earth," by their daily practice; and oh, that I could always do so! Spent some considerable time in a pleasant grove, in prayer and meditation. Oh, it is sweet to be thus weaned from friends and from myself, and dead to the present world, that so I may live wholly to and upon the blessed God! Saw myself little, low, and vile in myself.

In the afternoon, preached at Bethlehem, from Deuteronomy 8:2. God helped me to speak to the hearts of dear Christians. Blessed be the Lord for this season; I trust they and I shall rejoice on this account to all eternity. Dear Mr. Bellamy came in while I was making the first prayer (being returned home from a journey). After meeting, we walked away together and spent the evening in sweetly conversing on divine things, and praying together, with sweet and tender love to each other, and returned to rest with our hearts in a serious spiritual frame.

Saturday, October 23. Somewhat perplexed and confused

Rode this day from Bethlehem to Simsbury to see friends.

Lord's Day, October 24. Felt so vile and unworthy that I scarce knew how to converse with human creatures.

Monday, October 25. (At Turkey Hills) In the evening I enjoyed the divine presence in secret prayer. It was a sweet and comfortable season to me; my soul longed for God, for the living God; enjoyed a sweet solemnity of spirit, and longing desire after the recovery of the divine image in my soul. "Then shall I be satisfied, when I shall awake in God's likeness," and never before.

Tuesday, October 26. (At West Suffield) Underwent the most dreadful distresses, under a sense of my own unworthiness. It seemed to me I deserved rather to be driven out of the place than to have anybody treat me with any kindness, or come to hear me preach. Verily my spirits were so depressed at this time (as at many others) that it was impossible I should treat immortal souls with faithfulness. I could not deal closely and faithfully with them, I felt so infinitely vile in myself. Oh, what dust and ashes I am, to think of preaching the gospel to others! Indeed I never can be faithful for one moment, but shall certainly "daub with untempered mortar" if God do not grant me special help. In the evening I went to the meetinghouse, and it looked to me near as easy for one to rise out of the grave and preach, as for me. However, God afforded me some life and power, both in prayer and sermon, and was pleased to lift me up and show me that He could enable me to preach! Oh, the wonderful goodness of God to so vile a sinner! Returned to my quarters and enjoyed some sweetness in prayer alone, and mourned that I could not live more to God.

Wednesday, October 27. I spent the forenoon in prayer and meditation; was not a little concerned about preaching in the afternoon. Felt exceedingly without strength, and very helpless indeed; and went into the meetinghouse, ashamed to see any come to hear such an unspeakably worthless wretch. However, God enabled me to speak with clearness, power, and pungency. But there was some noise and tumult in the assembly, that I did not well like. I endeavored to bear public testimony against it with moderation and mildness, through the current of my discourse. In the evening, was enabled to be in some measure thankful and devoted to God.

Thursday, November 4. (At Lebanon) Saw much of my nothingness most of this day, but felt concerned that I had no more sense of my insufficiency and unworthiness. Oh, it is sweet lying in the dust! But it is distressing to feel in my soul that hell of corruption which still remains in me. In the afternoon, had a sense of the sweetness of a strict, close, and constant devotedness to God, and my soul was comforted with His consolations. My soul felt a pleasing, yet painful concern, lest I should spend some moments without God. Oh, may I always live to God! In the evening, I was visited by some friends and spent the time in prayer and such conversation as tended to our edification. It was a comfortable season to my soul; I felt an intense desire to spend every moment for God.

God is unspeakably gracious to me continually. In times past, He has given me inexpressible sweetness in the performances of duty. Frequently my soul has enjoyed much of God; but has been ready to say, "Lord, it is good to be here," and so to indulge sloth while I have lived on the sweetness of my feelings. But of late, God has been pleased to keep my soul hungry almost continually, so that I have been filled with a kind of pleasing pain. When I really enjoy God, I feel my desires of Him the more insatiable, and my thirstings after holiness the more unquenchable. And the Lord will not allow me to feel as though I were fully supplied and satisfied, but keeps me still reaching forward.

I feel barren and empty, as though I could not live without more of God; I feel ashamed and guilty before Him. Oh! I see that "the law is spiritual, but I am carnal." I do not, I cannot live to God. Oh, for holiness! Oh, for more of God in my soul! Oh, this pleasing pain! It makes my soul press after God; the language of it is, "I shall be satisfied, when I awake, with thy likeness" (Ps. 17:15); but never, never before. Consequently I am engaged to "press towards the mark," day by day. Oh, that I may feel this continual hunger, and not be retarded, but rather animated by every cluster from Canaan to reach forward in the narrow way, for the full enjoyment and possession of the heavenly inheritance! Oh, that I may never loiter in my heavenly journey!

Lord's Day, November 7. (At Millington) It seemed as if such an unholy wretch as I never could arrive at that blessedness, to be "holy, as God is holy." At noon, I longed for sanctification and conformity to God. Oh, that is the ALL, the ALL! The Lord help me to press after God forever.

Monday, November 8. Towards night, enjoyed much sweetness in secret prayer so that my soul longed for an arrival in the heavenly country, the blessed paradise of God. Through divine goodness I have scarce seen the day, for two months, but death has looked so pleasant to me at one time or other of the day that I could have rejoiced the present should be my last, notwithstanding my pressing inward trials and conflicts. I trust the Lord will finally make me a conqueror, and more than a conqueror; and that I shall be able to use that triumphant language, "O death, where is thy sting?" and, "O grave, where is thy victory?"

Friday, November 19. (At New Haven) Received a letter from the Reverend Mr. Pemberton of New York desiring me speedily to go down thither and consult about the Indian affairs in those parts; and to meet certain gentlemen there who were intrusted with those affairs. My mind was instantly seized with concern so I retired with two or three Christian friends and prayed. Indeed it was a sweet time with me. I was enabled to leave myself and all my concerns with God; and taking leave of friends, I rode to Ripton and was comforted in an opportunity to see and converse with dear Mr. Mills.

Wednesday, November 24. Came to New York; felt still much concerned about the importance of my business and put up many earnest requests to God for His help and direction. Was confused with the noise and tumult of the city;

enjoyed but little time alone with God, but my soul longed after Him.

Thursday, November 25. Spent much time in prayer and supplication; was examined by some gentlemen of my Christian experiences and my acquaintance with divinity and some other studies, in order to my improvement in that important affair of gospelizing the heathen. [These gentlemen, who examined Mr. Brainerd, were the correspondents in New York, New Jersey, and Pennsylvania, of the honorable society in Scotland for propagating Christian knowledge; to whom was committed the management of their affairs in those parts, and who were now met at New York.—J.E.] Thus I was made sensible of my great ignorance and unfitness for public service. I had the most abasing thoughts of myself, I think, that ever I had. I thought myself the worst wretch that ever lived; it hurt me and pained my very heart that anybody should show me any respect. Alas! methought, how sadly they are deceived in me! How miserably would they be disappointed if they knew my inside! Oh, my heart! And in this depressed condition I was forced to go and preach to a considerable assembly, before some grave and learned ministers; but felt such a pressure from a sense of my vileness, ignorance, and unfitness to appear in public that I was almost overcome with it. My soul was grieved for the congregation that they should sit there to hear such a dead dog as I preach. I thought myself infinitely indebted to the people and longed that God would reward them with the rewards of His grace. I spent much of the evening alone.

# PART IV

*1742, 1743*

FRIDAY, November 26. Had still a sense of my great vileness, and endeavored as much as I could to keep alone. Oh, what a nothing, what dust and ashes I am! Enjoyed some peace and comfort in spreading my complaints before the God of all grace.

Saturday, November 27. Committed my soul to God with some degree of comfort; left New York about nine in the morning; came away with a distressing sense still of my unspeakable unworthiness. Surely I may well love all my brethren, for none of them all is so vile as I. Whatever they do outwardly, yet it seems to me none is conscious of so much guilt before God. Oh, my leanness, my barrenness, my carnality, and past bitterness, and want of a gospel-temper! These things oppress my soul. Rode from New York, thirty miles, to White Plains, and most of the way continued lifting up my heart to God for mercy and purifying grace; spent the evening much dejected in spirit.

Wednesday, December 1. My soul breathed after God in sweet spiritual and longing desires of conformity to Him. My soul was brought to rest itself and all on His rich grace, and felt strength and encouragement to do or suffer anything that divine providence should allot me. Rode about twenty miles from Stratfield to Newton.

Saturday, December 11. Conversed with a dear friend to whom I had thought of giving a liberal education, and being at the whole charge of it, that he might be fitted for the gospel ministry.[1] I acquainted him with my thoughts in that matter, and so left him to consider it till I should see him again. Then I rode to Bethlehem, came to Mr. Bellamy's lodgings; and spent the evening with him in sweet conversation and prayer. We recommended the concern of sending my friend to college to the God of all grace. Blessed be the Lord for this evening's opportunity together.

Lord's Day, December 12. I felt, in the morning, as if I had little or no power either to pray or preach and felt a distressing need of divine help. I went to meeting trembling, but it pleased God to assist me in prayer and sermon. I think my soul scarce ever penetrated so far into the immaterial world in any one prayer that ever I made, nor were my devotions ever so free from gross conceptions and imaginations framed from beholding material objects. I preached with some sweetness, from Matthew 6:33, "But seek ye first the kingdom of God," and in the afternoon from Romans 15:30, "Now I beseech you, brethren . . ." There was much affection in the assembly. This has been a sweet Sabbath to me; and blessed be God, I have reason to think that my religion is become more spiritual, by means of my later inward conflicts. Amen. May I always be willing that God should use His own methods with me!

Monday, December 13. Joined in prayer with Mr. Bellamy and found sweetness and composure in parting with him, as he went a journey. Enjoyed some sweetness through the day, and just at night rode down to Woodbury.

---

[1] Mr. Brainerd, having now undertaken the business of a missionary to the Indians, and expecting in a little time to leave his native country, to go among the savages into the wilderness, far distant, and spend the remainder of his life among them—and having some estate left him by his father, and thinking he should have no occasion for it among them (though afterwards, as he told me, he found himself mistaken),—set himself to think which way he might spend it most to the glory of God; and no way presenting to his thoughts, wherein he could do more good with it, than by being at the charge of educating some young person for the ministry, who appeared to be of good abilities, and well disposed, he fixed upon the person here spoken of to this end. Accordingly he was soon put to learning; and Mr. Brainerd continued to be at the charge of his education from year to year, so long as he lived, which was till this young man was carried through his third year in college.—J. E.

Tuesday, December 14. Some perplexity hung on my mind.
I was distressed last night and this morning for the interest
of Zion, especially on account of the false appearances of
religion that do but rather breed confusion, especially in some
places. I cried to God for help to enable me to bear testimony
against those things which, instead of promoting, do but
hinder the progress of vital piety. In the afternoon, rode down
to Southbury, and conversed again with my friend about the
important affair of his pursuing the work of the ministry.
He appeared much inclined to devote himself to that work,
if God should succeed his attempts to qualify himself for so
great a work. In the evening I preached from I Thessalonians
4:8, "He therefore that despiseth . . ." and endeavored,
though with tenderness, to undermine false religion. The
Lord gave me some assistance, but I seemed so vile I was
ashamed to be seen when I came out of the meetinghouse.

Wednesday, December 15. Enjoyed something of God today, both in secret and social prayer; but was sensible of
much barrenness and defect in duty, as well as my inability
to help myself for the time to come, or to perform the work
and business I have to do. Afterwards, felt much of the sweetness of religion and the tenderness of the gospel temper. I
found a dear love to all mankind, and was much afraid lest
some motion of anger or resentment should, some time or
other, creep into my heart. Had some comforting soul-refreshing discourse with dear friends, just as we took our leave of
each other; and supposed it might be likely we should not
meet again till we came to the eternal world.[2] I doubt not,
through grace, but that some of us shall have a happy meeting there, and bless God for this season, as well as many
others. Amen.

Thursday. December 16. Rode down to Derby and had some
sweet thoughts on the road; especially on the essence of our

[2] It had been determined by the commissioners, who employed Mr. Brainerd as a
missionary, that he should go as soon as might be, conveniently, to the Indians living
near the Forks of Delaware River in Pennsylvania, and the Indians on Susquehanna
River; which being far off, where also he would be exposed to many hardships and
dangers, was the occasion of his taking leave of his friends in this manner.

salvation by Christ, from those words, "Thou shalt call his name Jesus."

Friday, December 17. Spent much time in sweet conversation on spiritual things with dear Mr. Humphreys. Rode to Ripton; spent some time in prayer with dear Christian friends.

Saturday, December 18. Spent much time in prayer in the woods and seemed raised above the things of the world. My soul was strong in the Lord of hosts but was sensible of great barrenness.

Lord's Day, December 19. At the sacrament of the Lord's Supper, I seemed strong in the Lord; and the world, with all its frowns and flatteries, in a great measure disappeared, so that my soul had nothing to do with them. I felt a disposition to be wholly and forever the Lord's. In the evening, enjoyed something of the divine presence; had a humbling sense of my vileness, barrenness, and sinfulness. Oh, it wounded me to think of the misimprovements of time! God be merciful to me a sinner.

Monday, December 20. Spent this day in prayer, reading, and writing, and enjoyed some assistance, especially in correcting some thoughts on a certain subject; but had a mournful sense of my barrenness.

Tuesday, December 21. Had a sense of my insufficiency for any public work and business, as well as to live to God. I rode over to Derby and preached there. It pleased God to give me very sweet assistance and enlargement and to enable me to speak with a soft, tender power and energy. We had afterwards a comfortable evening in singing and prayer. God enabled me to pray with as much spirituality and sweetness as I have done for some time. My mind seemed to be unclothed of sense and imagination and was in a measure let into the immaterial world of spirits. This day was, I trust, through infinite goodness, made very profitable to a number of us, to advance our souls in holiness and conformity to God; the glory be to Him forever. Amen. *How blessed it is to grow more and more like God!*

Wednesday, December 22. Enjoyed some assistance in

preaching at Ripton, but my soul mourned within me for my barrenness.

Thursday, December 23. Enjoyed, I trust, something of God this morning in secret. Oh, how divinely sweet is it to come into the secret of His presence and abide in His pavilion! Took an affectionate leave of friends, not expecting to see them again for a very considerable time, if ever in this world. Rode with Mr. Humphreys to his house at Derby; spent the time in sweet conversation; my soul was refreshed and sweetly melted with divine things. Oh, that I was always consecrated to God! Near night I rode to New Haven and there enjoyed some sweetness in prayer and conversation with some dear Christian friends. My mind was sweetly serious and composed; but, alas! I too much lost the sense of divine things.

Lord's Day, December 26. Felt much sweetness and tenderness in prayer, especially my whole soul seemed to love my worst enemies, and was enabled to pray for those that are strangers and enemies to God with a great degree of softness and pathetic fervor. In the evening, rode from New Haven to Branford, after I had kneeled down and prayed with a number of dear Christian friends in a very retired place in the woods, and so parted.

Monday, December 27. Enjoyed a precious season indeed; had a sweet melting sense of divine things, of the pure spirituality of the religion of Christ Jesus. In the evening, I preached from Matthew 6:33, "But seek ye first . . . ," with much freedom, and sweet power and pungency; the presence of God attended our meeting. Oh, the sweetness, the tenderness I felt in my soul! If ever I felt the temper of Christ, I had some sense of it now. Blessed be my God, I have seldom enjoyed a more comfortable and profitable day than this. Oh, that I could spend all my time for God!

Tuesday, December 28. Rode from Branford to Haddam. In the morning my clearness and sweetness in divine things continued; but afterwards my spiritual life sensibly declined.

Friday, January 14, 1743. My spiritual conflicts today were unspeakably dreadful, heavier than the mountains and overflowing floods. I seemed inclosed, as it were, in hell itself. I was deprived of all sense of God, even of the being of a God; and that was my misery. I had no awful apprehension of God as angry. This was distress, the nearest akin to the damned's torments that I ever endured. Their torment, I am sure, will consist much in a privation of God, and consequently of all good. This taught me the absolute dependence of a creature upon God the Creator, for every crumb of happiness it enjoys.

Oh! I feel that if there is no God, though I might live forever here, and enjoy not only this, but all other worlds, I should be ten thousand times more miserable than a toad. My soul was in such anguish I could not eat, but felt as I suppose a poor wretch would that is just going to the place of execution. I was almost swallowed up with anguish when I saw people gathering together to hear me preach. However, I went in that distress to the house of God, and found not much relief in the first prayer. It seemed as if God would let loose the people upon me to destroy me; nor were the thoughts of death distressing to me like my own vileness. But afterwards in my discourse from Deuteronomy 8:2, God was pleased to give me some freedom and enlargement, some power and spirituality; and I spent the evening somewhat comfortably.

Wednesday, January 19. (At Canterbury.) In the afternoon preached the lecture at the meetinghouse; felt some tenderness and something of the gospel temper. Exhorted the people to love one another and not to set up their own frames as a standard to try all their brethren by. But was much pressed, most of the day, with a sense of my own badness, inward impurity, and unspeakable corruption. Spent the evening in loving, Christian conversation.

Thursday, January 20. Rode to my brother's house between Norwich and Lebanon; and preached in the evening to a number of people. Enjoyed neither freedom nor spirituality, but saw myself exceeding unworthy.

Friday, January 21. Had great inward conflicts; enjoyed but little comfort. Went to see Mr. Williams of Lebanon and spent several hours with him and was greatly delighted with his serious, deliberate, and impartial way of discourse about religion.

Lord's Day, January 23. I scarce ever felt myself so unfit to exist as now. Saw I was not worthy of a place among the Indians, where I am going, if God permit. Thought I should be ashamed to look them in the face, and much more to have any respect shown me there. Indeed I felt myself banished from the earth, as if all places were too good for such a wretch. I thought I should be ashamed to go among the very savages of Africa. I appeared to myself a creature fit for nothing, neither heaven nor earth. None know, but those who feel it, what the soul endures that is sensibly shut out from the presence of God. Alas! it is more bitter than death.

Wednesday, January 26. Preached to a pretty large assembly at Mr. Fish's meetinghouse; insisted on humility and steadfastness in keeping God's commands; and that through humility we should prefer one another in love and not make our own frames the rule by which we judge others. I felt sweetly calm and full of brotherly love; and never more free from party spirit. I hope some good will follow; that Christians will be freed from false joy, and party zeal, and censuring one another.

Friday, January 28. Here I found some fallen into extravagances; too much carried away with a false zeal and bitterness. Oh, the want of a gospel temper is greatly to be lamented! Spent the evening in conversing about some points of conduct in both ministers and private Christians; but did not agree with them. God had not taught them with briers and thorns to be of a kind disposition towards mankind.

> On Saturday he rode to East Haddam, and spent the three following days there. In that space of time he speaks of his feeling weanedness from the world, a sense of the nearness of eternity, special assistance in praying for the enlargement of Christ's kingdom, times of spiritual comfort.—J. E.

Wednesday, February 2. Preached my farewell sermon last night at the house of an aged man who had been unable to attend on the public worship for some time. This morning, spent the time in prayer, almost wherever I went. Having taken leave of friends, I set out on my journey towards the Indians, though I was to spend some time at East Hampton on Long Island, by leave of the commissioners who employed me in the Indian affair;[3] and being accompanied by a messenger from East Hampton, we traveled to Lyme. On the road I felt an uncommon pressure of mind; I seemed to struggle hard for some pleasure in something here below and seemed loath to give up all for gone. Saw I was evidently throwing myself into all hardships and distresses in my present undertaking. I thought it would be less difficult to lie down in the grave; but yet I chose to go rather than stay. Came to Lyme that night.

> He waited the two next days for a passage over the Sound and spent much of the time in inward conflicts and dejection, but had some comfort.
> On Saturday he crossed the Sound, landed at Oyster Ponds on Long Island, and traveled from thence to East Hampton. And the seven following days he spent there, for the most part under extreme dejection and gloominess of mind, with great complaints of darkness and ignorance. Yet his heart appears to have been constantly engaged in the great business of religion, much concerned for the interest of religion in East Hampton, and praying and laboring much for it. —J. E.

Saturday, February 12. Enjoyed a little more comfort; was enabled to meditate with some composure of mind. Especially in the evening, found my soul more refreshed in prayer than at any time of late. My soul seemed to "take hold of God's strength" and was comforted with His consolations. Oh, how sweet are some glimpses of divine glory! how strengthening and quickening!

---

[3] The reason the commissioners or correspondents did not order Mr. Brainerd to go immediately to the Indians and enter on his business as a missionary, was that the winter was not judged to be a convenient season for him first to go out into the wilderness, and enter on the difficulties and hardships he must there be exposed to.

Lord's Day, February 13. At noon under a great degree of discouragement; knew not how it was possible for me to preach in the afternoon. I was ready to give up all for gone; but God was pleased to assist me in some measure. In the evening, my heart was sweetly drawn out after God and devoted to Him.

Tuesday, February 15. Early in the day I felt some comfort; afterwards I walked into a neighboring grove and felt more as a stranger on earth, I think, than ever before; dead to any of the enjoyments of the world as if I had been dead in a natural sense. In the evening, had divine sweetness in secret duty. God was then my portion, and my soul rose above those deep waters into which I have sunk so low of late. My soul then cried for Zion and had sweetness in so doing.

Thursday, February 17. In the morning, found myself comfortable and rested on God in some measure. Preached this day at a little village belonging to East Hampton. God was pleased to give me His gracious presence and assistance, so that I spake with freedom, boldness and some power. In the evening, spent some time with a dear Christian friend; and felt serious, as on the brink of eternity. My soul enjoyed sweetness in lively apprehensions of standing before the glorious God. Prayed with my dear friend with sweetness and discoursed with the utmost solemnity. And truly it was a little emblem of heaven itself. I find my soul is more refined and weaned from a dependence on my frames and spiritual feelings.

Friday, February 18. Felt something sweetly most of the day and found access to the throne of grace. Blessed be the Lord for any intervals of heavenly delight and composure, while I am engaged in the field of battle. Oh, that I might be serious, solemn, and always vigilant, while in an evil world! Had some opportunity alone today and found some freedom in study. Oh, I long to live to God!

Saturday, February 19. Was exceeding infirm today, greatly troubled with pain in my head and dizziness, scarce able to sit up. However, enjoyed something of God in prayer and performed some necessary studies. I exceedingly long to die; and yet, through divine goodness, have felt very willing to live, for two or three days past.

Lord's Day, February 20. I was perplexed on account of my carelessness; thought I could not be suitably concerned about the important work of the day, and so was restless with my easiness. Was exceeding infirm again today; but the Lord strengthened me, both in the outward and inward man. I preached with some life and spirituality, and was enabled to speak closely against selfish religion that loves Christ for His benefits, but not for Himself.

Monday, March 7. This morning when I arose, I found my heart go forth after God in longing desires of conformity to Him, and in secret prayer found myself sweetly quickened and drawn out in praises to God for all He had done to and for me, and for all my inward trials and distresses of late. My heart ascribed glory, glory, glory to the blessed God! and bid welcome to all inward distress again, if God saw meet to exercise me with it. Time appeared but an inch long, and eternity at hand. I thought I could with patience and cheerfulness bear anything for the cause of God; for I saw that a moment would bring me to a world of peace and blessedness. My soul, by the strength of the Lord, rose far above this lower world, and all the vain amusements and frightful disappointments of it. Afterwards, had some sweet meditation on Genesis 5:24, "And Enoch walked with God." This was a comfortable day to my soul.

Wednesday, March 9. Endeavored to commit myself and all my concerns to God. Rode sixteen miles to Mantauk, [the eastern cape or end of Long Island, inhabited chiefly by Indians.—J. E.] and had some inward sweetness on the road; but something of flatness and deadness after I came there and had seen the Indians. I withdrew and endeavored to pray, but found myself awfully deserted and left, and had an afflicting sense of my vileness and meanness. However, I went and preached from Isaiah 53:10, "Yet it pleased the Lord to bruise him." Had some assistance and, I trust, something of the divine presence was among us. In the evening I again prayed and exhorted among them, after having had a season alone, wherein I was so pressed with the blackness of my nature that I thought it was not fit for me to speak so much as to Indians.

> The next day he returned to East Hampton; was exceeding infirm in body through the remaining part of this week; but speaks of assistance and enlargement in study and religious exercises, and of inward sweetness and breathing after God.—J. E.

Lord's Day, March 13. At noon, I thought it impossible for me to preach, by reason of bodily weakness and inward deadness. In the first prayer I was so weak that I could hardly stand; but in the sermon God strengthened me so that I spake near an hour and a half with sweet freedom, clearness, and some tender power, from Genesis 5:24, "And Enoch walked with God." I was sweetly assisted to insist on a close walk with God, and to leave this as my parting advice to God's people here, that they should walk with God. May the God of all grace succeed my poor labors in this place!

Monday, March 14. In the morning, was very busy in preparation for my journey, and was almost continually engaged in ejaculatory prayer. About ten, took leave of the dear people of East Hampton. My heart grieved and mourned and rejoiced at the same time. Rode near fifty miles to a part of Brook Haven and lodged there, and had refreshing conversation with a Christian friend.

> In two days more he reached New York; but complains of much desertion and deadness on the road. He stayed one day in New York, and on Friday went to Mr. Dickinson's at Elisabeth Town. His complaints are the same as on the two preceding days.

Saturday, March 19. Was bitterly distressed under a sense of my ignorance, darkness, and unworthiness; got alone, and poured out my complaint to God in the bitterness of my soul. In the afternoon, rode to Newark and had some sweetness in conversation with Mr. Burr and in praying together. Oh, blessed be God for ever and ever for any enlivening and quickening seasons.

Lord's Day, March 20. Preached in the forenoon; God gave me some assistance and sweetness and enabled me to speak with real tenderness, love, and impartiality. In the evening, preached again; and, of a truth, God was pleased to assist a poor worm. Blessed be God, I was enabled to speak with life, power, and desire of the edification of God's people; and with some power to sinners. In the evening, I felt spiritual and watchful lest my heart should by any means be drawn away from God. Oh, when shall I come to that blessed world, where every power of my soul will be incessantly and eternally wound up in heavenly employments and enjoyments, to the highest degree!

# PART V

## FROM HIS BEGINNING TO INSTRUCT THE INDIANS AT KAUNAUMEEK, TO HIS ORDINATION

### *1743, 1744*

FRIDAY, April 1, 1743. I rode to Kaunaumeek, near twenty miles from Stockbridge, where the Indians live with whom I am concerned, and there lodged on a little heap of straw. I was greatly exercised with inward trials and distresses all day. In the evening, my heart was sunk and I seemed to have no God to go to. Oh, that God would help me!

Thursday, April 7. Appeared to myself exceeding ignorant, weak, helpless, unworthy, and altogether unequal to my work. It seemed to me I should never do any service or have any success among the Indians. My soul was weary of my life; I longed for death, beyond measure. When I thought of any godly soul departed, my soul was ready to envy him his privilege, thinking, "Oh, when will my turn come! must it be years first!" But I know these ardent desires, at this and other times, rose partly from want of resignation to God under all miseries, and so were but impatience. Towards night, I had the exercise of faith in prayer and some assistance in writing. Oh, that God would keep me near Him!

Friday, April 8. Was exceedingly pressed under a sense of my pride, selfishness, bitterness, and party spirit in times past, while I attempted to promote the cause of God. Its vile nature and dreadful consequences appeared in such odious colors to me that my very heart was pained. I saw how poor souls stumbled over it into everlasting destruction that I was constrained to make that prayer in the bitterness of my soul, "O Lord, deliver me from bloodguiltiness." I saw my desert of hell on this account. My soul was full of inward anguish and shame before God that I had spent so much time in conversation tending only to promote a party spirit.

Oh, I saw I had not suitably prized mortification, self-denial, resignation under all adversities, meekness, love, candor, and holiness of heart and life. This day was almost wholly spent in such bitter and soul-afflicting reflections on my past frames and conduct. Of late, I have thought much of having the kingdom of Christ advanced in the world; but now I saw I had enough to do within myself. The Lord be merciful to me a sinner, and wash my soul!

Saturday, April 9. Remained much in the same state as yesterday, excepting that the sense of my vileness was not so quick and acute.

Lord's Day, April 10. Rose early in the morning and walked out and spent a considerable time in the woods, in prayer and meditation. Preached to the Indians, both forenoon and afternoon. They behaved soberly in general; two or three in particular appeared under some religious concern, with whom I discoursed privately. One told me her heart had cried ever since she heard me preach first.

Tuesday, April 12. Was greatly oppressed with grief and shame, reflecting on my past conduct, my bitterness and party zeal. I was ashamed to think that such a wretch as I had ever preached. Longed to be excused from that work. And when my soul was not in anguish and keen distress, I felt senseless "as a beast before God," and felt a kind of guilty amusement with the least trifles; which still maintained a kind of stifled horror of conscience, so that I could not rest any more than a condemned malefactor.

Wednesday, April 13. My heart was overwhelmed within me; I verily thought I was the meanest, vilest, most helpless, guilty, ignorant, benighted creature living. And yet I knew what God had done for my soul, at the same time. Sometimes I was assaulted with damping doubts and fears whether it was possible for such a wretch as I to be in a state of grace.

Friday, April 15. In the forenoon, very disconsolate. In the afternoon, preached to my people and was a little encouraged in some hopes that God might bestow mercy on their souls. Felt somewhat resigned to God under all dispensations of His providence.

Saturday, April 16. Still in the depths of distress. In the afternoon, preached to my people, but was more discouraged with them than before. I feared that nothing would ever be done for them to any happy effect. I retired and poured out my soul to God for mercy, but without any sensible relief. Soon after came an Irishman and a Dutchman, with a design, as they said, to hear me preach the next day; but none can tell how I felt to hear their profane talk. Oh, I longed that some dear Christian knew my distress. I got into a kind of hovel and there groaned out my complaint to God; and withal felt more sensible gratitude and thankfulness to God that He had made me to differ from these men, as I knew through grace He had.

Lord's Day, April 17. In the morning was again distressed as soon as I waked, hearing much talk about the world and the things of it. I perceived the men were in some measure afraid of me. I discoursed something about sanctifying the Sabbath, if possible to solemnize their minds. But when they were at a little distance, they again talked freely about secular affairs. Oh, I thought what a hell it would be to live with such men to eternity! The Lord gave me some assistance in preaching all day, and some resignation and a small degree of comfort in prayer at night.

Tuesday, April 19. In the morning, I enjoyed some sweet repose and rest in God; felt some strength and confidence in Him, and my soul was in some measure refreshed and comforted. Spent most of the day in writing, and had some exercise of grace, sensible and comfortable. My soul seemed lifted above the deep waters wherein it has been so long almost drowned; felt some spiritual longings and breathings of soul after God and found myself engaged for the advancement of Christ's kingdom in my own soul.

Wednesday, April 20. Set apart this day for fasting and

prayer, to bow my soul before God for the bestowment of divine grace; especially that all my spiritual afflictions and inward distresses might be sanctified to my soul. And endeavored also to remember the goodness of God to me the year past, this day being my birthday. Having obtained help of God, I have hitherto lived and am now arrived at the age of twenty-five years. My soul was pained to think of my barrenness and deadness; that I have lived so little to the glory of the eternal God. I spent the day in the woods alone, and there poured out my complaint to God. Oh, that God would enable me to live to His glory for the future!

Thursday, April 21. Spent the forenoon in reading and prayer, and found myself engaged but still much depressed in spirit under a sense of my vileness and unfitness for any public service. In the afternoon, I visited my people and prayed and conversed with some about their souls' concerns. Afterwards found some ardor of soul in secret prayer. Oh, that I might grow up into the likeness of God!

Friday, April 22. Spent the day in study, reading, and prayer; and felt a little relieved of my burden that has been so heavy of late. But still was in some measure oppressed and had a sense of barrenness. Oh, my leanness testifies against me! My very soul abhors itself for its unlikeness to God, its inactivity and sluggishness. When I have done all, alas, what an unprofitable servant I am! My soul groans to see the hours of the day roll away because I do not fill them in spirituality and heavenly mindedness. And yet I long they should speed their pace to hasten me to my eternal Home, where I may fill up all my moments through eternity for God and His glory.

Lord's Day, May 1. Was at Stockbridge today. In the forenoon had some relief and assistance, though not so much as usual. In the afternoon, felt poorly in body and soul. While I was preaching I seemed to be rehearsing idle tales without the least life, fervor, sense, or comfort. Afterwards, at the sacrament, my soul was filled with confusion and the utmost anguish that ever I endured, under the feeling of my inexpressible vileness and meanness. It was a most bitter and distressing season to me, by reason of the view I had of my own heart and the secret abominations that lurk there. I thought the eyes of all in the house were upon me and I dared not look anyone in the face; for it verily seemed as if they saw the vileness of my heart and all the sins I had ever been guilty of.

And if I had been banished from the presence of all mankind, never to be seen any more or so much as thought of, still I should have been distressed with shame. I should have been ashamed to see the most barbarous people on earth because I was viler and seemingly more brutishly ignorant than they. "I am made to possess the sins of my youth."

Tuesday, May 10. Was in the same state, as to my mind, that I have been in for some time; extremely pressed with a sense of guilt, pollution, and blindness: "The iniquity of my heels has compassed me about; the sins of my youth have been set in order before me; they have gone over my head, as an heavy burden, too heavy for me to bear." Almost all the actions of my life past seem to be covered over with sin and guilt; and those of them that I performed in the most conscientious manner, now fill me with shame and confusion, that I cannot hold up my face. Oh! the pride, selfishness, hypocrisy, ignorance, bitterness, party zeal, and the want of love, candor, meekness, and gentleness that have attended my attempts to promote religion and virtue. And this when I have reason to hope I had real assistance from above, and some sweet intercourse with heaven! But, alas, what corrupt mixtures attended my best duties!

The next seven days, his gloom and distress continued for the most part, but he had some turns of relief and spiritual comfort. He gives an account of his spending part of this time in hard labor to build himself a little cottage to live in amongst the Indians, in which he might be by himself; having, it seems, hitherto lived with a poor Scotchman . . . and afterwards, before his own house was habitable, lived in a wigwam among the Indians.—J. E.

Wednesday, May 18. My circumstances are such, that I have no comfort of any kind but what I have in God. I live in the most lonesome wilderness; have but one single person to converse with, that can speak English.[1] Most of the talk I hear is either Highland Scotch or Indian. I have no fellow Christian to whom I might unbosom myself or lay open my spiritual sorrows; with whom I might take sweet counsel in conversation about heavenly things and join in social prayer. I live poorly with regard to the comforts of life. Most of my diet consists of boiled corn, hasty-pudding, etc. I lodge on a bundle of straw, my labor is hard and extremely difficult, and I have little appearance of success, to comfort me. The Indians have no land to live on but what the Dutch people lay claim to; and these threaten to drive them off. They have no regard to the souls of the poor Indians; and, by what I can learn, they hate me because I come to preach to them. But that which makes all my difficulties grievous to be borne is that God hides His face from me.

Thursday, May 19. Spent most of this day in close studies, but was sometimes so distressed that I could think of nothing but my spiritual blindness, ignorance, pride and misery. Oh, I have reason to make that prayer, "Lord, forgive my sins of youth, and former trespasses."

Friday, May 20. Was much perplexed, some part of the day; but towards night, had some comfortable meditations on Isaiah 40:1, "Comfort ye, comfort ye, . . ." and enjoyed some sweetness in prayer. Afterwards my soul rose so far above the deep waters that I dared to rejoice in God. I saw there was sufficient matter of consolation in the blessed God.

The next nine days, his burdens were for the most part alleviated, but with variety; at some times, having considerable consolation and at others, more depressed. The next

[1] This person was Mr. Brainerd's interpreter, who was an ingenious young Indian belonging to Stockbridge, whose name was John Wauwaumpequunnaunt. He had been instructed in the Christian religion by Mr. Sergeant; had lived with the Reverend Mr. Williams of Long Meadow; had been further instructed by him, at the charge of Mr. Hollis of London. He understood both English and Indian very well and wrote a good hand.

day, Monday, May 30, he set out on a journey to New Jersey to consult the commissioners who employed him about the affairs of his mission. . . . His business with the commissioners now was to obtain orders from them to set up a school among the Indians at Kaunaumeek, and that his interpreter might be appointed the schoolmaster, which was accordingly done.

The manner of his relief from his sorrow, once in particular, is worthy to be mentioned in his own words (Diary for July 25). "Had a little or no resolution for a life of holiness; was ready almost to renounce my hopes of living to God. And oh, how dark it looked, to think of being unholy forever! This I could not endure. The cry of my soul was Psalm 65:3, 'Iniquities prevail against me.' But was in some measure relieved by a comfortable meditation on God's eternity, that He never had a beginning. Whence I was led to admire His greatness and power in such a manner that I stood still and praised the Lord for His own glories and perfections. Though I was (and if I should forever be) an unholy creature, my soul was comforted to apprehend an eternal, infinite, powerful, holy God."—J. E.

Saturday, July 30. Just at night, moved into my own house [a little hut, which he made chiefly by his own hands, by long and hard labor], and lodged there that night; found it much better spending the time alone than in the wigwam where I was before.

Lord's Day, July 31. Felt more comfortably than some days past. Blessed be the Lord who has now given me a place of retirement. Oh, that I might find God in it and that He would dwell with me forever!

Monday, August 1. Was still busy in further labors on my house. Felt a little of the sweetness of religion and thought it was worth the while to follow after God through a thousand snares, deserts and death itself. Oh, that I might always follow after holiness, that I may be fully conformed to God! Had some degree of sweetness in secret prayer, though I had much sorrow.

Tuesday, August 2. Was still laboring to make myself more

comfortable with regard to my house and lodging. Labored under spiritual anxiety; it seemed to me I deserved to be kicked out of the world; yet found some comfort in committing my cause to God. It is good for me to be afflicted that I may die wholly to this world and all that is in it.

Wednesday, August 3. Spent most of the day in writing. Enjoyed some sense of religion. Through divine goodness I am now uninterruptedly alone and find my retirement comfortable. I have enjoyed more sense of divine things within a few days last past than for some time before. I longed after holiness, humility and meekness. Oh, that God would enable me to "pass the time of my sojourning here in his fear," and always live to Him!

Thursday, August 4. Was enabled to pray much, through the whole day; and through divine goodness found some intenseness of soul in the duty, as I used to do, and some ability to persevere in my supplications. I had some apprehensions of divine things that were engaging and which afforded me some courage and resolution. It is good, I find, to persevere in attempts to pray if I cannot pray with perseverance, that is, continue long in my addresses to the Divine Being. I have generally found that the more I do in secret prayer the more I have delighted to do, and have enjoyed more of a spirit of prayer; and frequently have found the contrary, when with journeying or otherwise I have been much deprived of retirement. A seasonable, steady performance of secret duties in their proper hours, and a careful improvement of all time, filling up every hour with some profitable labor, either of heart, head, or hands, are excellent means of spiritual peace and boldness before God. Christ, indeed, is our peace, and by Him we have boldness of access to God. But a good conscience void of offense is an excellent preparation for an approach into the divine presence.

There is a difference between self-confidence or a self-righteous pleasing of ourselves—as with our own duties, attainments, and spiritual enjoyments—which godly souls sometimes are guilty of, and that holy confidence arising from the testimony of a good conscience which good Hezekiah had when he says, "Remember, O Lord, I beseech thee, how I have walked before thee in truth, and with a perfect heart." Then, says the holy Psalmist, "shall I not be ashamed when I have respect to all thy commandments." Filling up our time with and for God is the way to rise up and lie down in peace.

> The next eight days, he continued for the most part in a very comfortable frame, having his mind fixed and sweetly engaged in religion; and more than once blessed God that He had given him a little cottage where he might live alone, and enjoy a happy retirement, free from noise and disturbance, and could at any hour of the day lay aside all studies and spend time in lifting up his soul to God for spiritual blessings.—J. E.

Saturday, August 13. Was enabled in secret prayer to raise my soul to God, with desire and delight. It was indeed a blessed season to my soul. I found the comfort of being a Christian and counted the sufferings of the present life not worthy to be compared with the glory of divine enjoyments even in this world. All my past sorrows seemed kindly to disappear, and I "remembered no more the sorrow, for joy." Oh, how kindly and with what a filial tenderness the soul confides in the Rock of ages at such a season, that He will "never leave it, nor forsake it," that He will cause all things to work together for its good! I longed that others should know how good a God the Lord is. My soul was full of tenderness and love, even to the most inveterate of my enemies. I longed they should share in the same mercy; and loved that God should do just as He pleased with me and everything else. I felt exceeding serious, calm, and peaceful, and encouraged to press after holiness as long as I live, whatever difficulties and trials may be in my way. May the Lord always help me so to do! Amen, and amen.

Lord's Day, August 14. I had much more freedom in public than in private. God enabled me to speak with some feeling sense of divine things, but I perceived no considerable effect.

Monday, August 15. Spent most of the day in labor to procure something to keep my horse on in the winter. Enjoyed not much sweetness in the morning; was very weak in body through the day, and thought this frail body would soon drop into the dust. Had some very realizing apprehensions of a speedy entrance into another world. And in this weak state of body I was not a little distressed for want of suitable food. I had no bread, nor could I get any. I am forced to go or send ten or fifteen miles for all the bread I eat, and sometimes it is moldy and sour before I eat it, if I get any considerable quantity.

And then again I have none for some days together for want of an opportunity to send for it, and cannot find my horse in the woods to go myself; and this was my case now. But through divine goodness I had some Indian meal, of which I made little cakes, and fried them. Yet felt contented with my circumstances and sweetly resigned to God. In prayer I enjoyed great freedom and blessed God as much for my present circumstances as if I had been a king and thought I found a disposition to be contented in any circumstances. Blessed be God.

> The rest of this week, he was exceeding weak in body, and much exercised with pain; yet obliged from day to day to labor hard to procure fodder for his horse. Except some part of the time, he was so very ill that he was neither able to work nor study; but speaks of longings after holiness and perfect conformity to God. He complains of enjoying but little of God; yet, he says, that little was better to him than all the world besides. In his diary for Saturday he says he was somewhat melancholy and sorrowful in mind, and adds, "I never feel comfortably, but when I find my soul going forth after God. If I cannot be holy, I must necessarily be miserable forever."—J. E.

Lord's Day, August 21. Was much straitened in the forenoon exercise; my thoughts seemed to be all scattered to the ends of the earth. At noon, I fell down before the Lord, groaned under my vileness, barrenness, and deadness. I felt as if I was guilty of soul murder, in speaking to immortal souls in such a manner as I had then done. In the afternoon, God was pleased to give me some assistance and I was enabled to set before my hearers the nature and necessity of true repentance. Afterwards, had some small degree of thankfulness. Was very ill and full of pain in the evening, and my soul mourned that I had spent so much time to so little profit.

Monday, August 22. Spent most of the day in study and found my bodily strength in a measure restored. Had some intense and passionate breathings of soul after holiness, and very clear manifestations of my utter inability to procure, or work it in myself; it is wholly owing to the power of God. Oh, with what tenderness the love and desire of holiness fills the soul! I wanted to wing out of myself to God, or rather to get a conformity to Him. But, alas! I cannot add to my stature in grace one cubit. However, my soul can never leave striving for it; or at least groaning, that it cannot strive for it and obtain more purity of heart. At night, I spent some time in instructing my poor people. Oh, that God would pity their souls!

Tuesday, August 23. Studied in the forenoon and enjoyed some freedom. In the afternoon, labored abroad. Endeavored to pray, but found not much sweetness or intenseness of mind. Towards night, was very weary and tired of this world of sorrow. The thoughts of death and immortality appeared very desirable and even refreshed my soul. Those lines turned in my mind with pleasure,

> "Come death, shake hands; I'll kiss thy bands:
> 'Tis happiness for me to die.
> What! dost thou think, that I will shrink?
> I'll go to immortality."

In evening prayer, God was pleased to draw near my soul, though very sinful and unworthy; was enabled to wrestle with God and to persevere in my requests for grace. I poured out my soul for all the world, friends and enemies. My soul was concerned, not so much for souls as such, but rather for

Christ's kingdom that it might appear in the world, that God might be known to be God in the whole earth. And oh, my soul abhorred the very thought of a party in religion! Let the truth of God appear, wherever it is, and God have the glory forever. Amen. This was indeed a comfortable season. I thought I had some small taste of, and real relish for the enjoyments and employments of the upper world. Oh, that my soul were more attempered to it!

Wednesday, August 24. Spent some time, in the morning, in study and prayer. Afterwards was engaged in some necessary business abroad. Towards night, found a little time for some particular studies. I thought, if God should say, "Cease making any provision for this life, for you shall in a few days go out of time into eternity," my soul would leap for joy. Oh, that I may both "desire to be dissolved, to be with Christ," and likewise "wait patiently all the days of my appointed time till my change come!" But, alas! I am very unfit for the business and blessedness of heaven. Oh, for more holiness!

Thursday, August 25. Part of the day was engaged in studies and part in labor abroad. I find it impossible to enjoy peace and tranquillity of mind without a careful improvement of time. This is really an imitation of God and Christ Jesus: "My Father worketh hitherto, and I work," says our Lord. But still, if we would be like God, we must see that we fill up our time for Him. I daily long to dwell in perfect light and love. In the meantime, my soul mourns that I make so little progress in grace and preparation for the world of blessedness. I see and know that I am a very barren tree in God's vineyard and that He might justly say, "Cut it down." Oh, that God would make me more lively and vigorous in grace, for His own glory! Amen.

Lord's Day, August 28. Was much perplexed with some irreligious Dutchmen. All their discourse turned upon the things of the world, which was no small exercise to my mind. Oh, what a hell it would be to spend an eternity with such men! Well might David say, "I beheld the transgressors, and was grieved." But adored be God, heaven is a place into which no unclean thing enters. Oh, I long for the holiness of that world! Lord prepare me for it.

> The next day, he set out on a journey to New York. Was somewhat dejected the two first days of his journey, but yet seems to have enjoyed some degree of the sensible presence of God.—J. E.

Wednesday, August 31. Rode down to Bethlehem; was in a sweet, serious, and, I hope, Christian frame, when I came there. Eternal things engrossed all my thoughts and I longed to be in the world of spirits. Oh, how happy is it to have all our thoughts swallowed up in that world; to feel one's self a serious, considerate stranger in this world, diligently seeking a road through it, the best, the sure road to the heavenly Jerusalem!

Thursday, September 1. Rode to Danbury. Was more dull and dejected in spirit than yesterday. Indeed, I always feel comfortably when God realizes death and the things of another world to my mind. Whenever my mind is taken off from the things of this world and set on God, my soul is then at rest.

## He Visits New Haven

> He went forward on his journey and came to New York on the next Monday. After tarrying there two or three days, he set out from the city towards New Haven, intending to be there at the commencement; and on Friday came to Horse Neck. In the meantime he complains much of dullness and want of fervor in religion. But yet, from time to time, speaks of his enjoying spiritual warmth and sweetness in conversation with Christian friends, assistance in public services.—J. E.

Saturday, September 10. Rode six miles to Stanwich and preached to a considerable assembly of people. Had some assistance and freedom, especially towards the close. Endeavored much afterwards, in private conversation, to establish holiness, humility, and meekness as the essence of true religion, and to moderate some noisy sort of persons that appeared to me to be actuated by unseen spiritual pride. Alas, what extremes men incline to run into! Returned to Horse Neck and felt some seriousness and sweet solemnity in the evening.

Lord's Day, September 11. In the afternoon, I preached from Titus 3:8, "This is a faithful saying, and these things . . ." I think God never helped me more in painting true religion and in detecting clearly and tenderly discountenancing false appearances of religion, wildfire party zeal and spiritual pride as well as a confident dogmatical spirit, and its spring, namely, ignorance of the heart. In the evening, took much pains in private conversation to suppress some confusions that I perceived were amongst that people.

Monday, September 12. Rode to Mr. Mills' at Ripton. Had some perplexing hours, but was some part of the day very comfortable. It is "through great trials," I see, "that we must enter the gates of paradise." If my soul could but be holy that God might not be dishonored, methinks I could bear sorrows.

Tuesday, September 13. Rode to New Haven. Was sometimes dejected; not in the sweetest frame. Lodged at ____. Had some profitable Christian conversation. I find, though my inward trials were great and a life of solitude gives them greater advantage to settle and penetrate to the very inmost recesses of the soul, yet it is better to be alone than incumbered with noise and tumult. I find it very difficult maintaining any sense of divine things while removing from place to place, diverted with new objects and filled with care and business. A settled steady business is best adapted to a life of strict religion.

Wednesday, September 14. This day I ought to have taken my degree (this being my commencement day); but God sees fit to deny it me. And though I was greatly afraid of being overwhelmed with perplexity and confusion when I should see my classmates take theirs; yet, at the very time, God enabled me with calmness and resignation to say, "The will of the Lord be done." Indeed, through divine goodness, I have scarcely felt my mind so calm, sedate and comfortable for some time. I have long feared this season and expected my humility, meekness, patience, and resignation would be much tried [2]: but found much more pleasure and divine comfort than I expected. Felt spiritually serious, tender and affectionate in private prayer with a dear Christian friend today.

Thursday, September 15. Had some satisfaction in hearing the ministers discourse. It is always a comfort to me to hear religious and spiritual discourse. Oh, that ministers and people were more spiritual and devoted to God! Towards night, with the advice of Christian friends, I offered the following reflections in writing, to the rector and trustees of the college—which are for substance the same that I had freely offered to the rector before, and intreated him to accept—that if possible I might cut off all occasion of offense from those who seek occasion. What I offered, is as follows:

"Whereas I have said before several persons, concerning Mr. Whittelsey, one of the tutors of Yale College, that I did not believe he had any more grace than the chair I then leaned upon: I humbly confess, that herein I have sinned against God, and acted contrary to the rules of His Word, and have injured Mr. Whittelsey. I had no right to make thus free with his character; and had no just reason to say as I did concerning him. My fault herein was the more aggravated, in that I said this concerning one that was so much my superior, and one that I was obliged to treat with special respect and honor, by reason of the relation I stood in to him in the college. Such a manner of behavior, I confess, did not become a Christian; it was taking too much upon me, and did not savor of that humble respect, that I ought to have expressed towards Mr. Whittelsey.

"I have long since been convinced of the falseness of those apprehensions by which I then justified such a conduct. I have often reflected on this act with grief; I hope, on account of

[2] His trial was the greater, in that, had it not been for the displeasure of the governors of the college, he would not only on that day have shared with his classmates in the public honors which they then received, but would on that occasion have appeared at the head of that class; which, if he had been with them, would have been the most numerous of any that ever had been graduated at that college.

the sin of it: and am willing to lie low and be abased before God and man for it. And humbly ask the forgiveness of the governors of the college, and of the whole society; but of Mr. Whittelsey in particular. And whereas I have been accused by one person of saying concerning the reverend rector of Yale College, that I wondered he did not expect to drop down dead for fining the scholars that followed Mr. Tennent to Milford; I seriously profess, that I do not remember my saying anything to this purpose. But if I did, which I am not certain I did not, I utterly condemn it, and detest all such kind of behavior; and especially in an undergraduate towards the rector.

"And I now appear to judge and condemn myself for going once to the separate meeting in New Haven, a little before I was expelled, though the rector had refused to give me leave. For this I humbly ask the rector's forgiveness. And whether the governors of the college shall ever see cause to remove the academical censure I lie under, or no, or to admit me to the privileges I desire; yet I am willing to appear, if they think fit, openly to own, and to humble myself for those things I have herein confessed."

God has made me willing to do anything that I can do, consistent with truth, for the sake of peace, and that I might not be a stumbling block to others. For this reason I can cheerfully forego and give up what I verily believe, after the most mature and impartial search, is my right, in some in-stances. God has given me that disposition that, if this were the case that a man has done me an hundred injuries and I (though ever so much provoked to it) have done him one, I feel disposed and heartily willing humbly to confess my fault to him, and on my knees to ask forgiveness of him; though at the same time he should justify himself in all the injuries he has done me and should only make use of my humble confession to blacken my character the more and represent me as the only person guilty.

Yea, though he should as it were insult me and say, he knew all this before, and that I was making work for repent-ance. Though what I said concerning Mr. Whittelsey was only spoken in private, to a friend or two; and being partly overheard, was related to the rector, and by him extorted from my friends; yet, seeing it was divulged and made public, I was willing to confess my fault therein publicly. But I trust, God will plead my cause.[3]

Monday, September 19. In the afternoon, rode to Bethlehem, and there preached. Had some measure of assistance, both in prayer and preaching. I felt serious, kind and tender towards all mankind and longed that holiness might flourish.

Tuesday, September 20. Had thoughts of going forward on my journey to my Indians; but towards night was taken with a hard pain in my teeth, and shivering cold; and could not possibly recover a comfortable degree of warmth the whole night following. I continued very full of pain all night; and in the morning had a very hard fever and pains almost over my whole body. I had a sense of the divine goodness in appointing this to be the place of my sickness, namely, among my friends who were very kind to me. I should probably have perished if I had first got home to my own house in the wilderness where I have none to converse with but the poor, rude, ignorant Indians. Here I saw was mercy in the midst of affliction.

I continued thus, mostly confined to my bed, till Friday

---

[3] I was witness to the very Christian spirit Mr. Brainerd showed at that time, being then at New Haven and one that he thought fit to consult on that occasion. This was the first time that ever I had an opportunity of personal acquaintance with him. There truly appeared in him a great degree of calmness and humility; without the least appearance of rising of spirit for any ill treatment he supposed he had suffered, or the least backwardness to abase himself before them who, as he thought, had wronged him. What he did was without any objection or appearance of reluctance, even in private to his friends, to whom he freely opened himself. Earnest application was made on his behalf to the authority of the college that he might have his degree then given him; and particularly by the Reverend Mr. Burr of Newark, one of the correspondents of the honorable society in Scotland; he being sent from New Jersey to New Haven, by the rest of the commissioners, for that end; and many arguments were used, but without success.
Indeed the governors of the college were so far satisfied with the reflections Mr. Brainerd had made on himself, that they appeared willing to admit him again into college; but not to give him his degree, till he should have remained there, at least twelve months, which being contrary to what the correspondents, to whom he was now engaged, had declared to be their mind, he did not consent to it. He desired his degree, as he thought it would tend to his being more extensively useful; but still when he was denied it, he manifested no disappointment or resentment.—J. Edwards.

night, very full of pain most of the time; but through divine goodness not afraid of death. Then the extreme folly of those appeared to me who put off their turning to God till a sickbed. Surely this is not a time proper to prepare for eternity. On Friday evening my pains went off somewhat suddenly; I was exceeding weak and almost fainted, but was very comfortable the night following. These words, Psalm 118:17, "I shall not die, but live," I frequently revolved in my mind; and thought we were to prize the continuation of life only on this account, that we may "show forth God's goodness and works of grace."

## He Returns to Kaunaumeek

From this time he gradually recovered; and on the next Tuesday was so well as to be able to go forward on his journey homewards; but it was not till the Tuesday following that he reached Kaunaumeek. And seems, great part of this time, to have had a very deep and lively sense of the the vanity and emptiness of all things here below, and of the reality, nearness, and vast importance of eternal things.
—J. E.

Tuesday, October 4. This day rode home to my own house and people. The poor Indians appeared very glad of my return. Found my house and all things in safety. I presently fell on my knees and blessed God for my safe return after a long and tedious journey, and a season of sickness in several places where I had been, and after I had been ill myself. God has renewed His kindness to me, in preserving me one journey more. I have taken many considerable journeys since this time last year, and yet God has never suffered one of my bones to be broken, or any distressing calamity to befall me, excepting the ill turn I had in my last journey. I have been often exposed to cold and hunger in the wilderness where the comforts of life were not to be had; have frequently been lost in the woods; and sometimes obliged to ride much of the night; and once lay out in the woods all night. Yet, blessed be God, He has preserved me!

Lord's Day, October 16. In the evening, God was pleased to give me a feeling sense of my own unworthiness; but, through divine goodness, such as tended to draw me to, rather than drive me from, God; it filled me with solemnity. I retired alone (having at this time a friend with me) and poured out my soul to God with much freedom; and yet in anguish, to find myself so unspeakably sinful and unworthy before a holy God. Was now much resigned under God's dispensations towards me, though my trials had been very great. But thought whether I could be resigned if God should let the French Indians come upon me and deprive me of life, or carry me away captive (though I knew of no special reason then to propose this trial to myself, more than any other). My soul seemed so far to rest and acquiesce in God that the sting and terror of these things seemed in a great measure gone. Presently after I came to the Indians, whom I was teaching to sing psalm tunes that evening, I received the following letter from Stockbridge, by a messenger sent on the Sabbath on purpose, which made it appear of greater importance:

> "Sir—Just now received advices from Col. Stoddard, that there is the utmost danger of a rupture with France. He has received the same from His Excellency our governor, ordering him to give notice to all the exposed places, that they may secure themselves the best they can against any sudden invasion. We thought best to send directly to Kaunaumeek, that you may take the prudentest measures for your safety that dwell there. I am, Sir, etc."

I thought, upon reading the contents, it came in a good season; for my heart seemed fixed on God, and therefore I was not much surprised. This news only made me more serious and taught me that I must not please myself with any of the comforts of life which I had been preparing. Blessed be God, who gave me any intenseness and fervency this evening!

Monday, October 17. Had some rising hopes, that "God would arise and have mercy on Zion speedily." My heart is indeed refreshed, when I have any prevailing hopes of Zion's prosperity. Oh, that I may see the glorious day when Zion shall become the joy of the whole earth! Truly there is nothing that I greatly value in this lower world.

> On Tuesday, he rode to Stockbridge; complains of being much diverted and having but little life. On Wednesday, he expresses some solemn sense of divine things, and a longing to be always doing for God with a godly frame of spirit.
> —J. E.

Thursday, October 20. Had but little sense of divine things this day. Alas, that so much of my precious time is spent with so little of God! Those are tedious days.

Friday, October 21. Returned home to Kaunaumeek; was glad to get alone in my little cottage and to cry to that God who seeth in secret and is present in a wilderness.

Saturday, October 22. Had but little sensible communion with God. This world is a dark, cloudy mansion. Oh, when will the Sun of Righteousness shine on my soul without intermission!

Lord's Day, October 23. In the morning, I had a little dawn of comfort arising from hopes of seeing glorious days in the Church of God. Was enabled to pray for such a glorious day with some courage and strength of hope. In the forenoon, treated on the glories of heaven. In the afternoon on the miseries of hell and the danger of going there. Had some freedom and warmth both parts of the day, and my people were very attentive. In the evening, two or three came to me under concern for their souls; to whom I was enabled to discourse closely, and with some earnestness and desire. Oh, that God would be merciful to their poor souls!

> He seems, through the whole of this week, to have been greatly engaged to fill up every inch of time in the service of God, and to have been most diligently employed in study, prayer, and instructing the Indians. From time to time expresses longings of soul after God, and the advancement of His kingdom, and spiritual comfort and refreshment.—J. E.

Lord's Day, October 30. In the morning, I enjoyed some fixedness of soul in prayer, which was indeed sweet and desirable. Was enabled to leave myself with God, and to acquiesce in Him. At noon my soul was refreshed with reading Revelation 3, more especially the eleventh and twelfth verses. Oh, my soul longed for that blessed day, when I should "dwell in the temple of God," and "go no more out" of His immediate presence!

Monday, October 31. Rode to Kinderhook, about fifteen miles from my place. While riding, I felt some divine sweetness in the thoughts of being "a pillar in the temple of God" in the upper world, and being no more deprived of His blessed presence and the sense of His favor, which is better than life. My soul was so lifted up to God that I could pour out my desires to Him, for more grace and further degrees of sanctification, with abundant freedom. Oh, I longed to be more abundantly prepared for that blessedness with which I was then in some measure refreshed! Returned home in the evening; but took an extremely bad cold by riding in the night.

Tuesday, November 1. Was very much disordered in body, and sometimes full of pain in my face and teeth. Was not able to study much and had not much spiritual comfort. Alas! when God is withdrawn, all is gone. Had some sweet thoughts, which I could not but write down, on the design, nature, and end of Christianity.

Wednesday, November 2. Was still more indisposed in body, and in much pain most of the day. I had not much comfort; was scarcely able to study at all; and still entirely alone in the wilderness. But blessed be the Lord, I am not exposed in the open air. I have a house and many of the comforts of life to support me. I have learned, in a measure, that all good things, relating both to time and eternity, come from God. In the evening, I had some degree of quickening in prayer. I think God gave me some sense of His presence.

Thursday, November 3. Spent this day in secret fasting and prayer, from morning till night. Early in the morning, I had some small degree of assistance in prayer. Afterwards, read the story of Elijah the prophet, I Kings 17, 18, and 19, and also II Kings 2 and 4. My soul was much moved observing the faith, zeal, and power of that holy man and how he wrestled with God in prayer. My soul then cried with Elisha, "Where is the Lord God of Elijah!" Oh, I longed for more faith! My soul breathed after God and pleaded with Him that a "double portion of that spirit," which was given to Elijah, might "rest on me."

That which was divinely refreshing and strengthening to my soul was that I saw that God is the same as He was in the days of Elijah. Was enabled to wrestle with God by prayer in a more affectionate, fervent, humble, intense, and importunate manner than I have for many months past. Nothing seemed too hard for God to perform; nothing too great for me to hope for from Him.

I had for many months entirely lost all hopes of being made instrumental of doing any special service for God in the world. It has appeared entirely impossible that one so black and vile should be thus employed for God. But at this time God was pleased to revive this hope.

Afterwards read the third chapter of Exodus and on to the twentieth, and saw more of the glory and majesty of God discovered in those chapters than ever I had seen before. Frequently in the meantime I fell on my knees and cried to God for the faith of Moses and for a manifestation of the divine glory. Especially the third and fourth, and part of the fourteenth and fifteenth chapters, were unspeakably sweet to my soul. My soul blessed God that He had shown Himself so gracious to His servants of old. The fifteenth chapter seemed to be the very language which my soul uttered to God in the season of my first spiritual comfort, when I had just got through the Red Sea, by a way that I had no expectation of.

Oh, how my soul then rejoiced in God! And now those things came fresh and lively to my mind. Now my soul blessed God afresh that He had opened that unthought-of way to deliver me from the fear of the Egyptians, when I almost despaired of life.

Afterwards read the story of Abraham's pilgrimage in the land of Canaan; my soul was melted in observing his faith, how he leaned on God; how he communed with God and what a stranger he was here in the world. After that, read the story of Joseph's sufferings and God's goodness to him. Blessed God for these examples of faith and patience. My soul was ardent in prayer, was enabled to wrestle ardently for myself, for Christian friends, and for the Church of God. Felt more desire to see the power of God in the conversion of souls than I have done for a long season. Blessed be God for this season of fasting and prayer! May His goodness always abide with me and draw my soul to Him!

Friday, November 4. Rode to Kinderhook; went quite to Hudson's River, about twenty miles from my house; performed some business and returned home in the evening to my own house. I had rather ride hard and fatigue myself to get home, than to spend the evening and night amongst those who have no regard for God.

> The two next days, he was very ill and full of pain, probably through his riding in the night, after a fatiguing day's journey on Thursday; but yet seems to have been diligent in business.

Monday, November 7. This morning the Lord afforded me some special assistance in prayer; my mind was solemn, fixed, affectionate, and ardent in desires after holiness. Felt full of tenderness and love, and my affections seemed to be dissolved into kindness. In the evening I enjoyed the same comfortable assistance in prayer as in the morning. My soul longed after God and cried to Him with a filial freedom, reverence, and boldness. Oh, that I might be entirely devoted to God!

Thursday, November 10. Spent this day in fasting and prayer alone. In the morning was very dull and lifeless, melancholy and discouraged. But after some time, while reading II Kings 19, my soul was moved and affected; especially reading verse 14 and onward. I saw there was no other way for the afflicted children of God to take but to go to God with all their sorrows. Hezekiah in his great distress went and spread his complaint before the Lord. I was then enabled to see the mighty power of God and my extreme need of that power. Was enabled to cry to Him affectionately and ardently for His power and grace to be exercised towards me.

Afterwards, read the story of David's trials, and observed the course he took under them, how he strengthened his hands in God; whereby my soul was carried out after God, enabled to cry to Him and rely upon Him, and felt strong in the Lord. Was afterwards refreshed, observing the blessed temper that was wrought in David by his trials. All bitterness, and desire of revenge seemed wholly taken away so that he mourned for the death of his enemies (II Sam. 1:17 and 4:9, to the end). Was enabled to bless God that He had given me something of this divine temper, that my soul freely forgives and heartily loves my enemies.

> It appears by his diary for the remaining part of this week and for the two following weeks, that great part of the time he was very ill and full of pain; and yet obliged, through his circumstances, in this ill state of body, to be at great fatigues, in labor and traveling day and night, and to expose himself in stormy and severe seasons. He from time to time, within this space, speaks of outgoings of soul after God; his heart strengthened in God; seasons of divine sweetness and comfort; his heart affected with gratitude for mercies. And yet there are many complaints of lifelessness, weakness of grace, distance from God, and great unprofitableness. But still there appears a constant care, from day to day not to lose time but to improve it all for God.—J. E.

Lord's Day, November 27. In the evening, I was greatly affected in reading an account of the very joyful death of a pious gentleman, which seemed to invigorate my soul in God's ways. I felt courageously engaged to pursue a life of holiness and self-denial as long as I live; and poured out my soul to God for His help and assistance in order thereto. Eternity then seemed near, and my soul rejoiced and longed to meet it. I trust that will be a blessed day that finishes my toil here.

Monday, November 28. In the evening, I was obliged to spend time in company and conversation that was unprofitable. Nothing lies heavier upon me than the misimprovement of time.

Tuesday, November 29. Began to study the Indian tongue with Mr. Sergeant at Stockbridge.[4] Was perplexed for want of more retirement. I love to live alone in my own little cottage where I can spend much time in prayer.

Wednesday, November 30. Pursued my study of Indian but was very weak and disordered in body; was troubled in mind at the barrenness of the day, that I had done so little for God. I had some enlargement in prayer at night. Oh, a barn, or stable, hedge, or any other place is truly desirable, if God is there!

Thursday, December 1. Both morning and evening, I enjoyed some intenseness of soul in prayer and longed for the enlargement of Christ's kingdom in the world. My soul seems, of late, to wait on God for His blessing on Zion. Oh, that religion might powerfully revive!

Friday, December 2. Enjoyed not so much health of body, or fervor of mind, as yesterday. If the chariot wheels move with ease and speed at any time, for a short space, yet by and by they drive heavily again. "Oh, that I had the wings of a dove! that I might fly away" from sin and corruption, and be at rest in God!

Saturday, December 3. Rode home to my house and people. Suffered much with the extreme cold. I trust I shall ere long arrive safe at my journey's end, where my toils shall cease.

Lord's Day, December 4. Had but little sense of divine and heavenly things. My soul mourns over my barrenness. Oh, how sad is spiritual deadness!

---

[4] The commissioners who employed him, had directed him to spend much time this winter with Mr. Sergeant, to learn the language of the Indians; which necessitated him very often to ride, backwards and forwards, twenty miles through the uninhabited woods between Stockbridge and Kaunaumeek; which many times exposed him to extreme hardship in the severe seasons of the winter.

Monday, December 5. Rode to Stockbridge. Was almost outdone with the extreme cold. Had some refreshing meditations by the way, but was barren, wandering, and lifeless much of the day. Thus my days roll away, with but little done for God; and this is my burden.

Tuesday, December 6. Was perplexed to see the vanity and levity of professed Christians. Spent the evening with a Christian friend, who was able in some measure to sympathize with me in my spiritual conflicts. Was a little refreshed to find one with whom I could converse of inward trials.

Wednesday, December 7. Spent the evening in perplexity, with a kind of guilty indolence. When I have no heart or resolution for God and the duties incumbent on me, I feel guilty of negligence and misimprovement of time. Certainly I ought to be engaged in my work and business to the utmost extent of my strength and ability.

Thursday, December 8. My mind was much distracted with different affections. I seemed to be at an amazing distance from God, and looking round in the world to see if there was not some happiness to be derived from it. God and certain objects in the world seemed each to invite my heart and affections; and my soul seemed to be distracted between them. I have not been so much beset with the world for a long time; and that with relation to some particular objects which I thought myself most dead to. But even while I was desiring to please myself with anything below, guilt, sorrow, and perplexity attended the first motions of desire. Indeed I cannot see the appearance of pleasure and happiness in the world, as I used to do; and blessed be God for any habitual deadness to the world. I found no peace or deliverance from this distraction and perplexity of mind till I found access to the throne of grace. As soon as I had any sense of God and things divine, the allurements of the world vanished, and my heart was determined for God. But my soul mourned over my folly, that I should desire any pleasure but only in God. God forgive my spiritual idolatry.

Thursday, December 22. Spent this day alone in fasting and

prayer and reading in God's Word the exercises and deliverances of His children. Had, I trust, some exercises of faith and realizing apprehension of divine power, grace, and holiness; and also of the unchangeableness of God, that He is the same as when He delivered His saints of old out of great tribulation. My soul was sundry times in prayer enlarged for God's Church and people. Oh, that Zion might become the "joy of the whole earth"! It is better to wait upon God with patience than to put confidence in anything in this lower world. "My soul, wait thou on the Lord;" for from Him comes thy salvation.

Friday, December 23. Felt a little more courage and resolution in religion, than at some other times.

Saturday, December 24. Had some assistance and longing desires after sanctification in prayer this day, especially in the evening. Was sensible of my own weakness and spiritual impotency; saw plainly I should fall into sin if God of His abundant mercy did not "uphold my soul, and withhold me from evil." Oh, that God would uphold me by His free Spirit, and save me from the hour of temptation!

Lord's Day, December 25. Prayed much in the morning, with a feeling sense of my own spiritual weakness and insufficiency for any duty. God gave me some assistance in preaching to the Indians; especially in the afternoon, when I was enabled to speak with uncommon plainness, freedom, and earnestness. Blessed be God for any assistance granted to one so unworthy.

Monday, December 26. Rode down to Stockbridge. Was very much fatigued with my journey, wherein I underwent great hardships; was much exposed and very wet by falling into a river. Spent the day and evening without much sense of divine and heavenly things, but felt guilty, grieved, and perplexed with wandering, careless thoughts.

Tuesday, December 27. Had a small degree of warmth in secret prayer in the evening; but, alas! had but little spiritual life and consequently but little comfort. Oh, the pressure of a body of death!

Wednesday. December 28. Rode about six miles to the ordination of Mr. Hopkins. At the solemnity I was somewhat affected with a sense of the greatness and importance of the work of a minister of Christ. Afterwards was grieved to see the vanity of the multitude. In the evening, spent a little time with some Christian friends, with some degree of satisfaction; but most of the time, I had rather have been alone.

Thursday, December 29. Spent the day mainly in conversing with friends; yet enjoyed little satisfaction, because I could find but few disposed to converse of divine and heavenly things. Alas, what are the things of this world, to afford satisfaction to the soul! Near night, returned to Stockbridge; in secret, I blessed God for retirement and that I am not always exposed to the company and conversation of the world. Oh, that I could live "in the secret of God's presence!"

Friday, December 30. Was in a solemn, devout frame in the evening. Wondered that earth, with all its charms, should ever allure me in the least degree. Oh, that I could always realize the being and holiness of God!

Saturday, December 31. Rode from Stockbridge home to my house. The air was clear and calm, but as cold as ever I felt it, or near. I was in great danger of perishing by the extremity of the season. Was enabled to meditate much on the road.

Lord's Day, January 1, 1744. In the morning, had some small degree of assistance in prayer. Saw myself so vile and unworthy that I could not look my people in the face when I came to preach. Oh, my meanness, folly, ignorance, and inward pollution! In the evening, had a little assistance in prayer so that the duty was delightful, rather than burdensome. Reflected on the goodness of God to me in the past year. Of a truth God has been kind and gracious to me, though He has caused me to pass through many sorrows. He has provided for me bountifully so that I have been enabled, in about fifteen months past, to bestow to charitable uses about an hundred pounds New England money, that I can now remember. Blessed be the Lord, that has so far used me as His steward to distribute a portion of His goods. May I always remember that all I have comes from God. Blessed be the Lord that has carried me through all the toils, fatigues, and hardships of the year past, as well as the spiritual sorrows and conflicts that have attended it. Oh, that I could begin this year with God and spend the whole of it to His glory, either in life or death!

Monday, January 2. Had some affecting sense of my own impotency and spiritual weakness. It is nothing but the power of God that keeps me from all manner of wickedness. I see I am nothing and can do nothing without help from above. Oh, for divine grace! In the evening, had some ardor of soul in prayer, and longing desires to have God for my guide and safeguard at all times.

Tuesday, January 3. Was employed much of the day in writing and spent some time in other necessary employment. But my time passes away so swiftly that I am astonished when I reflect on it and see how little I do. My state of solitude does not make the hours hang heavy upon my hands. Oh, what reason of thankfulness have I on account of this retirement! I find that I do not, and it seems I cannot, lead a Christian life when I am abroad and cannot spend time in devotion, Christian conversation and serious meditation, as I should do. Those weeks that I am obliged now to be from home, in order to learn the Indian tongue, are mostly spent in perplexity and barrenness, without much sweet relish of divine things. I feel myself a stranger at the throne of grace for want of more frequent and continued retirement. When I return home and give myself to meditation, prayer and fasting, a new scene opens to my mind and my soul longs for mortification, self-denial, humility and divorcement from all the things of the world. This evening my heart was somewhat warm and fervent in prayer and meditation, so that I was loath to indulge sleep. Continued in those duties till about midnight.

Wednesday, January 4. Was in a resigned and mortified temper of mind, much of the day. Time appeared a moment, life a vapor, and all its enjoyments as empty bubbles and fleeting blasts of wind.

Thursday, January 5. Had a humbling and pressing sense of my unworthiness. My sense of the badness of my own heart filled my soul with bitterness and anguish, which was ready to sink as under the weight of a heavy burden. Thus I spent the evening, till late. Was somewhat intense and ardent in prayer.

Friday, January 6. Feeling and considering my extreme weakness and want of grace, the pollution of my soul and danger of temptations on every side, I set apart this day for fasting and prayer, neither eating nor drinking from evening to evening, beseeching God to have mercy on me. My soul intensely longed that the dreadful spots and stains of sin might be washed away from it. Saw something of the power and all-sufficiency of God. My soul seemed to rest on His power and grace. I longed for resignation to His will and mortification to all things here below.

My mind was greatly fixed on divine things; my resolutions for a life of mortification, continual watchfulness, self-denial, seriousness, and devotion were strong and fixed. My desires were ardent and intense; my conscience tender and afraid of every appearance of evil. My soul grieved with reflection on past levity and want of resolution for God. I solemnly renewed my dedication of myself to God and longed for grace to enable me always to keep covenant with Him. Time appeared very short, eternity near; and a great name, either in or after life, together with all earthly pleasures and profits, but an empty bubble, a deluding dream.

Saturday, January 7. Spent this day in seriousness, with steadfast resolutions for God and a life of mortification. Studied closely, till I felt my bodily strength fail. Felt some degree of resignation to God, with an acquiescence in His dispensations. Was grieved that I could do so little for God before my bodily strength failed. In the evening, though tired, was enabled to continue instant in prayer for some time. Spent the time in reading, meditation, and prayer, till the evening was far spent. Was grieved to think that I could not watch unto prayer the whole night. But blessed be God, heaven is a place of continual and incessant devotion, though the earth is dull.

Saturday, January 14. This morning, enjoyed a most solemn season in prayer. My soul seemed enlarged, and assisted to pour out itself to God for grace and for every blessing I wanted, for myself, my dear Christian friends and for the Church of God. I was so enabled to see Him who is invisible that my soul rested upon Him for the performance of everything I asked agreeable to His will. It was then my happiness to "continue instant in prayer," and was enabled to continue in it for near an hour. My soul was then "strong in the Lord and in the power of his might." Longed exceedingly for angelic holiness and purity and to have all my thoughts, at all times, employed in divine and heavenly things. Oh, how blessed is an heavenly temper! Oh, how unspeakably blessed it is, to feel a measure of that rectitude, in which we were at first created! Felt the same divine assistance in prayer sundry times in the day. My soul confided in God for myself and for His Zion; trusted in divine power and grace that He would do glorious things in His Church on earth, for His own glory.

Monday, January 23. I think I never felt more resigned to God, nor so much dead to the world, in every respect, as now; was dead to all desire of reputation and greatness, either in life, or after death. All I longed for was to be holy, humble, crucified to the world.

Tuesday, January 24. Near noon, rode over to Canaan. In the evening, I was unexpectedly visited by a considerable number of people, with whom I was enabled to converse profitably of divine things. Took pains to describe the difference between a *regular* and *irregular* self-love; the one consisting with a supreme love to God, but the other not; the former uniting God's glory and the soul's happiness that they become one common interest, but the latter disjoining and separating God's glory and man's happiness, seeking the latter with a neglect of the former. Illustrated this by that genuine love that is founded between the sexes, which is diverse from that which is wrought up towards a person only by rational argument, or hope of self-interest. Love is a pleasing passion;

it affords pleasure to the mind where it is; but yet, genuine love is not, nor can be placed upon any object with that design of pleasure itself.

> On Wednesday he rode to Sheffield; the next day, to Stockbridge; and on Saturday, home to Kaunaumeek, though the season was cold and stormy; which journey was followed with illness and pain. It appears by this diary that he spent the time while riding in profitable meditations and in lifting up his heart to God. He speaks of assistance, comfort, and refreshment, but still complains of barrenness. His diary for the five next days is full of the most heavy, bitter complaints; and he expresses himself as full of shame and self-loathing for his lifeless temper of mind and sluggishness of spirit, and as being in perplexity and extremity, and appearing to himself unspeakably vile and guilty before God, on account of some inward workings of corruption he found in his heart.—J. E.

Thursday, February 2. Spent this day in fasting and prayer, seeking the presence and assistance of God, that He would enable me to overcome all my corruptions and spiritual enemies.

Friday, February 3. Enjoyed more freedom and comfort than of late; was engaged in meditation upon the different whispers of the various powers and affections of a pious mind, exercised with a great variety of dispensations. I could but write, as well as meditate, on so entertaining a subject. I hope the Lord gave me some true sense of divine things this day; but alas, how great and pressing are the remains of indwelling corruption! I am now more sensible than ever that God alone is "the author and finisher of our faith," that is, that the whole and every part of sanctification and every good word, work, or thought found in me, is the effect of His power and grace. "Without him I can do nothing," in the strictest sense, and "he works in us to will and to do of his own good pleasure," and from no other motive. Oh, how amazing it is that people can talk so much about men's power and goodness when, if God did not hold us back every moment, we should be devils incarnate! This my bitter experience for several days last past has abundantly taught me concerning myself.

Lord's Day, February 5. Was enabled in some measure to rest and confide in God and to prize His presence and some glimpses of the light of His countenance, above my necessary food. Thought myself, after the season of weakness, temptation, and desertion I endured the last week, to be somewhat like Samson when his locks began to grow again. Was enabled to preach to my people with more life and warmth than I have for some weeks past.

Monday, February 6. This morning my soul again was strengthened in God, and I found some sweet repose in Him in prayer; longing especially for the complete mortification of sensuality and pride, and for resignation to God's dispensations, at all times, as through grace I felt it at this time. I did not desire deliverance from any difficulty that attends my circumstances, unless God was willing. Oh, how comfortable is this temper! Spent most of the day in reading God's Word, in writing and prayer. Enjoyed repeated and frequent comfort and intenseness of soul in prayer through the day. In the evening, spent some hours in private conversation with my people; afterwards, felt some warmth in secret prayer.

Tuesday, February 7. Was much engaged in some sweet meditations on the powers and affections of godly souls in their pursuit of their beloved Object. Wrote something of the native language of spiritual sensation, in its soft and tender whispers; declaring, that it now "feels and tastes that the Lord is gracious; that He is the supreme good, the only soul-satisfying happiness: that He is a complete, sufficient, and almighty portion: saying,

"Whom have I in heaven but Thee? and there is none upon earth that I desire besides this blessed portion. Oh, I feel it is heaven to please Him, and to be just what He would have me to be! Oh, that my soul were holy as He is holy! Oh, that it were pure, even as Christ is pure; and perfect, as my Father in heaven is perfect! These, I feel, are the sweetest commands in God's Book, comprising all others. And shall I break them? Must I break them? Am I under a necessity of it as long as I live in the world? O my soul, woe, woe is me that I am a sinner, because I now necessarily grieve and offend this blessed God, who is infinite in goodness and grace!

"Oh, methinks if He would punish me for my sins, it would not wound my heart so deep to offend Him; but though I sin continually, yet He continually repeats His kindness to me! Oh, methinks I could bear any sufferings; but how can I bear to grieve and dishonor this blessed God? How shall I yield ten thousand times more honor to Him? What shall I do to glorify and worship this Best of beings? Oh, that I could consecrate myself, soul and body, to His service forever! Oh, that I could give up myself to Him, so as never more to attempt to be my own, or to have any will or affection that are not perfectly conformed to him!

"But, alas, alas! I find I cannot be thus entirely devoted to God; I cannot live and not sin. O ye angels, do ye glorify Him incessantly; and if possible, prostrate yourselves lower before the blessed King of heaven? I long to bear a part with you; and, if it were possible, to help you. Oh, when we have done all that we can, to all eternity, we shall not be able to offer the ten thousandth part of the homage that the glorious God deserves!"

Felt something spiritual, devout, resigned and mortified to the world, much of the day, especially towards and in the evening. Blessed be God that He enables me to love Him for Himself.

Wednesday, February 8. Was in a comfortable frame of soul, most of the day; though sensible of and restless under spiritual barrenness. I find that both mind and body are quickly tired with intenseness and fervor in the things of God. Oh, that I could be as incessant as angels in devotion and spiritual fervor!

Thursday, February 9. Observed this day as a day of fasting and prayer, intreating of God to bestow upon me His blessing and grace; especially to enable me to live a life of mortification to the world, as well as of resignation and patience.

Friday, February 10. Was exceedingly oppressed, most of the day, with shame, grief, and fear, under a sense of my past folly, as well as present barrenness and coldness. When God sets before me my past misconduct, especially any instances of misguided zeal, it sinks my soul into shame and confusion, makes me afraid of a shaking leaf. My fear is such as the prophet Jeremiah complains of (Jer. 20:10). I have no confidence to hold up my face, even before my fellow worms; but only when my soul confides in God, and I find the sweet temper of Christ, the spirit of humility, solemnity, and mortification, and resignation, alive in my soul. But, in the evening, was unexpectedly refreshed in pouring out my complaint to God; my shame and fear was turned into a sweet composure and acquiescence in God.

Lord's Day, February 12. My soul seemed to confide in God and to repose itself on Him; and had outgoings of soul after God in prayer. Enjoyed some divine assistance, in the forenoon, in preaching; but in the afternoon, was more perplexed with shame. Afterwards, found some relief in prayer; loved, as a feeble, afflicted, despised creature, to cast myself on a God of infinite grace and goodness, hoping for no happiness but from Him.

Monday, February 13. Was calm and sedate in morning devotions; and my soul seemed to rely on God. Rode to Stockbridge and enjoyed some comfortable meditations by the way. Had a more refreshing taste and relish of heavenly blessedness than I have enjoyed for many months past. I have many times, of late, felt as ardent desires of holiness as ever, but not so much sense of the sweetness and unspeakable pleasure of the enjoyments and employments of heaven. My soul longed to leave earth and bear a part with angels in their celestial employments. My soul said, "Lord, it is good to be here"; and it appeared to be better to die than to lose the relish of these heavenly delights.

A sense of divine things seemed to continue with him, in a lesser degree, through the next day. On Wednesday he was, by some discourse that he heard, cast into a melancholy gloom that operated much in the same manner as his melancholy had formerly done when he came first to Kaunaumeek; the effects of which seemed to continue in some degree the six following days.—J. E.

Thursday, February 23. Was frequent in prayer, and enjoyed some assistance. There is a God in heaven who overrules all things for the best; and this is the comfort of my soul: "I had fainted, unless I had believed to see the goodness of God in the land of the living," notwithstanding present sorrows. In the evening, enjoyed some freedom in prayer, for myself, friends, and the Church of God.

Friday, March 2. Was most of the day employed in writing on a divine subject. Was frequent in prayer and enjoyed some small degree of assistance. But in the evening, God was pleased to grant me a divine sweetness in prayer; especially in the duty of intercession. I think I never felt so much kindness and love to those whom I have reason to think are my enemies—though at that time I found such a disposition to think the best of all that I scarce knew how to think that any such thing as enmity and hatred lodged in any soul. It seemed as if all the world must needs be friends—and never prayed with more freedom and delight, for myself, or dearest friend, than I did now for my enemies.

Saturday, March 3. In the morning spent (I believe) an hour in prayer, with great intenseness and freedom, and with the most soft and tender affection towards mankind. I longed that those who, I have reason to think, owe me ill will, might be eternally happy. It seemed refreshing to think of meeting them in heaven, how much soever they had injured me on earth. I had no disposition to insist upon any confession from them in order to reconciliation and the exercise of love and kindness to them.

Oh, it is an emblem of heaven itself to love all the world

with a love of kindness, forgiveness, and benevolence; to feel
our souls sedate, mild, and meek; to be void of all evil sur-
misings and suspicions and scarce able to think evil of any
man upon any occasion; to find our hearts simple, open and
free, to those that look upon us with a different eye! Prayer
was so sweet an exercise to me, that I knew not how to cease,
lest I should lose the spirit of prayer. Felt no disposition to
eat or drink for the sake of the pleasure of it, but only to support my nature and fit me for divine service. Could not be
content without a very particular mention of a great number
of dear friends at the throne of grace; as also the particular
circumstances of many, so far as they were known.

Lord's Day, March 4. In the morning, enjoyed the same
intenseness in prayer as yesterday morning, though not in so
great a degree. Felt the same spirit of love, universal benevolence, forgiveness, humility, resignation, mortification to
the world, and composure of mind, as then. My soul rested in
God and I found I wanted no other refuge or friend. While my
soul thus trusts in God, all things seem to be at peace with
me, even the stones of the earth; but when I cannot apprehend
and confide in God, all things appear with a different aspect.

Saturday, March 10. In the morning, felt exceeding dead to
the world and all its enjoyments. I thought I was ready and
willing to give up life and all its comforts, as soon as called
to it; and yet then had as much comfort of life as almost ever
I had. Life itself now appeared but an empty bubble; the
riches, honors, and common enjoyments of life appeared extremely tasteless. I longed to be perpetually and entirely
crucified to all things here below, by the cross of Christ. My
soul was sweetly resigned to God's disposal of me, in every
regard; and I saw there had nothing happened but what was
best for me. I confided in God that He would never leave me,
though I should "walk through the valley of the shadow of
death." It was then my meat and drink to be holy, to live
to the Lord, and die to the Lord.

And I thought that I then enjoyed such a heaven as far
exceeded the most sublime conceptions of an unregenerate

soul; and even unspeakably beyond what I myself could conceive of at another time. I did not wonder that Peter said, "Lord, it is good to be here," when thus refreshed with divine glories. My soul was full of love and tenderness in the duty of intercession; especially felt a most sweet affection to some precious godly ministers of my acquaintance. Prayed earnestly for dear Christians and for those I have reason to fear are my enemies; and could not have spoken a word of bitterness, or entertained a bitter thought, against the vilest man living. Had a sense of my own great unworthiness.

My soul seemed to breathe forth love and praise to God afresh, when I thought He would let His children love and receive me as one of their brethren and fellow citizens. When I thought of their treating me in that manner, I longed to lie at their feet and could think of no way to express the sincerity and simplicity of my love and esteem of them, as being much better than myself. Towards night, was very sorrowful; seemed to myself the worst creature living and could not pray, nor meditate, nor think of holding up my face before the world. Was a little relieved in prayer in the evening, but longed to get on my knees and ask forgiveness of everybody that ever had seen anything amiss in my past conduct, especially in my religious zeal. Was afterwards much perplexed, so that I could not sleep quietly.

Lord's Day, March 11. My soul was in some measure strengthened in God in morning devotion so that I was released from trembling fear and distress. Preached to my people from the Parable of the Sower, Matthew 13, and enjoyed some assistance, both parts of the day. Had some freedom, affection and fervency in addressing my poor people; longed that God should take hold of their hearts, and make them spiritually alive. And indeed I had so much to say to them that I knew not how to leave off speaking.[5]

---

[5] This was the last Sabbath that ever he performed public service at Kaunaumeek, and these the last sermons that ever he preached there. It appears by his diary, that while he continued with these Indians he took great pains with them, and did it with much discretion; but the particular manner how, has been omitted for brevity's sake.

Monday, March 12. In the morning, was in a devout, tender, and loving frame of mind. I was enabled to cry to God, I hope, with a childlike spirit, with importunity, and resignation, and composure of mind. My spirit was full of quietness, and love to mankind, and I longed that peace should reign on the earth; was grieved at the very thoughts of a fiery, angry and intemperate zeal in religion; mourned over past follies in that regard. My soul confided in God for strength and grace sufficient for my future work and trials. Spent the day mainly in hard labor, making preparation for my intended journey.

Tuesday, March 13. Felt my soul going forth after God sometimes; but not with such ardency as I longed for. In the evening, was enabled to continue instant in prayer, for some considerable time together; and especially had respect to the journey I designed to enter upon, with the leave of divine providence, on the morrow. Enjoyed some freedom and fervency, intreating that the divine presence might attend me in every place where my business might lead me; had a particular reference to the trials and temptations that I apprehended I might be more eminently exposed to in particular places. Was strengthened and comforted, although I was before very weary. Truly the joy of the Lord is strength and life.

Wednesday, March 14. Enjoyed some intenseness of soul in prayer, repeating my petitions for God's presence in every place where I expected to be in my journey. Besought the Lord that I might not be too much pleased and amused with dear friends and acquaintance, in one place and another. Near ten set out on my journey; and near night came to Stockbridge.

## He Leaves Kaunaumeek

Thursday, March 15. Rode down to Sheffield. Here I met a messenger from East Hampton on Long Island who, by the unanimous vote of that large town, was sent to invite me thither, in order to settle with that people where I had been before frequently invited. Seemed more at a loss what was my duty than before. When I heard of the great difficulties of that place, I was much concerned and grieved, and felt some desires to comply with their request; but knew not what to do; endeavored to commit the case to God.

Lord's Day, March 18. (At Salisbury.) Was exceeding weak and faint so that I could scarce walk. But God was pleased to afford me much freedom, clearness and fervency in preaching. I have not had the like assistance in preaching to sinners for many months past. Here another messenger met me and informed me of the vote of another congregation to give me an invitation to come among them upon probation for settlement. Was something exercised in mind with a weight and burden of care. Oh, that God would "send forth faithful laborers into his harvest!"

> After this, he went forward on his journey towards New York and New Jersey, in which he proceeded slowly, performing his journey under great degrees of bodily indisposition. However, he preached several times by the way, being urged by friends; in which he had considerable assistance. He speaks of comfort in conversation with Christian friends, from time to time, and of various things in the exercises and frames of his heart that show much of a divine influence on his mind in this journey. But complains of the things that he feared, namely, a decline of his spiritual life, or vivacity in religion, by means of his constant removal from place to place, and want of retirement. Complains bitterly of his unworthiness and deadness. He came to New York on Wednesday, March 28, and to Elisabeth Town on the Saturday following, where it seems he waited till the commissioners came together.—J. E.

Thursday, April 5. Was again much exercised with weakness, and with pain in my head. Attended on the commissioners in their meeting.[6] Resolved to go on still with the

---

[6] The Indians at Kaunaumeek being but few in number, and Mr. Brainerd having now been laboring among them about a year, and having prevailed upon them to be willing to leave Kaunaumeek and remove to Stockbridge, to live constantly under Mr. Sergeant's ministry; he thought he might now do more service for Christ among

Indian affair, if divine providence permitted; although I had before felt some inclination to go to East Hampton, where I was solicited to go. (See Appendix II.)

> After this, he continued two or three days in the Jerseys, very ill; and then returned to New York; and from thence into New England; and went to his native town of Haddam, where he arrived on Saturday, April 14. . . . He spent some days among his friends at East Hampton and Millington.—J. E.

Tuesday, April 17. Rode to Millington again and felt perplexed when I set out; was feeble in body and weak in faith. I was going to preach a lecture and feared I should never have assistance enough to get through. But contriving to ride alone, at a distance from the company that was going, I spent the time in lifting my heart to God. Had not gone far before my soul was abundantly strengthened with those words, "If God be for us, who can be against us?" I went on, confiding in God and fearing nothing so much as self-confidence. In this frame I went to the house of God and enjoyed some assistance. Afterwards felt the spirit of love and meekness in conversation with some friends. Then rode home. . . .

In the evening, singing hymns with friends, my soul seemed to melt, and in prayer afterwards enjoyed the exercise of faith and was enabled to be fervent in spirit. Found more of God's presence than I have done any time in my late wearisome journey. Eternity appeared very near; my nature was very weak and seemed ready to be dissolved, the sun declining, and the shadows of the evening drawing on apace. Oh, I longed to fill up the remaining moments all for God! Though my body was so feeble, and wearied with preaching and much private conversation, yet I wanted to sit up all night to do something for God. To God, the giver of these refreshments, be glory for ever and ever. Amen.

---

the Indians elsewhere. Therefore went this journey to New Jersey to lay the matter before the commissioners who met at Elisabeth Town on this occasion, and determined that he should forthwith leave Kaunaumeek and go to the Delaware Indians.

Wednesday, April 18. Was very weak and enjoyed but little spiritual comfort. Was exercised with one who caviled against original sin. May the Lord open his eyes to see the fountain of sin in himself!

> After this, he visited several ministers in Connecticut; and then traveled towards Kaunaumeek, and came to Mr. Sergeant's at Stockbridge, Thursday, April 26. He performed this journey in a very weak state of body.—J. E.

Friday and Saturday, April 27 and 28. Spent some time in visiting friends and discoursing with my people (who were now moved down from their own place to Mr. Sergeant's), and found them very glad to see me returned. Was exercised in my mind with a sense of my own unworthiness.

Lord's Day, April 29. Preached for Mr. Sergeant, both parts of the day, from Revelation 14:4, "These are they which were not defiled . . ." Enjoyed some freedom in preaching, though not much spirituality. In the evening, my heart was in some measure lifted up in thankfulness to God for any assistance.

Monday, April 30. Rode to Kaunaumeek, but was extremely ill; did not enjoy the comfort I hoped for in my own house.

Tuesday, May 1. Having received new orders to go to a number of Indians on Delaware River in Pennsylvania, and my people here being mostly removed to Mr. Sergeant's, I this day took all my clothes and books and disposed of them, and set out for the Delaware River. But made it my way to return to Mr. Sergeant's; which I did this day, just at night. Rode several hours in the rain through the howling wilderness, although I was so disordered in body, that little or nothing but blood came from me.

Tuesday, May 8. Set out from Sharon in Connecticut and traveled about forty-five miles to a place called the Fish-kit [a place so called in New York Government, near Hudson's River on the west side]; and lodged there. Spent much of my time, while riding, in prayer that God would go with me to

Delaware. My heart sometimes was ready to sink with the thoughts of my work, and going alone in the wilderness, I knew not where. But still it was comfortable to think that others of God's children had "wandered about in caves and dens of the earth," and Abraham, when he was called to go forth, "went out, not knowing whither he went." Oh, that I might follow after God!

> The next day, he went forward on his journey; crossed Hudson's River, and went to Goshen in the Highlands; and so traveled across the woods, from Hudson's River to Delaware, about a hundred miles, through a desolate and hideous country above New Jersey, where were few settlements; in which journey he suffered much fatigue and hardship. He visited some Indians in the way, and discoursed with them concerning Christianity. Was considerably melancholy and disconsolate, being alone in a strange wilderness. On Saturday, he came to a settlement of Irish and Dutch people, about twelve miles above the Forks of Delaware.—J. E.

Lord's Day, May 13. Rose early; felt very poorly after my long journey, and after being wet and fatigued. Was very melancholy; have scarce ever seen such a gloomy morning in my life. There appeared to be no Sabbath; the children were all at play. I was a stranger in the wilderness and knew not where to go, and all circumstances seemed to conspire to render my affairs dark and discouraging. Was disappointed respecting an interpreter, and heard that the Indians were much scattered.

Oh, I mourned after the presence of God and seemed like a creature banished from His sight! Yet He was pleased to support my sinking soul amidst all my sorrows so that I never entertained any thought of quitting my business among the poor Indians; but was comforted to think that death would ere long set me free from these distresses. Rode about three or four miles to the Irish people, where I found some that appeared sober and concerned about religion. My heart then began to be a little encouraged. Went and preached first

to the Irish and then to the Indians; and in the evening was a
little comforted. My soul seemed to rest on God and take
courage. Oh, that the Lord would be my support and comforter in an evil world!

Tuesday, May 15. Still much engaged in my studies and enjoyed more health than I have for some time past. But was
something dejected in spirit with a sense of my meanness;
seemed as if I could never do anything at all to any good purpose by reason of ignorance and folly. Oh, that a sense of
these things might work more habitual humility in my soul!

Thursday, May 17. In the afternoon, met with the Indians,
according to appointment, and preached to them. While
riding to them my soul seemed to confide in God; afterwards
had some relief and enlargement of soul in prayer and some
assistance in the duty of intercession. Vital piety and holiness
appeared sweet to me and I longed for the perfection of it.

Friday, May 18. Felt again something of the sweet spirit
of religion; and my soul seemed to confide in God, that He
would never leave me. But oftentimes saw myself so mean a
creature that I knew not how to think of preaching. Oh, that
I could always live *to* and *upon* God!

Saturday, May 19. Was, some part of the time, greatly oppressed with the weight and burden of my work. It seemed
impossible for me ever to go through with the business I had
undertaken. Towards night was very calm and comfortable,
and I think my soul trusted in God for help.

Lord's Day, May 20. Preached twice to the poor Indians,
and enjoyed some freedom in speaking, while I attempted to
remove their prejudices against Christianity. My soul longed
for assistance from above, all the while; for I saw I had no
strength sufficient for that work. Afterwards, preached to the
Irish people; was much assisted in the first prayer, and something in sermon. Several persons seemed much concerned for
their souls, with whom I discoursed afterwards with much
freedom and some power. Blessed be God for any assistance
afforded to an unworthy worm.

Lord's Day, May 27. Visited my Indians in the morning,

and attended upon a funeral among them; was affected to see their heathenish practices. Oh, that they might be "turned from darkness to light"! Afterwards got a considerable number of them together and preached to them; and observed them very attentive. After this, preached to the white people from Hebrews 2:3, "How shall we escape, if we neglect . . ." Was enabled to speak with some freedom and power. Several people seemed much concerned for their souls, especially one who had been educated a Roman Catholic. Blessed be the Lord for any help.

Monday, May 28. Set out from the Indians above the Forks of Delaware, on a journey towards Newark in New Jersey, according to my orders. Rode through the wilderness and was much fatigued with the heat; lodged at a place called Black River; was exceedingly tired and worn out.

Monday, June 11. This day the Presbytery met together at Newark, in order to my ordination. Was very weak and disordered in body; yet endeavored to repose my confidence in God. Spent most of the day alone, especially the forenoon. At three in the afternoon preached my probation sermon, from Acts 26:17, 18, "Delivering thee from the people, and from the Gentiles . . ." being a text given me for that end. Felt not well, either in body or mind; however, God carried me through comfortably. Afterwards, passed an examination before the Presbytery. Was much tired and my mind burdened with the greatness of that charge [which] I was in the most solemn manner about to take upon me. My mind was so pressed with the weight of the work incumbent upon me that I could not sleep this night.

Tuesday, June 12. Was this morning further examined, respecting my experimental acquaintance with Christianity.[7]

[7] Mr. Pemberton, in a letter to the honorable society in Scotland that employed Mr. Brainerd, which he wrote concerning him (published in Scotland, in the *Christian Monthly History*), writes thus: "We can with pleasure say, that Mr. Brainerd passed through his ordination trial, to the universal approbation of the Presbytery, and appeared uncommonly qualified for the work of the ministry. He seems to be armed with a great deal of self-denial, and animated with a noble zeal to propagate the gospel among those barbarous nations, who have long dwelt in darkness."

At ten o'clock my ordination was attended; the sermon preached by Mr. Pemberton. At this time I was affected with a sense of the important trust committed to me; yet was composed and solemn, without distraction. I hope that then, as many times before, I gave myself up to God, to be for Him and not for another. Oh, that I might always be engaged in the service of God, and duly remember the solemn charge I have received, in the presence of God, angels and men. Amen. May I be assisted of God for this purpose. Towards night, rode to Elisabeth Town.

# PART VI

FROM HIS ORDINATION, TILL HE FIRST BEGAN TO PREACH TO
THE INDIANS AT CROSSWEEKSUNG, AMONG WHOM HE HAD HIS
MOST REMARKABLE SUCCESS

### 1744, 1745

WEDNESDAY, June 13, 1744. Spent some considerable time in writing an account of the Indian affairs to go to Scotland; some, in conversation with friends; but enjoyed not much sweetness and satisfaction.

Thursday, June 14. Received some particular kindness from friends, and wondered that God should open the hearts of any to treat me with kindness. Saw myself to be unworthy of any favor from God, or any of my fellow men. Was much exercised with pain in my head; however I determined to set out on my journey towards Delaware in the afternoon. But when the afternoon came, my pain increased exceedingly, so that I was obliged to betake myself to bed. The night following, I was greatly distressed with pain and sickness; was sometimes almost bereaved of the exercise of reason by the extremity of pain. Continued much distressed till Saturday, when I was somewhat relieved by an emetic. Was unable to walk abroad till the Monday following in the afternoon, and still remained very feeble.

I often admired the goodness of God that He did not suffer me to proceed on my journey from this place where I was so tenderly used, and to be sick by the way among strangers. God is very gracious to me, both in health and sickness, and intermingles much mercy with all my afflictions and toils. Enjoyed some sweetness in things divine, in the midst of my pain and weakness. Oh, that I could praise the Lord!

165

On Tuesday, June 19, he set out on his journey home, and in three days reached his place, near the Forks of Delaware. Performed the journey under much weakness of body, but had comfort in his soul from day to day. Both his weakness of body and consolation of mind continued through the week.—J. E.

Lord's Day, June 24. Extremely feeble, scarce able to walk. However visited my Indians and took much pains to instruct them; labored with some that were much disaffected to Christianity. My mind was much burdened with the weight and difficulty of my work. My whole dependence and hope of success seemed to be on God, who alone I saw could make them willing to receive instruction. My heart was much engaged in prayer, sending up silent requests to God even while I was speaking to them. Oh, that I could always go in the strength of the Lord!

Monday, June 25. Was something better in health than of late; was able to spend a considerable part of the day in prayer and close studies. Had more freedom and fervency in prayer than usual of late. Especially longed for the presence of God in my work and that the poor heathen might be converted. And in evening prayer my faith and hope in God were much raised. To an eye of reason, everything that respects the conversion of the heathen is as dark as midnight; and yet I cannot but hope in God for the accomplishment of something glorious among them.

Tuesday, June 26. In the morning, my desires seemed to rise and ascend up freely to God. Was busy most of the day in translating prayers into the language of the Delaware Indians; met with great difficulty by reason that my interpreter was altogether unacquainted with the business. But though I was much discouraged with the extreme difficulty of that work, yet God supported me; and especially in the evening, gave me sweet refreshment.

In prayer my soul was enlarged, and my faith drawn into sensible exercise. Was enabled to cry to God for my poor Indians; though the work of their conversion appeared impossible with man, yet with God I saw all things were possible. My faith was much strengthened by observing the wonderful assistance God afforded His servants Nehemiah and Ezra in reforming His people and re-establishing His ancient church. I was much assisted in prayer for dear Christian friends and for others that I apprehended to be Christless. But was more especially concerned for the poor heathen and those of my own charge. Was enabled to be instant in prayer for them and hoped that God would bow the heavens and come down for their salvation. It seemed to me there could be no impediment sufficient to obstruct that glorious work, seeing the living God, as I strongly hoped, was engaged for it.

I continued in a solemn frame, lifting up my heart to God for assistance and grace that I might be more mortified to this present world; that my whole soul might be taken up continually in concern for the advancement of Christ's kingdom. Longed that God would purge me more that I might be as a chosen vessel to bear His name among the heathens. Continued in this frame till I dropped asleep.

Wednesday, June 27. Felt something of the same solemn concern and spirit of prayer that I enjoyed last night, soon after I rose in the morning. In the afternoon, rode several miles to see if I could procure any lands for the poor Indians, that they might live together and be under better advantages for instruction. While I was riding, had a deep sense of the greatness and difficulty of my work. My soul seemed to rely wholly upon God for success, in the diligent and faithful use of means. Saw, with greatest certainty, that the arm of the Lord must be revealed for the help of these poor heathen, if ever they were delivered from the bondage of the powers of darkness. Spent most of the time, while riding, in lifting up my heart for grace and assistance.

Thursday, June 28. Spent the morning in reading several parts of the Holy Scripture, and in fervent prayer for my Indians that God would set up His kingdom among them and bring them into His Church. About nine, I withdrew to my usual place of retirement in the woods and there again enjoyed some assistance in prayer. My great concern was for the conversion of the heathen to God; and the Lord helped me to plead with Him for it. Towards noon, rode up to the Indians in order to preach to them. While going, my heart went up to God in prayer for them; could freely tell God He knew that the cause was not mine which I was engaged in; but it was His own cause and it would be for His own glory to convert the poor Indians. Blessed be God, I felt no desire of their conversion that I might receive honor from the world, as being the instrument of it. Had some freedom in speaking to the Indians.

Saturday, June 30. My soul was very solemn in reading God's Word; especially the ninth chapter of Daniel. I saw how God had called out His servants to prayer and made them wrestle with Him when He designed to bestow any great mercy on His Church. And, alas! I was ashamed of myself, to think of my dullness and inactivity when there seemed to be so much to do for the upbuilding of Zion. Oh, how does Zion lie waste!

Lord's Day, July 1. In the morning, was perplexed with wandering vain thoughts; was much grieved, judged and condemned myself before God. And oh, how miserable did I feel because I could not live to God! At ten, rode away with a heavy heart, to preach to my Indians. Upon the road I attempted to lift up my heart to God; but was infested with an unsettled wandering frame of mind. Was exceeding restless and perplexed and filled with shame and confusion before God. I seemed to myself to be "more brutish than any man"; and thought none deserved to be "cast out of God's presence" so much as I. If I attempted to lift up my heart to God, as I frequently did by the way, on a sudden, before I was aware, my thoughts were wandering "to the ends of the earth"; and my soul was filled with surprise and anxiety, to find it thus. Thus also after I came to the Indians my mind was confused. I felt nothing sensibly of that sweet reliance on God that my soul has been comforted with in days past. Spent the forenoon in this posture of mind and preached to the Indians without any heart.

In the afternoon, I felt still barren when I began to preach, and after about half an hour I seemed to myself to know nothing and to have nothing to say to the Indians; but soon after, I found in myself a spirit of love, and warmth, and power, to address the poor Indians. God helped me to plead with them to "turn from all the vanities of the heathen to the living God." I am persuaded the Lord touched their consciences for I never saw such attention raised in them before. And when I came away from them, I spent the whole time, while I was riding to my lodgings three miles distant, in prayer and praise to God.

After I rode more than two miles, it came into my mind to dedicate myself to God again; which I did with great solemnity and unspeakable satisfaction. Especially gave up myself to Him renewedly in the work of the ministry. And this I did by divine grace, I hope, without any exception or reserve; not in the least shrinking back from any difficulties that might attend this great and blessed work. I seemed to be most free, cheerful and full in this dedication of myself. My whole soul cried: "Lord, to Thee I dedicate myself! Oh, accept of me and let me be Thine forever. Lord, I desire nothing else; I desire nothing more. Oh, come, come, Lord, accept a poor worm. 'Whom have I in heaven but Thee? and there is none upon earth, that I desire besides Thee.' "

After this, was enabled to praise God with my whole soul that He had enabled me to devote and consecrate all my powers to Him in this solemn manner. My heart rejoiced in my particular work as a missionary; rejoiced in my necessity of self-denial in many respects. I still continued to give up myself to God and implore mercy of Him, praying incessantly, every moment, with sweet fervency. My nature being very weak of late, and much spent, was now considerably overcome. My fingers grew very feeble and somewhat numb, so that I could scarcely stretch them out straight. When I lighted from my horse I could hardly walk, my joints seemed all to be loosed. But I felt abundant strength in the inner man. Preached to the white people. God helped me much, especially in prayer. Sundry of my poor Indians were so moved as to come to meeting also; and one appeared much concerned.

Tuesday, July 3. Was still very weak. This morning, was enabled to pray under a feeling sense of my need of help from God, and, I trust, had some faith in exercise. Blessed be God, was enabled to plead with Him a considerable time. Truly God is good to me. But my soul mourned and was grieved at my sinfulness and barrenness, and longed to be more engaged for God. Near nine, withdrew again for prayer and through divine goodness had the blessed spirit of prayer. My soul loved the duty and longed for God in it. Oh, it is sweet to be the Lord's, to be sensibly devoted to Him! What a blessed portion is God! How glorious, how lovely in Himself! Oh, my soul longed to improve time wholly for God! Spent most of the day in translating prayers into Indian. In the evening, was enabled again to wrestle with God in prayer with fervency. Was enabled to maintain a self-diffident and watchful frame of spirit in the evening, and was jealous and afraid lest I should admit carelessness and self-confidence.

Friday, July 6. Awoke this morning in the fear of God. Soon called to mind my sadness in the evening past and spent my first waking minutes in prayer for sanctification, that my soul may be washed from its exceeding pollution and defilement. After I arose, I spent some time in reading God's Word and in prayer. I cried to God under a sense of my great indigency. I am, of late, most of all concerned for ministerial qualifications and the conversion of the heathen. Last year, I longed to be prepared for a world of glory and speedily to depart out of this world; but of late all my concern almost is for the conversion of the heathen, and for that end I long to live.

But blessed be God, I have less desire to live for any of the pleasures of the world, than ever I had. I long and love to be a pilgrim, and want grace to imitate the life, labors and sufferings of Paul among the heathen. And when I long for holiness now it is not so much for myself as formerly; but rather that thereby I may become an "able minister of the New Testament," especially to the heathen. Spent about two hours this morning in reading and prayer by turns. Was in a watchful tender frame, afraid of everything that might cool my affections and draw away my heart from God. Was a little strengthened in my studies; but near night was very weak and weary.

Saturday, July 7. Was very much disordered this morning, and my vigor all spent and exhausted. Was affected and refreshed in reading the sweet story of Elijah's translation, and enjoyed some affection and fervency in prayer. Longed much for ministerial gifts and graces that I might do something in the cause of God. Afterwards was refreshed and invigorated while reading Mr. Joseph Alleine's first case of conscience, and enabled then to pray with some ardor of soul; was afraid of carelessness and self-confidence, and longed for holiness.

Lord's Day, July 8. Was ill last night, not able to rest quietly. Had some small degree of assistance in preaching to the Indians. Afterwards was enabled to preach to the white people with some power, especially in the close of my discourse, from Jeremiah 3:23, "Truly in vain is salvation hoped for from the hills." The Lord also assisted me in some measure in the first prayer, blessed be His name. Near night, though very weary, was enabled to read God's Word with some sweet relish of it, and to pray with affection, fervency, and I trust with faith. My soul was more sensibly dependent on God than usual. Was watchful, tender, and jealous of my own heart, lest I should admit carelessness and vain thoughts, and grieve the blessed Spirit, so that He should withdraw His sweet, kind, and tender influences. Longed to "depart and be with Christ," more than at any time of late. My soul was exceedingly united to the saints of ancient times, as well as those now living; especially my soul melted for the society of Elijah and Elisha.

Monday, July 9. Was under much illness of body most of the day and not able to sit up the whole day. Towards night, felt a little better. Then spent some time in reading God's Word and prayer; enjoyed some degree of fervency and affection; was enabled to plead with God for His cause and kingdom. Through divine goodness, it was apparent to me that it was His cause I pleaded for, and not my own; and was enabled to make this an argument with God to answer my requests.

Tuesday, July 10. Was very ill, and full of pain, and very dull and spiritless. In the evening, had an affecting sense of my ignorance, and of my need of God at all times, to do everything for me; and my soul was humbled before God.

Wednesday, July 11. Was still exercised with illness and pain. Had some degree of affection and warmth in prayer and reading God's Word. Longed for Abraham's faith and fellowship with God and felt some resolution to spend all my time for God and to exert myself with more fervency in His service. But I found my body weak and feeble. In the afternoon, though very ill, was enabled to spend some considerable time in prayer; spent indeed most of the day in that exercise. My soul was diffident, watchful, and tender lest I should offend my blessed Friend, in thought or behavior. I am persuaded my soul confided in and leaned upon the blessed God. Oh, what need did I see myself to stand in of God at all times to assist me and lead me! Found a great want of strength and vigor, both in the outward and inner man.

Saturday, July 21. This morning, I was greatly oppressed with guilt and shame, from a sense of inward vileness and pollution. About nine, withdrew to the woods for prayer, but had not much comfort. I appeared to myself the vilest, meanest creature upon earth, and could scarcely live with myself. So mean and vile I appeared that I thought I should never be able to hold up my face in heaven, if God of His infinite grace should bring me thither. Towards night my burden respecting my work among the Indians began to increase much and was aggravated by hearing sundry things that looked very discouraging. In particular, that they intended to meet together the next day for an idolatrous feast and dance. Then I began to be in anguish. I thought I must in conscience go and endeavor to break them up, and knew not how to attempt such a thing.

However, I withdrew for prayer, hoping for strength from above. And in prayer I was exceedingly enlarged and my soul was as much drawn out as ever I remember it to have been in my life, or near. I was in such anguish and pleaded with so much earnestness and importunity that when I rose from my knees, I felt extremely weak and overcome—I could scarcely walk straight. My joints were loosed, the sweat ran down my face and body, and nature seemed as if it would dissolve. So far as I could judge, I was wholly free from selfish ends in my fervent supplications for the poor Indians. I knew they were met together to worship devils and not God. This made me cry earnestly that God would now appear and help me in my attempts to break up this idolatrous meeting. My soul pleaded long; and I thought God would hear and would go with me to vindicate His own cause. I seemed to confide in God for His presence and assistance. Thus I spent the evening, praying incessantly for divine assistance, and that I might not be self-dependent, but still have my whole dependence upon God.

Lord's Day, July 22. When I waked, my soul was burdened with what seemed to be before me. I cried to God before I could get out of my bed. As soon as I was dressed I withdrew into the woods to pour out my burdened soul to God, especially for assistance in my great work, for I could scarcely think of anything else. I enjoyed the same freedom and fervency as the last evening, and did with unspeakable freedom give up myself afresh to God, for life or death, for all hardships He should call me to among the heathen. I felt as if nothing could discourage me from this blessed work. I had a strong hope that God would "bow the heavens and come down" and do some marvelous work among the heathen. And when I was riding to the Indians, three miles, my heart was continually going up to God for His presence and assistance; and hoping, and almost expecting, that God would make this the day of His power and grace amongst the poor Indians.

When I came to them, I found them engaged in their frolic. Through divine goodness I got them to break up and attend to my preaching, yet still there appeared nothing of the special power of God among them. Preached again to them in the afternoon and observed the Indians were more sober than before, but still saw nothing special among them. From whence Satan took occasion to tempt and buffet me with these cursed suggestions, There is no God, or if there be, He is not able to convert the Indians, before they have more knowledge. I was very weak and weary, and my soul borne down with perplexity; but was mortified to all the world, and was determined still to wait upon God for the conversion of the heathen, though the Devil tempted me to the contrary.

Monday, July 23. Retained still a deep and pressing sense of what lay with so much weight upon me yesterday, but was more calm and quiet. Enjoyed freedom and composure after the temptations of the last evening. Had sweet resignation to the divine will and desired nothing so much as the conversion of the heathen to God, and that His kingdom might come in my own heart and the hearts of others. Rode to a settlement of Irish people, about fifteen miles southwestward; spent my time in prayer and meditation by the way. Near night, preached from Matthew 5:3, "Blessed are the poor in spirit." God was pleased to afford me some degree of freedom and fervency. Blessed be God for any measure of assistance.

Tuesday, July 24. Rode about seventeen miles westward, over a hideous mountain, to a number of Indians. Got together near thirty of them; preached to them in the evening, and lodged among them. Was weak, and felt in some degree disconsolate; yet could have no freedom in the thought of any other circumstances or business in life. All my desire was the conversion of the heathen and all my hope was in God. God does not suffer me to please or comfort myself with hopes of seeing friends, returning to my dear acquaintance, and enjoying worldly comforts.

Saturday, September 1. Was so far strengthened, after a season of great weakness, that I was able to spend two or three hours in writing on a divine subject. Enjoyed some comfort and sweetness in things divine and sacred. As my bodily strength was in some measure restored, so my soul seemed to be somewhat vigorous, and engaged in the things of God.

Lord's Day, September 2. Was enabled to speak to my poor Indians with much concern and fervency. I am persuaded God enabled me to exercise faith in Him, while I was speaking to them. I perceived that some of them were afraid to hearken to and embrace Christianity, lest they should be enchanted and poisoned by some of the powwows [probably, here, Indian priests or medicine men]; but I was enabled to plead with them not to fear these; and confiding in God for safety and deliverance, I bid a challenge to all these powers of darkness, to do their worst upon me first. I told my people I was a Christian, and asked them why the powwows did not bewitch and poison me. I scarcely ever felt more sensible of my own unworthiness than in this action. I saw that the honor of God was concerned in the affair, and I desired to be preserved, not from selfish views, but for a testimony of the divine power and goodness and of the truth of Christianity, and that God might be glorified. Afterwards, I found my soul rejoiced in God for His assisting grace. [After this, he went on a journey into New England, and was absent from the place of his abode, at the Forks of the Delaware, about three weeks.]

Wednesday, September 26. Rode home to the Forks of the Delaware. What reason have I to bless God, who has preserved me in riding more than four hundred and twenty miles, and has "kept all my bones, that not one of them has been broken"! My health likewise is greatly recovered. Oh, that I could dedicate my all to God! This is all the return I can make to Him.

Thursday, September 27. Was somewhat melancholy; had not much freedom and comfort in prayer. My soul is disconsolate when God is withdrawn.

Friday, September 28. Spent the day in prayer, reading, and writing. Felt some small degree of warmth in prayer and some desires of the enlargement of Christ's kingdom by the conversion of the heathen, and that God would make me a "chosen vessel, to bear his name before them." Longed for grace to enable me to be faithful.

Monday, October 1. Was engaged this day in making preparation for my intended journey to Susquehannah. Withdrew several times to the woods for secret duties and endeavored to plead for the divine presence to go with me to the poor pagans, to whom I was going to preach the gospel. Towards night, rode about four miles, and met Brother Byram [minister at a place called Rockciticus about forty miles from Mr. Brainerd's lodgings]; who was come, at my desire, to be my companion in travel to the Indians. I rejoiced to see him; and, I trust, God made his conversation profitable to me. I saw him, as I thought, more dead to the world, its anxious cares and alluring objects, than I was. This made me look within myself and gave me a greater sense of my guilt, ingratitude, and misery.

### He Visits the Indians on the Susquehannah

Tuesday, October 2. Set out on my journey, in company with dear Brother Byram and my interpreter, and two chief Indians from the Forks of Delaware. Traveled about twenty-five miles, and lodged in one of the last houses on our road; after which there was nothing but a hideous and howling wilderness.

Wednesday, October 3. We went on our way into the wilderness and found the most difficult and dangerous traveling, by far, that ever any of us had seen. We had scarce anything else but lofty mountains, deep valleys, and hideous rocks, to make our way through. However, I felt some sweetness in divine things part of the day, and had my mind intensely engaged in meditation on a divine subject. Near night, my beast that I rode upon, hung one of her legs in the rocks, and fell down under me; but through divine goodness, I was not hurt. However, she broke her leg; and being in such a hideous place, and near thirty miles from any house, I saw nothing that could be done to preserve her life, and so was obliged to kill her, and to prosecute my journey on foot. This accident made me admire the divine goodness to me, that my bones were not broken, and the multitude of them filled with strong pain. Just at dark, we kindled a fire, cut up a few bushes, and made a shelter over our heads, to save us from the frost, which was very hard that night. Committing ourselves to God by prayer, we lay down on the ground and slept quietly.

Friday, October 5. We arrived at Susquehannah River, at a place called Opeholhaupung and found there twelve Indian houses. After I had saluted the king in a friendly manner, I told him my business, and that my desire was to teach them Christianity. After some consultation, the Indians gathered, and I preached to them. And when I had done, I asked if they would hear me again. They replied that they would consider of it, and soon after sent me word that they would immediately attend, if I would preach; which I did, with freedom, both times. When I asked them again whether they would hear me further, they replied they would the next day. I was exceeding sensible of the impossibility of doing anything for the poor heathen without special assistance from above. My soul seemed to rest on God and leave it to Him to do as He pleased in that which I saw was His own cause. Indeed, through divine goodness, I had felt something of this frame most of the time while I was traveling thither, and in some measure before I set out.

Saturday, October 6. Rose early and besought the Lord for help in my great work. Near noon, preached again to the Indians. In the afternoon, visited them from house to house and invited them to come and hear me again the next day, and put off their hunting design, which they were just entering upon, till Monday. "This night," I trust, "the Lord stood by me," to encourage and strengthen my soul. I spent more than an hour in secret retirement and was enabled to "pour out my heart before God," for the increase of grace in my soul, for ministerial endowments, for success among the poor Indians, for God's ministers and people and for distant dear friends. Blessed be God!

Monday, October 8. Visited the Indians with a design to take my leave of them, supposing they would this morning go out to hunting early. But beyond my expectation and hope, they desired to hear me preach again. I gladly complied with their request, and afterwards endeavored to answer their objections against Christianity; then they went away. We spent the rest of the afternoon in reading and prayer, intending to go homeward very early the next day. My soul was in some measure refreshed in secret prayer and meditation. Blessed be the Lord for all His goodness.

Tuesday, October 9. We rose about four in the morning, and commending ourselves to God by prayer and asking His special protection, we set out on our journey homewards about five. We traveled with great steadiness till past six at night and then made us a fire and a shelter of barks, and so rested. I had some clear and comfortable thoughts on a divine subject, by the way, towards night. In the night, the wolves howled around us; but God preserved us.

## He Renews His Labors at Crossweeksung

Friday, October 12. Rode home to my lodgings where I poured out my soul to God in secret prayer and endeavored to bless Him for His abundant goodness to me in my late journey. I scarce ever enjoyed more health, at least of later years; and God marvelously, and almost miraculously, supported me under the fatigues of the way, and traveling on foot. Blessed be the Lord, who continually preserves me in all my ways.

Lord's Day, October 14. Was much confused and perplexed in my thoughts; could not pray and was almost discouraged, thinking I should never be able to preach any more. Afterwards, God was pleased to give me some relief from these confusions. But still I was afraid and even trembled before God. I went to the place of public worship, lifting up my heart to God for assistance and grace in my great work

God was gracious to me, helping me to plead with Him for holiness, and to use the strongest arguments with Him, drawn from the incarnation and sufferings of Christ for this very end, that men might be made holy.

Afterwards, I was much assisted in preaching. I know not that ever God helped me to preach in a more close and distinguishing manner for the trial of men's state. Through the infinite goodness of God, I felt what I spoke. He enabled me to treat on divine truth with uncommon clearness; and yet I was so sensible of my defects in preaching that I could not be proud of my performance, as at some times. Blessed be the Lord for this mercy. In the evening, I longed to be entirely alone to bless God for help in a time of extremity. I longed for great degrees of holiness that I might show my gratitude to God.

Friday, October 19. Felt an abasing sense of my own impurity and unholiness and felt my soul melt and mourn that I had abused and grieved a very gracious God who was still kind to me, notwithstanding all my unworthiness. My soul enjoyed a sweet season of bitter repentance and sorrow that I had wronged that blessed God, who, I was persuaded, was reconciled to me in His dear Son. My soul was now tender, devout, and solemn. I was afraid of nothing but sin, and afraid of that in every action and thought.

Wednesday, October 24. Near noon, rode to my people; spent some time and prayed with them. I felt the frame of a pilgrim on earth and longed much to leave this gloomy mansion, but yet found the exercise of patience and resignation. As I returned home from the Indians, spent the whole time in lifting up my heart to God. In the evening, enjoyed a blessed season alone in prayer and was enabled to cry to God with a childlike spirit, for the space of near an hour. I enjoyed a sweet freedom in supplicating for myself, for dear friends, ministers, and some who are preparing for that work, and for the Church of God; longed to be as lively myself in God's service as the angels.

Thursday, October 25. Was busy in writing. Was very sensible of my absolute dependence on God in all respects; saw that I could do nothing, even in those affairs that I have sufficient natural faculties for, unless God should smile upon my attempt. "Not that we are sufficient of ourselves, to think anything, as of ourselves," I saw was a sacred truth.

Friday, October 26. In the morning, my soul was melted with a sense of divine goodness and mercy to such a vile, unworthy worm. I delighted to lean upon God and place my whole trust in Him. My soul was exceedingly grieved for sin, and prized, and longed after holiness. It wounded my heart deeply, yet sweetly, to think how I had abused a kind God. I longed to be perfectly holy that I might not grieve a gracious God, who will continue to love, notwithstanding His love is abused! I longed for holiness more for this end than I did for my own happiness' sake. Yet this was my greatest happiness, never more to dishonor, but always to glorify, the blessed God.

Friday, November 2. Was filled with sorrow and confusion in the morning, and could enjoy no sweet sense of divine things, nor get any relief in prayer. Saw I deserved that every one of God's creatures should be let loose, to be the executioners of His wrath against me. Yet therein saw I deserved what I did not fear as my portion. About noon, rode up to the Indians and, while going, could feel no desires for them, and even dreaded to say anything to them. But God was pleased to give me some freedom and enlargement, and made the season comfortable to me. In the evening, had enlargement in prayer.

But, alas! what comforts and enlargements I have felt for these many weeks past have been only transient and short. The greater part of my time has been filled up with deadness, or struggles with deadness, and bitter conflicts with corruption. I have found myself exercised sorely with some particular things that I thought myself most of all freed from. And thus I have ever found it, when I have thought the battle was over and the conquest gained and so let down my watch, the enemy has risen up and done me the greatest injury.

Saturday, November 3. I read the life and trials of a godly

man, and was much warmed by it. I wondered at my past deadness and was more convinced of it than ever. Was enabled to confess and bewail my sin before God, with self-abhorrence.

Lord's Day, November 4. Had, I think, some exercise of faith in prayer, in the morning; longed to be spiritual. Had considerable help in preaching to my poor Indians; was encouraged with them, and hoped that God designed mercy for them.

Wednesday, November 21. Rode from Newark to Rockciticus in the cold, and was almost overcome with it. Enjoyed some sweetness in conversation with dear Mr. Jones, while I dined with him. My soul loves the people of God, and especially the ministers of Jesus Christ who feel the same trials that I do.

Thursday, November 22. Came on my way from Rockciticus to Delaware River. Was very much disordered with a cold and pain in my head. About six at night, I lost my way in the wilderness, and wandered over rocks and mountains, down hideous steeps, through swamps, and most dreadful and dangerous places. The night being dark, so that few stars could be seen, I was greatly exposed. I was much pinched with cold, and distressed with an extreme pain in my head, attended with sickness at my stomach, so that every step I took was distressing to me. I had little hope for several hours together, but that I must lie out in the woods all night, in this distressed case. But about nine o'clock, I found a house, through the abundant goodness of God, and was kindly entertained. Thus I have frequently been exposed, and sometimes lain out the whole night; but God has hitherto preserved me. Blessed be His name.

Such fatigues and hardships as these serve to wean me more from the earth, and, I trust, will make heaven the sweeter. Formerly, when I was thus exposed to cold and rain, I was ready to please myself with the thoughts of enjoying a comfortable house, a warm fire, and other outward comforts. But now these have less place in my heart (through the grace of God), and my eye is more to God for comfort. In this world I expect tribulation; and it does not now, as formerly, appear strange to me. I do not in such seasons of difficulty flatter myself that it will be better hereafter, but rather think, how much worse it might be; how much greater trials others of God's children have endured; and how much greater are yet perhaps reserved for me. Blessed be God, that He makes the thoughts of my journey's end and of my dissolution a great comfort to me, under my sharpest trials, and scarce ever lets these thoughts be attended with terror or melancholy; but they are attended frequently with great joy.

Friday, November 23. Visited a sick man; discoursed and prayed with him. Then visited another house, where was one dead and laid out. I looked on the corpse and longed that my time might come to depart, that I might be with Christ. Then went home to my lodgings, about one o'clock. Felt poorly; but was able to read most of the afternoon.

> Within the space of the next twelve days, he passed under many changes in the frames and exercises of his mind . . . He spent much time, within this space, in hard labor, with others, to make for himself a little cottage or hut, to live in by himself through the winter. Yet he frequently preached to the Indians, and speaks of special assistance he had from time to time, in addressing himself to them, and of his sometimes having considerable encouragement from the attention they gave.—J. E.

Thursday, December 6. I now have a happy opportunity of being retired in a house of my own, which I have lately procured and moved into. It is now a long time since I have been able, either on account of bodily weakness, or for want of retirement, or some other difficulty, to spend any time in secret fasting and prayer. Considering the greatness of my work and the extreme difficulties that attend it; and that my poor Indians are now worshiping devils notwithstanding all the pains I have taken with them—which almost overwhelms my spirit; moreover, considering my extreme barrenness, spiritual deadness and dejection, of late, as also the power of some particular corruptions, I set apart this day for secret prayer and fasting, to implore the blessing of God on myself, on my poor people, on my friends, and on the Church of God.

At first, I felt a great backwardness to the duties of the day, on account of the seeming impossibility of performing them. But the Lord helped me to break through this difficulty. God was pleased by the use of means, to give me some clear conviction of my sinfulness, and a discovery of the plague of my own heart, more affecting than what I have of late had . . . Toward night, I felt my soul rejoice that God is unchangeably happy and glorious; that He will be glorified, whatever becomes of His creatures. I was enabled to persevere in prayer till sometime in the evening, at which time I saw so much need of divine help, in every respect, that I knew not how to leave off, and had forgot that I needed food. This evening, I was much assisted in meditating on Isaiah 52:3, "For thus saith the Lord, Ye have sold yourselves for nought." Blessed be the Lord for any help in the past day.

Friday, December 7. Spent some time in prayer, in the morning, and enjoyed some freedom and affection in the duty, and had longing desires of being made "faithful to the death." Spent a little time in writing on a divine subject; then visited the Indians and preached to them, but under inexpressible dejection. I had no heart to speak to them, and could not do it but as I forced myself. I knew they must hate to hear me, as having but just got home from their idolatrous feast and devil-worship. In the evening, had some freedom in prayer and meditation.

Saturday, December 8. Have been uncommonly free this day from dejection, and from that distressing apprehension that I could do nothing. I was enabled to pray and study with some comfort, and especially was assisted in writing on a divine subject. In the evening, my soul rejoiced in God, and I blessed His name for shining on my soul. Oh, the sweet and blessed change I then felt, when God "brought me out of darkness into his marvelous light"!

Lord's Day, December 9. Preached both parts of the day at a place called Greenwich, in New Jersey, about ten miles from my own house. In the first discourse I had scarce any warmth or affectionate longing for souls. In the intermediate season I got alone among the bushes and cried to God for pardon of my deadness, and was in anguish and bitterness that I could not address souls with more compassion and tender affection. I judged and condemned myself for want of this divine temper, though I saw I could not get it as of myself any more than I could make a world. In the latter exercise, blessed be the Lord, I had some fervency, both in prayer and preaching. Especially in the application of my discourse I was enabled to address precious souls with affection, concern, tenderness, and importunity. The Spirit of God, I think, was there as the effects were apparent—tears running down many cheeks.

Monday, December 10. Near noon I preached again. God gave me some assistance and enabled me to be in some degree faithful, so that I had peace in my own soul and a very comfortable composure, "although Israel should not be gathered." Came away from Greenwich and rode home, arriving just in the evening. By the way my soul blessed God for His goodness. I rejoiced that so much of my work was done, and I so much nearer my blessed reward. Blessed be God for grace to be faithful.

Tuesday, December 11. Felt very poorly in body, being much tired and worn out the last night. I was assisted in some measure in writing on a divine subject, but was so feeble and sore in my breast that I had not much resolution in my work. Oh, how I long for that world "where the weary are at rest"! and yet through the goodness of God I do not now feel impatient.

Wednesday, December 12. I was again very weak, but somewhat assisted in secret prayer and enabled with pleasure and sweetness to cry, "Come, Lord Jesus! come, Lord Jesus! come quickly." My soul "longed for God, for the living God." Oh, how delightful it is to pray under such sweet influences! Oh, how much better is this than one's necessary food! I had at this time no disposition to eat (though late in the morning), for earthly food appeared wholly tasteless. Oh, how

much "better is thy love than wine," than the sweetest wine!
I visited and preached to the Indians in the afternoon, but
under much dejection. Found my interpreter under some concern for his soul, which was some comfort to me; and yet
filled me with new care. I longed greatly for his conversion
and lifted up my heart to God for it while I was talking to
him. Coming home, I poured out my soul to God for him:
enjoyed some freedom in prayer, and was enabled, I think, to
leave all with God.

Thursday, December 13. Endeavored to spend the day in
fasting and prayer, to implore the divine blessing, more especially on my poor people. In particular, I sought for converting grace for my interpreter, and three or four more under
some concern for their souls. I was much disordered in the
morning when I arose, but having determined to spend the
day in this manner, I attempted it. Some freedom I had in
pleading for these poor concerned souls, several times. When
interceding for them I enjoyed greater freedom from wandering and distracting thoughts than in any part of my supplications.

But, in general, I was greatly exercised with wanderings
so that in the evening it seemed as if I had need to pray for
nothing so much as for the pardon of sins committed in the
day past and the vileness I then found in myself. The sins I
had most sense of were pride, and wandering thoughts,
whereby I mocked God. The former of these cursed iniquities
excited me to think of writing, preaching, or converting
heathens, or performing some other great work, that my
name might live when I should be dead. My soul was in
anguish and ready to drop into despair, to find so much of
that cursed temper. With this and the other evil I labored
under, namely wandering thoughts, I was almost overwhelmed, and even ready to give over striving after a spirit
of devotion. Oftentimes I was sunk into a considerable degree
of despondency and thought I was "more brutish than any
man." Yet after all my sorrows, I trust, through grace, this
day and the exercises of it have been for my good, and taught

me more of my corruption and weakness without Christ than I knew before.

Friday, December 14. Near noon, went to the Indians, but knew not what to say to them and was ashamed to look them in the face. I felt I had no power to address their consciences, and therefore had no boldness to say anything. Much of the day I was in a great degree of despair about ever doing or seeing any good "in the land of the living."

Lord's Day, December 16. Was so overwhelmed with dejection that I knew not how to live. I longed for death exceedingly; my soul was sunk into deep waters and the floods were ready to drown me. I was so much oppressed that my soul was in a kind of horror. I could not keep my thoughts fixed in prayer for the space of one minute, without fluttering and distraction. It made me exceedingly ashamed that I did not live to God. I had no distressing doubt about my own state, but I would have cheerfully ventured (as far as I could possibly know) into eternity. While I was going to preach to the Indians, my soul was in anguish. I was so overborne with discouragement that I despaired of doing any good, and was driven to my wit's end. I knew nothing what to say, nor what course to take.

But at last I insisted on the evidence we have of the truth of Christianity from the miracles of Christ, many of which I set before them. God helped me to make a close application to those who refused to believe the truth of what I taught them. Indeed I was enabled to speak to the consciences of all, in some measure, and was somewhat encouraged to find that God enabled me to be faithful once more.

Monday, December 17. I was comfortable in mind most of the day, and was enabled to pray with some freedom, cheerfulness, composure, and devotion. I had also some assistance in writing on a divine subject.

Tuesday, December 18. Went to the Indians and discoursed to them near an hour, without any power to come close to their hearts. But at last I felt some fervency, and God helped me to speak with warmth. My interpreter also was amazingly assisted, and I doubt not but "the Spirit of God was upon him" (though I had no reason to think he had any true and saving grace, but was only under conviction of his lost state). Presently upon this most of the grown persons were much affected, and the tears ran down their cheeks.

One old man (I suppose, an hundred years old) was so affected that he wept and seemed convinced of the importance of what I taught them. I stayed with them a considerable time, exhorting and directing them, and came away, lifting up my heart to God in prayer and praise, and encouraged and exhorted my interpreter to "strive to enter in at the strait gate." Coming home, I spent most of the evening in prayer and thanksgiving and found myself much enlarged and quickened. Was greatly concerned that the Lord's work, which seemed to be begun, might be carried on with power, to the conversion of poor souls and the glory of divine grace.

Tuesday, December 25. Enjoyed very little quiet sleep last night, by reason of bodily weakness and the closeness of my studies yesterday. Yet my heart was somewhat lively in prayer and praise. I was delighted with the divine glory and happiness, and rejoiced that God was God and that He was unchangeably possessed of glory and blessedness. Though God held my eyes waking, yet He helped me to improve my time profitably amidst my pains and weakness, in continued meditations on Luke 13:7, "Behold, these three years I come seeking fruit." My meditations were sweet and I wanted to set before sinners their sin and danger.

> He continued in a very low state, as to his bodily health, for some days; which seems to have been a great hindrance to him in his religious exercises and pursuits. But yet he expresses some degree of divine assistance, from day to day, through the remaining part of this week. He preached several times this week to his Indians. There appeared still some concern amongst them for their souls. On Saturday, he rode to the Irish settlement, about fifteen miles from his lodgings, in order to spend the Sabbath there.—J. E.

Lord's Day, December 30. Discoursed, both parts of the day, from Mark 8:34, "Whosoever will come after me . . ." God gave me very great freedom and clearness and (in the afternoon especially) considerable warmth and fervency. In the evening also had very great clearness while conversing with friends on divine things. I do not remember ever to have had more clear apprehensions of religion in my life, but found a struggle, in the evening, with spiritual pride.

> On Monday, he preached again in the same place with freedom and fervency. He rode home to his lodging and arrived in the evening under a considerable degree of bodily illness, which continued the two next days.—J. E.

Thursday, January 3, 1745. Being sensible of the great want of divine influences and the outpouring of God's Spirit, I spent this day in fasting and prayer to seek so great a mercy for myself, my poor people in particular, and the Church of God in general. In the morning, I was very lifeless in prayer and could get scarce any sense of God. Near noon, I enjoyed some sweet freedom to pray that the will of God might in every respect become mine, and I am persuaded it was so at that time in some good degree. In the afternoon, I was exceeding weak and could not enjoy much fervency in prayer, but felt a great degree of dejection which, I believe, was very much owing to my bodily weakness and disorder.

Friday, January 4. I rode up to the Indians, near noon, and spent some time under great disorder. My soul was sunk down into deep waters and I was almost overwhelmed with melancholy.

Lord's Day, January 6. Was still distressed with vapory disorders. Preached to my poor Indians, but had little heart or life. Towards night, my soul was pressed under a sense of my unfaithfulness. Oh, the joy and peace that arises from a sense of "having obtained mercy of God to be faithful"! And oh, the misery and anguish that spring from an apprehension of the contrary!

Wednesday, January 9. In the morning, God was pleased to

remove the gloom which has of late oppressed my mind and gave me freedom and sweetness in prayer. I was encouraged, strengthened, and enabled to plead for grace for myself and mercy for my poor Indians. I was sweetly assisted in my intercessions with God for others. Blessed be His holy name for ever and ever. Amen and amen. Those things that of late appeared most difficult and almost impossible now appeared not only possible, but easy.

My soul so much delighted to continue instant in prayer at this blessed season that I had no desire for my necessary food. I even dreaded leaving off praying at all, lest I should lose this spirituality and this blessed thankfulness to God which I then felt. I felt now quite willing to live and undergo all trials that might remain for me in a world of sorrow, but I still longed for heaven that I might glorify God in a perfect manner. Oh, "come, Lord Jesus, come quickly." Spent the day in reading a little and in some diversions, which I was necessitated to take by reason of much weakness and disorder. In the evening, I enjoyed some freedom and intenseness in prayer.

Monday, January 14. Spent this day under a great degree of bodily weakness and disorder. I had very little freedom, either in my studies or devotions; in the evening, I was much dejected and melancholy. It pains and distresses me that I live so much of my time for nothing. I long to do much in a little time, and if it might be the Lord's will, to finish my work speedily in this tiresome world. I am sure I do not desire to live for anything in this world. Through grace I am not afraid to look the king of terrors in the face. I know, I shall be afraid, if God leaves me; and therefore I think it always my duty to lay in for that solemn hour.

But for a very considerable time past, my soul has rejoiced to think of death in its nearest approaches, even when I have been very weak and seemed nearest eternity. "Not unto me, not unto me, but to God be the glory." I feel that which convinces me, that if God do not enable me to maintain a holy dependence upon Him, death will easily be a terror to me.

But at present I must say, "I long to depart, and to be with Christ," which is the best of all. When I am in a sweet, resigned frame of soul, I am willing to tarry a while in a world of sorrow; I am willing to be from home as long as God sees fit it should be so; but when I want the influence of this temper, I am then apt to be impatient to be gone. Oh, when will the day appear, that I shall be perfect in holiness, and in the enjoyment of God!

Lord's Day, January 27. Had the greatest degree of inward anguish that almost ever I endured. I was perfectly overwhelmed and so confused, that after I began to discourse to the Indians, before I could finish a sentence I sometimes forgot entirely what I was aiming at. If, with much difficulty, I had recollected what I had before designed, still it appeared strange and like something I had long forgotten and had now but an imperfect remembrance of. I know it was a degree of distraction occasioned by vapory disorders, melancholy, spiritual desertion, and some other things that particularly pressed upon me with an uncommon weight this morning, the principal of which respected my Indians.

This distressing gloom never went off the whole day, but was so far removed that I was enabled to speak with some freedom and concern to the Indians, at two of their settlements. I think there was some appearance of the presence of God with us, some seriousness and seeming concern among the Indians, at least a few of them. In the evening, this gloom continued still, till family prayer,[1] about nine o'clock, and almost through this, until I came near the close, when I was praying (as I usually do) for the illumination and conversion of my poor people. Then the cloud was scattered so that I enjoyed sweetness and freedom, and conceived hopes that God designed mercy for some of them.

The same I enjoyed afterwards in secret prayer; in which precious duty I had for a considerable time sweetness and

---

[1] Though Mr. Brainerd now dwelt by himself in the aforementioned little cottage, which he had built for his own use, yet that was near to a family of white people with whom he had lived before, and with whom he still attended family prayer.

freedom, and (I hope) faith, in praying for myself, my poor
Indians, and dear friends and acquaintances in New England,
and elsewhere, and for the dear interest of Zion in general.
"Bless the Lord, O my soul, and forget not all his benefits."

Lord's Day, February 3. In the morning, I was somewhat
relieved of that gloom and confusion which have greatly
exercised my mind of late. I was enabled to pray with some
composure and comfort. However, I went to my Indians
trembling, for my soul "remembered the wormwood and the
gall" (I might almost say the hell) of Friday last; and I was
greatly afraid I should be obliged again to drink of that cup
of trembling, which was inconceivably more bitter than
death, and made me long for the grave more, unspeakably
more, than for hid treasures; yea, inconceivably more than the
men of this world long for such treasures.

But God was pleased to hear my cries, and to afford me
great assistance so that I felt peace in my own soul. I was
satisfied that if not one of the Indians should be profited by
my preaching but should all be damned, yet I should be accepted and rewarded as faithful, for I am persuaded God
enabled me to be so. Had some good degree of help afterwards, at another place, and much longed for the conversion
of the poor Indians. I was somewhat refreshed, and comfortable towards night and in the evening. Oh that my soul
might praise the Lord for His goodness! Enjoyed some freedom, in the evening, in meditation on Luke 13:24: "Strive to
enter in at the strait gate."

> On the next Sabbath, he preached at Greenwich in New
> Jersey. In the evening, he rode eight miles to visit a sick man
> at the point of death, and found him speechless and sense-
> less.—J. E.

Monday, February 11. About break of day, the sick man
died. I was affected at the sight and spent the morning with
the mourners. After prayer, and some discourse with them, I
returned to Greenwich, and preached again from Psalm 89:15,
"Blessed is the people that know . . ." The Lord gave me

assistance; I felt a sweet love to souls and to the kingdom of Christ, and longed that poor sinners might know the joyful sound. Several persons were much affected. After meeting, I was enabled to discourse, with freedom and concern, to some persons that applied to me under spiritual trouble. Left the place sweetly composed and rode home to my house about eight miles distant. Discoursed to friends and inculcated divine truths upon some.

In the evening, was in the most solemn frame that almost I ever remember to have experienced. I know not that ever death appeared more real to me, or that ever I saw myself in the condition of a dead corpse, laid out, and dressed for a lodging in the silent grave, so evidently as at this time . . . I spent most of the evening in conversing with a dear Christian friend. Blessed be God, it was a comfortable evening to us both. What are friends? What are comforts? What are sorrows? What are distresses? "The time is short: it remains, that they which weep, be as though they wept not; and they which rejoice, as though they rejoiced not: for the fashion of this world passeth away. O come, Lord Jesus, come quickly. Amen." Blessed be God for the comforts of the past day.

Friday, February 15. Was engaged in writing again almost the whole day. In the evening was much assisted in meditating on that precious text, John 7:37, "Jesus stood and cried . . ." I had then a sweet sense of the free grace of the gospel. My soul was encouraged, warmed, and quickened. My desires were drawn out after God in prayer and my soul was watchful, afraid of losing so sweet a Guest as I then entertained. I continued long in prayer and meditation, intermixing one with the other, and was unwilling to be diverted by anything at all from so sweet an exercise. I longed to proclaim the grace I then meditated upon, to the world of sinners. Oh, how quick and powerful is the Word of the blessed God!

Lord's Day, February 17. Preached to the white people (my interpreter being absent) in the wilderness upon the sunny side of a hill. Had a considerable assembly consisting of people who lived (at least many of them) not less than thirty miles away. Some of them came near twenty miles. I discoursed to them, all day, from John 7:37, "Jesus stood and cried, saying, If any man thirst . . ." In the afternoon, it pleased God to grant me great freedom and fervency in my discourse. I was enabled to imitate the example of Christ in the text, who stood and cried.

I think, I was scarce ever enabled to offer the free grace of God to perishing sinners with more freedom and plainness in my life. Afterwards, I was enabled earnestly to invite the children of God to come renewedly and drink of this fountain of water of life, from whence they have heretofore derived unspeakable satisfaction. It was a very comfortable time to me. There were many tears in the assembly and I doubt not but that the Spirit of God was there, convincing poor sinners of their need of Christ. In the evening I felt composed and comfortable, though much tired. I had some sweet sense of the excellency and glory of God; and my soul rejoiced that He was "God over all, blessed forever"; but was too much crowded with company and conversation and longed to be more alone with God. Oh, that I could forever bless God for the mercy of this day, who "answered me in the joy of my heart."

Lord's Day, February 24. In the morning, was much perplexed. My interpreter being absent, I knew not how to perform my work among the Indians. However, I rode to them, got a Dutchman to interpret for me, though he was but poorly qualified for the business. Afterwards, I came and preached to a few white people from John 6:67, "Then said Jesus unto the twelve . . ." Here the Lord seemed to unburden me in some measure, especially towards the close of my discourse. I felt freedom to open the love of Christ to His own dear disciples. When the rest of the world forsakes Him and are forsaken by Him that He calls them no more, He then turns to His own and says, Will ye also go away? I had a sense of the free grace of Christ to His own people in such seasons of general apostasy, and when they themselves in some measure backslide with the world.

Oh, the free grace of Christ that He seasonally reminds His people of their danger of backsliding, and invites them to persevere in their adherence to Himself! I saw that backsliding souls, who seemed to be about to go away with the world, might return, and welcome, to Him immediately; without anything to recommend them, notwithstanding all their former backslidings. And thus my discourse was suited to my own soul's case. For of late I have found a great want of this sense and apprehension of divine grace; and have often been greatly distressed in my own soul, because I did not suitably apprehend this "fountain to purge away sin." I have been too much laboring for spiritual life, peace of conscience, and progressive holiness, in my own strength; but now God showed me, in some measure, the arm of all strength, and the fountain of all grace. In the evening, I felt solemn, devout, and sweet, resting on free grace for assistance, acceptance, and peace of conscience.

Wednesday, March 6. Spent most of the day in preparing for a journey to New England. Spent some time in prayer, with a special reference to my intended journey. Was afraid I should forsake the Fountain of living waters, and attempt to derive satisfaction from broken cisterns, my dear friends and acquaintance, with whom I might meet in my journey. I looked to God to keep me from this vanity, as well as others. Towards night was visited by some friends, some of whom, I trust, were real Christians. They discovered an affectionate regard to me and seemed grieved that I was about to leave them, especially seeing I did not expect to make any considerable stay among them, if I should live to return from New England.[2] Oh, how kind has God been to me! How has He raised up friends in every place where His providence has called me! Friends are a great comfort, and it is God that gives

---

[2] It seems he had a design, by what afterwards appears, to remove and live among the Indians at Susquehannah River.

them; it is He makes them friendly to me. "Bless the Lord, O my soul, and forget not all his benefits."

## He Requests a Colleague

The next day he set out on his journey and it was about five weeks before he returned. The special design of this journey, he himself declares afterwards, in his diary for March 21, where, speaking of his conversing with a certain minister in New England, he says, "Contrived with him how to raise some money among Christian friends, in order to support a colleague with me in the wilderness—I having spent two years in a very solitary manner—that we might be together; as Christ sent out His disciples two and two. As this was the principal concern I had in view in taking this journey, so I took pains in it and hope God will succeed it, if for His glory."

He first went into various parts of New Jersey, and visited several ministers there; then went to New York; and from thence into New England, going to various parts of Connecticut. He then returned into New Jersey and met a number of ministers at Woodbridge, "who," he says, "met there to consult about the affairs of Christ's kingdom, in some important articles." He seems, for the most part, to have been free from melancholy in this journey; and many times to have had extraordinary assistance in public ministrations, and his preaching sometimes attended with very hopeful appearances of a good effect on the auditory. He also had many seasons of special comfort and spiritual refreshment, in conversation with ministers and other Christian friends, and also in meditation and prayer when alone.

—J. E.

Saturday, April 13. Rode home to my own house at the Forks of Delaware. Was enabled to remember the goodness of the Lord, who has now preserved me while riding full six hundred miles in this journey; has kept me that none of my bones has been broken. Blessed be the Lord, who has preserved me in this tedious journey, and returned me in safety to my own house. Verily it is God that has upheld me, and guarded my goings.

Lord's Day, April 14. Was disordered in body with the fatigues of my late journey, but was enabled however to preach to a considerable assembly of white people, gathered from all parts round about, with some freedom, from Ezekiel 33:11, "As I live, saith the Lord God . . ." Had much more assistance than I expected.

> This week, he went a journey to Philadelphia, in order to engage the governor there to use his interest with the chief man of the Six Nations, with whom he maintained a strict friendship, that he would give him leave to live at Susquehannah, and instruct the Indians that are within their territories. The Indians at Susquehannah are a mixed company of many nations, speaking various languages, and few of them properly of the Six Nations. But yet the country having formerly been conquered by the Six Nations, they claim the land, and the Susquehannah Indians are a kind of vassals to them. In his way to and from thence, he lodged with Mr. Beaty, a young Presbyterian minister. He speaks of seasons of sweet spiritual refreshment that he enjoyed at his lodgings.—J. E.

Saturday, April 20. Rode with Mr. Beaty to Abington, to attend Mr. Treat's administration of the sacrament, according to the method of the Church of Scotland. When we arrived, we found Mr. Treat preaching. Afterwards I preached a sermon from Matthew 5:3, "Blessed are the poor in spirit." God was pleased to give me great freedom and tenderness, both in prayer and sermon. The assembly was sweetly melted and scores were all in tears. It was, as then I hoped, and was afterwards abundantly satisfied by conversing with them, a "word spoken in season to many weary souls." I was extremely tired, and my spirits much exhausted, so that I could scarcely speak loud; yet I could not help rejoicing in God.

Lord's Day, April 21. In the morning, was calm and composed, and had some outgoings of soul after God in secret duties and longing desires of His presence in the sanctuary and at His Table, that His presence might be in the assembly;

and that His children might be entertained with a feast of fat things. In the forenoon Mr. Treat preached. I felt some affection and tenderness during the administration of the ordinance. Mr. Beaty preached to the multitude abroad, who could not half have crowded into the meeting house. In the season of the communion, I had comfortable and sweet apprehensions of the blissful communion of God's people, when they shall meet at their Father's Table in His kingdom, in a state of perfection. In the afternoon, I preached abroad to the whole assembly, from Revelation 14:4, "These are they that follow the Lamb." God was pleased again to give me very great freedom and clearness, but not so much warmth as before. However, there was a most amazing attention in the whole assembly. I was informed afterwards that this was a sweet season to many.

Monday, April 22. I enjoyed some sweetness in retirement, in the morning. At eleven o'clock, Mr. Beaty preached with freedom and life. Then I preached from John 7:37, "In the last day . . ." and concluded the solemnity. Had some freedom but not equal to what I had enjoyed before. Yet in the prayer the Lord enabled me to cry, I hope, with a childlike temper, with tenderness and brokenness of heart. Came home with Mr. Beaty to his lodgings and spent the time, while riding and afterwards, very agreeably on divine things.

Tuesday, April 23. Left Mr. Beaty's and returned home to the Forks of Delaware. Enjoyed some sweet meditations on the road and was enabled to lift up my heart to God in prayer and praise.

Friday, April 26. Conversed with a Christian friend with some warmth; felt a spirit of mortification to the world in a very great degree. Afterwards was enabled to pray fervently, and to rely on God sweetly for "all things pertaining to life and godliness." Just in the evening was visited by a dear Christian friend, with whom I spent an hour or two in conversation, on the very soul of religion. There are many with whom I can talk *about religion;* but alas! I find few with whom I can talk *religion itself.* But, blessed be the Lord, there are some that love to feed on the kernel, rather than the shell.

Tuesday, April 30. Was scarce able to walk about and was obliged to betake myself to bed, much of the day. Spent away the time in a very solitary manner, being neither able to read, meditate, nor pray, and had none to converse with in that wilderness. Oh, how heavily does time pass away when I can do nothing to any good purpose but seem obliged to trifle away precious time! But of late, I have seen it my duty to divert myself by all lawful means, that I may be fit, at least some small part of my time, to labor for God.

And here is the difference between my present diversions and those I once pursued, when in a natural state: Then I made a god of diversions, delighted in them with a neglect of God, and drew my highest satisfaction from them; now I use them as means to help me in living to God, fixedly delighting in Him. Then they were my all; now they are only means leading to my all. And those things that are the greatest diversion, when pursued with this view, do not tend to hinder, but promote my spirituality; I see now, more than ever, that they are absolutely necessary.

Wednesday, May 1. Was not able to sit up more than half the day, and yet had such recruits of strength sometimes that I was able to write a little on a divine subject. Was grieved that I could no more live to God. In the evening, had some sweetness and intenseness in secret prayer.

Friday, May 3. Felt a little vigor of body and mind, in the morning; had some freedom, strength, and sweetness in prayer. Rode to, and spent some time with my Indians. In the evening, again retiring into the woods, I enjoyed some sweet meditations on Isaiah 53:10, "Yet it pleased the Lord to bruise him."

Tuesday, May 7. Spent the day mainly in making preparation for a journey into the wilderness. Was still weak and concerned how I should perform so difficult a journey. Spent some time in prayer for the divine blessing, direction, and protection in my intended journey, but wanted bodily strength to spend the day in fasting and prayer.

## He Revisits the Susquehannah

The next day he set out on his journey to Susquehannah, with his interpreter. He endured great hardships and fatigues in his way thither through a hideous wilderness; where, after having lodged one night in the open woods, he was overtaken with a northeasterly storm, in which he was almost ready to perish. Having no manner of shelter, and not being able to make a fire in so great a rain, he could have no comfort if he stopped; therefore he determined to go forward in hopes of meeting with some shelter, without which he thought it impossible to live the night through; but their horses—happening to have eaten poison [for want of other food] at a place where they lodged the night before—were so sick that they could neither ride nor lead them, but were obliged to drive them and travel on foot; until, through the mercy of God, just at dusk, they came to a bark hut, where they lodged that night.

After he came to Susquehannah, he traveled about a hundred miles on the river, and visited many towns and settlements of the Indians; saw some of seven or eight distinct tribes; and preached to different nations, by different interpreters. He was sometimes much discouraged, and sunk in his spirits, through the opposition that appeared in the Indians to Christianity. At other times, he was encouraged by the disposition that some of these people manifested to hear, and willingness to be instructed. He here met with some that had formerly been his hearers at Kaunaumeek and had removed hither, who saw and heard him again with great joy.

He spent a fortnight among the Indians on this river, and passed through considerable labors and hardships, frequently lodging on the ground, and sometimes in the open air. At length he fell extremely ill, as he was riding in the wilderness, being seized with an ague, followed with a burning fever, and extreme pains in his head and bowels, attended with a great evacuation of blood. He thought he would perish in the wilderness.

But at last coming to an Indian trader's hut, he got leave to stay there; and though without physic or food proper for him, it pleased God, after about a week's distress, to relieve him so far that he was able to ride. He returned homewards from Juneauta, an island far down the river, where was a considerable number of Indians who appeared more free from prejudices against Christianity than most of the other Indians. He arrived at the Forks of Delaware on Thursday, May 30, after having ridden in this journey about three hundred and forty miles. He came home in a very weak state and under dejection of mind, which was a great hindrance to him in religious exercises. However on the Sabbath, after having preached to the Indians, he preached to the white people, with some success, from Isaiah 53:10, "Yet it pleased the Lord to bruise him." Some were awakened by his preaching. The next day, he was much exercised for want of spiritual life and fervency.—J. E.

## Editor's Note

Up to this point, the record has been taken from "Brainerd's Life and Diary." The next sections, following in chronological order and covering the period from June 19, 1745, to June 19, 1746, are taken from his "Journal," which was "kept by order of the Honorable Society (in Scotland) for Propagating Christian Knowledge," which directed and supported David Brainerd's work among the American Indians.
—P. E. H., Jr.

# BRAINERD'S
# JOURNAL

# THE RISE AND PROGRESS OF A REMARKABLE
# WORK OF GRACE

## Brainerd's Journal, Part I

*From June 19 to November 4, 1745, at Crossweeksung and the
Forks of Delaware*

CROSSWEEKSUNG, IN NEW JERSEY, JUNE, 1745.

JUNE 19. Having spent most of my time for more than a
year past among the Indians in the Forks of Delaware in
Pennsylvania; and having in that time made two journeys to
Susquehannah River, far back in that province, in order to
treat with the Indians there respecting Christianity; and not
having had any considerable appearance of special success in
either of those places, which damped my spirits and was not a
little discouraging to me; upon hearing that there was a
number of Indians in and about a place called (by the Indians) Crossweeksung in New Jersey, near fourscore miles
southeastward from the Forks of Delaware, I determined to
make them a visit, and see what might be done towards the
Christianizing of them; and accordingly arrived among them
this day.

I found very few persons at the place I visited, and perceived
the Indians in these parts were very much scattered, there
being not more than two or three families in a place, and
these small settlements six, ten, fifteen, twenty, and thirty
miles, and some more, from the place I was then at. However,
I preached to those few I found, who appeared well disposed
and not inclined to object and cavil, as the Indians had frequently done elsewhere.

When I had concluded my discourse, I informed them (there

being none but a few women and children) that I would willingly visit them again the next day. Whereupon they readily set out, and traveled ten or fifteen miles, in order to give notice to some of their friends at that distance. These women, like the woman of Samaria, seemed desirous that others might "see the man that told them what they had done" in their lives past, and the misery that attended their idolatrous ways.

June 20. Visited and preached to the Indians again as I proposed. Numbers more were gathered at the invitations of their friends, who heard me the day before. These also appeared as attentive, orderly, and well disposed as the others. And none made any objection, as Indians in other places have usually done.

June 22. Preached to the Indians again. Their number which at first consisted of about seven or eight persons, was now increased to near thirty. There was not only a solemn attention among them, but some considerable impressions, it was apparent, were made upon their minds by divine truths. Some began to feel their misery and perishing state, and appeared concerned for a deliverance from it.

Lord's Day, June 23. Preached to the Indians and spent the day with them. Their number still increased; and all with one consent seemed to rejoice in my coming among them. Not a word of opposition was heard from any of them against Christianity, although in times past they had been as opposite to anything of that nature, as any Indians whatsoever. And some of them not many months before were enraged with my interpreter, because he attempted to teach them something of Christianity.

June 24. Preached to the Indians at their desire, and upon their own motion. To see poor pagans desirous of hearing the gospel of Christ, animated me to discourse to them, although I was now very weakly and my spirits much exhausted. They attended with the greatest seriousness and diligence, and there was some concern for their souls' salvation apparent among them.

June 27. Visited and preached to the Indians again. Their number now amounted to about forty persons. Their solemnity and attention still continued, and a considerable concern for their souls became very apparent among sundry of them.

June 28. The Indians being now gathered, a considerable number of them, from their several and distant habitations, requested me to preach twice a day to them, being desirous to hear as much as they possibly could while I was with them. I cheerfully complied with their motion, and could not but admire the goodness of God, who, I was persuaded, had inclined them thus to inquire after the way of salvation.

June 29. Preached again twice to the Indians. Saw, as I thought, the hand of God very evidently, and in a manner somewhat remarkable, making provision for their subsistence together, in order to their being instructed in divine things. For this day and the day before, with only walking a little way from the place of our daily meeting, they killed three deer, which were a seasonable supply for their wants, and without which, it seems, they could not have subsisted together in order to attend the means of grace.

Lord's Day, June 30. Preached twice this day also. Observed yet more concern and affection among the poor heathens than ever; so that they even constrained me to tarry yet longer with them; although my constitution was exceedingly worn out, and my health much impaired by my late fatigues and labors, and especially by my late journey to Susquehannah in May last, in which I lodged on the ground for several weeks together.

July 1. Preached again twice to a very serious and attentive assembly of Indians, they having now learned to attend the worship of God with Christian decency in all respects. There were now between forty and fifty persons of them present, old and young. I spent some considerable time in discoursing with them in a more private way, inquiring of them what they remembered of the great truths that had been taught them from day to day; and may justly say, it was amazing to see how they had received and retained the instructions given them, and what a measure of knowledge some of them had acquired in a few days.

July 2. Was obliged to leave these Indians at Crossweek-sung, thinking it my duty, as soon as health would admit, again to visit those at the Forks of Delaware. When I came to take leave of them, and spoke something particularly to each of them, they all earnestly inquired when I would come again, and expressed a great desire of being further instructed. And of their own accord agreed, that when I should come again, they would all meet and live together during my continuance with them; and that they would do their utmost endeavors to gather all the other Indians in these parts that were yet further remote. And when I parted, one told me with many tears, "She wished God would change her heart"; another, that "she wanted to find Christ"; and an old man that had been one of their chiefs, wept bitterly with concern for his soul. I then promised them to return as speedily as my health, and business elsewhere would admit, and felt not a little concerned at parting, lest the good impressions then apparent upon numbers of them, might decline and wear off, when the means came to cease; and yet could not but hope that He who, I trusted, had begun a good work among them, and who I knew did not stand in need of means to carry it on, would maintain and promote it.

At the same time, I must confess that I had often seen encouraging appearances among the Indians elsewhere prove wholly abortive; and it appeared the favor would be so great, if God should now, after I had passed through so considerable a series of almost fruitless labors and fatigues, and after my rising hopes had been so often frustrated among these poor pagans, give me any special success in my labors with them. I could not believe, and scarce dared to hope that the event would be so happy, and scarce ever found myself more suspended between hope and fear, in any affair, or at any time, than this.

This encouraging disposition and readiness to receive instruction, now apparent among these Indians, seems to have been the happy effect of the conviction that one or two of them met with some time since at the Forks of Delaware, who have since endeavored to show their friends the evil of idolatry. And although the other Indians seemed but little to regard, but rather to deride them, yet this, perhaps, has put them into a thinking posture of mind, or at least, given them some thoughts about Christianity, and excited in some of them a curiosity to hear, and so made way for the present encouraging attention. An apprehension that this might be the case here, has given me encouragement that God may in such a manner bless the means I have used with Indians in other places, where there is as yet no appearance of it. If so, may His name have the glory of it; for I have learned by experience that He only can open the ear, engage the attention, and incline the heart of poor benighted, prejudiced pagans to receive instruction.

FORKS OF DELAWARE, IN PENNSYLVANIA, JULY, 1745.

Lord's Day, July 14. Discoursed to the Indians twice, several of whom appeared concerned, and were, I have reason to think, in some measure convinced by the Divine Spirit of their sin and misery; so that they wept much the whole time of divine service. Afterwards discoursed to a number of white people then present.

July 18. Preached to my people, who attended diligently, beyond what had been common among these Indians: and some of them appeared concerned for their souls.

Lord's Day, July 21. Preached to the Indians first, then to a number of white people present, and in the afternoon to the Indians again. Divine truth seemed to make very considerable impressions upon several of them, and caused the tears to flow freely. Afterwards I baptized my interpreter and his wife, who were the first I baptized among the Indians.

They are both persons of some experimental knowledge in religion; have both been awakened to a solemn concern for their souls; have to appearance been brought to a sense of their misery and undoneness in themselves; have both appeared to be comforted with divine consolations; and it is apparent both have passed a great, and I cannot but hope a saving, change.

It may perhaps be satisfactory and agreeable that I should give some brief relation of the man's exercise and experience since he has been with me, especially seeing he is employed as my interpreter to others. When I first employed him in this business in the beginning of summer, 1744, he was well fitted for his work in regard of his acquaintance with the Indian and English language, as well as with the manners of both nations; and in regard of his desire that the Indians should conform to the customs and manners of the English, and especially to their manner of living.

But he seemed to have little or no impression of religion upon his mind, and in that respect was very unfit for his work, being incapable of understanding and communicating to others many things of importance; so that I labored under great disadvantages in addressing the Indians, for want of his having an experimental, as well as more doctrinal acquaintance with divine truths; and, at times, my spirits sank, and were much discouraged under this difficulty, especially when I observed that divine truths made little or no impressions upon his mind for many weeks together.

He indeed behaved soberly after I employed him (although, before, he had been a hard drinker), and seemed honestly engaged as far as he was capable in the performance of his work; and especially he appeared very desirous that the Indians should renounce their heathenish notions and practices, and conform to the customs of the Christian world. But still he seemed to have no concern about his own soul, till he had been with me a considerable time.

Near the latter end of July, 1744, I preached to an assembly of white people, with more freedom and fervency than I could possibly address the Indians with, without their having first attained a greater measure of doctrinal knowledge. At this time he was present, and was somewhat awakened to a concern for his soul; so that the next day he discoursed freely with me about his spiritual concerns, and gave me an opportunity to use further endeavors to fasten the impressions of his perishing state upon his mind. I could plainly perceive for some time after this, that he addressed the Indians with more concern and fervency than he had formerly done.

But these impressions seemed quickly to decline, and he remained in a great measure careless and secure, until some time late in the fall of the year following, at which time he fell into a weak and languishing state of body, and continued much disordered for several weeks together. At this season divine truth took hold of him and made deep impressions upon his mind. He was brought under great concern for his soul, and his exercise was not now transient and unsteady, but constant and abiding, so that his mind was burdened from day to day. It was now his great inquiry, "What he should do to be saved?" His spiritual trouble prevailed, till at length his sleep, in a measure, departed from him, and he had little rest day or night; but walked about under a great pressure of mind (for he was still able to walk), and appeared like another man to his neighbors, who could not but observe his behavior with wonder.

After he had been some time under this exercise, while he was striving to obtain mercy, he says, there seemed to be an impassable mountain before him. He was pressing towards heaven, as he thought, but "his way was hedged up with thorns, that he could not stir an inch further." He looked this way and that way, but could find no way at all. He thought, if he could but make his way through these thorns and briers, and climb up the first steep pitch of the mountain, that then there might be hope for him; but no way or means could he find to accomplish this.

Here he labored for a time, but all in vain; he saw it was impossible, he says, for him ever to help himself through this insupportable difficulty. He felt it signified nothing, "it signified just nothing at all for him to strive and struggle any more." And here, he says, he gave over striving, and felt that it was a gone case with him, as to his *own* power; and that

all his attempts were, and forever would be, vain and fruitless. And yet was more calm and composed under this view of
things, than he had been while striving to help himself.

While he was giving this account of his exercises, I was not
without fears that what he related was but the working of
his own imagination, and not the effect of any divine illumination of mind. But before I had time to discover [disclose]
my fears, he added, that at this time he felt himself in a
miserable and perishing condition; that he saw plainly what
he had been doing all his days, and that he had never done
one good thing, as he expressed it. He knew, he said, he was
not guilty of some wicked actions that he knew some others
guilty of. He had not been used to steal, quarrel, and murder;
the latter of which vices are common among the Indians. He
likewise knew that he had done many things that were right;
he had been kind to his neighbors, and so on.

But still his cry was that he "had never done one good
thing." "I knew," said he, "that I had not been so bad as
some others in some things, and that I had done many things
which folks call good; but all this did me no good now. I saw
that all was bad, and that I never had done one good thing"
—meaning that he had never done anything from a right
principle and with a right view, though he had done many
things that were materially good and right. "And now I
thought," said he, "that I must sink down to hell, that there
was no hope for me, because I never could do anything that
was good; and if God let me alone never so long, and I should
try never so much, still I should do nothing but what is bad."

This further account of his exercise satisfied me that it was
not the mere working of his imagination, since he appeared
so evidently to die to himself, and to be divorced from a
dependence upon his own righteousness and good deeds,
which mankind, in a fallen state, are so much attached to,
and inclined to hope for salvation upon.

There was one thing more in his view of things at this time
that was very remarkable. He not only saw, he says, what a
miserable state he himself was in, but he likewise saw the

world around him, in general, were in the same perishing circumstances, notwithstanding the profession many of them
made of Christianity, and the hope they entertained of obtaining everlasting happiness. And this he saw clearly, as if
he "was now awaked out of sleep, or had a cloud taken from
before his eyes." He saw that the life he had lived was the
way to eternal death, that he was now on the brink of end-
less misery; and when he looked round, he saw multitudes
of others who had lived the same life with himself, persons
who had no more goodness than he, and yet dreamed that
they were safe enough, as he had formerly done. He was fully
persuaded by their conversation and behavior, that they had
never felt their sin and misery, as he now felt his.

After he had been for some time in this condition, sensible
of the impossibility of his helping himself by anything he
could do, or of being delivered by any created arm, so that he
"had given up all for lost" as to his own attempts, and was
become more calm and composed; then, he says, it was borne
in upon his mind as if it had been audibly spoken to him,
"There is hope, there is hope." Whereupon his soul seemed to
rest and be in some measure satisfied, though he had no considerable joy.

He cannot here remember distinctly any views he had of
Christ, or give any clear account of his soul's acceptance of
Him, which makes his experience appear the more doubtful,
and renders it less satisfactory to himself and others, than it
might be, if he could remember distinctly the apprehensions
and actings of his mind at this season.

But these exercises of soul were attended and followed with
a very great change in the man, so that it might justly be
said, he was become another man, if not a new man. His
conversation and deportment were much altered, and even the
careless world could not but admire what had befallen him
to make so great a change in his temper, discourse, and behavior. And especially there was a surprising alteration in his
public performances. He now addressed the Indians with admirable fervency, and scarce knew when to leave off; and

sometimes when I had concluded my discourse, and was returning homeward, he would tarry behind to repeat and inculcate what had been spoken.

His change is abiding, and his life, so far as I know, unblemished to this day, though it is now more than six months
since he experienced this change; in which space of time he
has been as much exposed to strong drink, as possible, in
divers places where it has been moving free as water; and yet
has never, that I know of, discovered any hankering desire
after it. He seems to have a very considerable experience of a
spiritual exercise, and discourses feelingly of the conflicts and
consolations of a real Christian. His heart echoes to the soul-
humbling doctrines of grace, and he never appears better
pleased than when he hears of the absolute sovereignty of
God, and the salvation of sinners in a way of mere free grace.
He has likewise of late had more satisfaction respecting his
own state, has been much enlivened and assisted in his work,
so that he has been a great comfort to me.

And upon a view and strict observation of his serious and
savory conversation, his Christian temper, and unblemished
behavior for so considerable a time, as well as his experience
I have given an account of, I think that I have reason to hope
that he is "created anew in Christ Jesus to good works." His
name is Moses Tinda Tautamy; he is about fifty years of age,
and is pretty well acquainted with the pagan notions and
customs of his countrymen, and so is the better able now to
expose them. He has, I am persuaded, already been, and I
trust will yet be a blessing to the other Indians.

July 23. Preached to the Indians, but had few hearers; those
who are constantly at home seem of late to be under some
serious impressions of a religious nature.

July 26. Preached to my people, and afterwards baptized
my interpreter's children.

Lord's Day, July 28. Preached again, and perceived my
people, at least some of them, more thoughtful than ever
about their souls' concerns. I was told by some that their

seeing my interpreter and others baptized made them more concerned than anything they had ever seen or heard before. There was indeed a considerable appearance of divine power among them when that ordinance was administered. May that divine influence spread and increase more abundantly!

July 30. Discoursed to a number of my people, and gave them some particular advice and direction, being now about to leave them for the present, in order to renew my visit to the Indians in New Jersey. They were very attentive to my discourse, and earnestly desirous to know when I designed to return to them again.

CROSSWEEKSUNG, IN NEW JERSEY, AUGUST, 1745.

August 3. I visited the Indians in these parts in June last, and tarried with them some considerable time, preaching almost daily; at which season God was pleased to pour upon them a spirit of awakening and concern for their souls, and surprisingly to engage their attention to divine truths. I now found them serious, and a number of them under deep concern for an interest in Christ. Their convictions of their sinful and perishing state having, in my absence from them, been much promoted by the labors and endeavors of the Rev. Mr. William Tennent, to whom I had advised them to apply for direction, and whose house they frequented much while I was gone. I preached to them this day with some view to Revelation 22:17, "And whosoever will, let him take the water of life freely," though I could not pretend to handle the subject methodically among them.

The Lord, I am persuaded, enabled me, in a manner somewhat uncommon, to set before them the Lord Jesus Christ as a kind and compassionate Saviour, inviting distressed and perishing sinners to accept everlasting mercy. And a surprising concern soon became apparent among them. There were about twenty adult persons together (many of the Indians at remote places not having as yet had time to come since my return hither), and not above two that I could see with dry eyes.

Some were much concerned, and discovered vehement longings of soul after Christ, to save them from the misery they
felt and feared.

Lord's Day, August 4. Being invited by a neighboring
minister to assist in the administration of the Lord's Supper,
I complied with his request, and took the Indians along with
me; not only those that were together the day before, but
many more that were coming to hear me; so that there were
near fifty in all, old and young. They attended the several
discourses of the day, and some of them that could understand
English, were much affected, and all seemed to have their
concern in some measure raised.

Now a change in their manners began to appear very visible.
In the evening when they came to sup together, they would
not taste a morsel till they had sent to me to come and ask a
blessing on their food; at which time sundry of them wept,
especially when I minded them how they had in times past
eaten their feasts in honor to devils, and neglected to thank
God for them.

August 5. After a sermon had been preached by another
minister, I preached, and concluded the public work of the
solemnity from John 7:37, "In the last day . . ." In my discourse addressed the Indians in particular, who sat by themselves in a part of the house; at which time one or two of
them were struck with deep concern, as they afterwards told
me, who had been little affected before; others had their concern increased to a considerable degree. In the evening (the
greater part of them being at the house where I lodged) I
discoursed to them, and found them universally engaged about
their souls' concern, inquiring, "What they should do to be
saved?" And all their conversation among themselves turned
upon religious matters, in which they were much assisted by
my interpreter, who was with them day and night.

This day there was one woman, who had been much concerned for her soul ever since she first heard me preach in June
last, who obtained comfort, I trust, solid and well grounded.
She seemed to be filled with love to Christ, at the same time

behaved humbly and tenderly, and appeared afraid of nothing so much as of grieving and offending Him whom her soul loved.

August 6. In the morning I discoursed to the Indians at the house where we lodged. Many of them were then much affected and appeared surprisingly tender, so that a few words about their souls' concerns would cause the tears to flow freely, and produce many sobs and groans.

In the afternoon, they being returned to the place where I had usually preached among them, I again discoursed to them there. There were about fifty-five persons in all, about forty that were capable of attending divine service with understanding. I insisted upon I John 4:10, "Herein is love." They seemed eager of hearing; but there appeared nothing very remarkable, except their attention, till near the close of my discourse. Then divine truths were attended with a surprising influence, and produced a great concern among them. There were scarce three in forty that could refrain from tears and bitter cries.

They all, as one, seemed in an agony of soul to obtain an interest in Christ; and the more I discoursed of the love and compassion of God in sending His Son to suffer for the sins of men; and the more I invited them to come and partake of His love, the more their distress was aggravated, because they felt themselves unable to come. It was surprising to see how their hearts seemed to be pierced with the tender and melting invitations of the gospel, when there was not a word of terror spoken to them.

There were this day two persons that obtained relief and comfort, which (when I came to discourse with them particularly) appeared solid, rational, and scriptural. After I had inquired into the grounds of their comfort and said many things I thought proper to them, I asked them what they wanted God to do further for them. They replied, "They wanted Christ should wipe their hearts, quite clean." Surprising were now the doings of the Lord, that I can say no less of this day (and I need say no more of it) than that the arm of the Lord was powerfully and marvelously revealed in it.

August 7. Preached to the Indians from Isaiah 53:3–10. There was a remarkable influence attending the Word, and great concern in the assembly; but scarce equal to what appeared the day before, that is, not quite so universal. However, most were much affected, and many in great distress for their souls; and some few could neither go nor stand, but lay flat on the ground, as if pierced at heart, crying incessantly for mercy. Several were newly awakened, and it was remarkable that as fast as they came from remote places round about the Spirit of God seemed to seize them with concern for their souls.

After public service was concluded, I found two persons more that had newly met with comfort, of whom I had good hopes; and a third that I could not but entertain some hopes of, whose case did not appear so clear as the others; so that there were now six in all that had got some relief from their spiritual distresses, and five whose experience appeared very clear and satisfactory. And it is worthy of remark, that those who obtained comfort first were in general deeply affected with concern for their souls when I preached to them in June last.

August 8. In the afternoon I preached to the Indians; their number was now about sixty-five persons, men, women, and children. I discoursed from Luke 14:16–23 and was favored with uncommon freedom in my discourse. There was much visible concern among them while I was discoursing publicly; but afterwards when I spoke to one and another more particularly, whom I perceived under much concern, the power of God seemed to descend upon the assembly "like a rushing mighty wind," and with an astonishing energy bore down all before it.

I stood amazed at the influence that seized the audience almost universally, and could compare it to nothing more aptly than the irresistible force of a mighty torrent, or swelling deluge, that with its insupportable weight and pressure bears down and sweeps before it whatever is in its way. Almost all persons of all ages were bowed down with concern together, and scarce one was able to withstand the shock of this surprising operation. Old men and women, who had been drunken wretches for many years, and some little children, not more than six or seven years of age, appeared in distress for their souls, as well as persons of middle age. And it was apparent these children (some of them at least) were not merely frightened with seeing the general concern; but were made sensible of their danger, the badness of their hearts, and their misery without Christ, as some of them expressed it.

The most stubborn hearts were now obliged to bow. A principal man among the Indians, who before was most secure and self-righteous and thought his state good because he knew more than the generality of the Indians had formerly done, and who with a great degree of confidence the day before, told me, "he had been a Christian more than ten years," was now brought under solemn concern for his soul, and wept bitterly. Another man advanced in years, who had been a murderer, a powwow (or conjurer) and a notorious drunkard, was likewise brought now to cry for mercy with many tears, and to complain much that he could be no more concerned when he saw his danger so very great.

They were almost universally praying and crying for mercy, in every part of the house, and many out of doors, and numbers could neither go nor stand. Their concern was so great, each one for himself, that none seemed to take any notice of those about them, but each prayed freely for himself. And, I am to think, they were to their own apprehension as much retired as if they had been, individually, by themselves in the thickest desert; or, I believe rather, that they thought nothing about any but themselves, and their own states, and so were everyone praying apart, although all together.

It seemed to me there was now an exact fulfillment of that prophecy, Zechariah 12: 10, 11, 12; for there was now "a great mourning, like the mourning of Hadadrimmon"; and each seemed to "mourn apart." Methought this had a near resemblance to the day of God's power, mentioned in Joshua 10:14. I must say I never saw any day like it in all respects. It was a day wherein I am persuaded the Lord did much to destroy the kingdom of darkness among this people today.

This concern in general was most rational and just. Those who had been awakened any considerable time complained more especially of the badness of their hearts. Those newly awakened, of the badness of their lives and actions past; all were afraid of the anger of God and of everlasting misery as the desert of their sins. Some of the white people who came out of curiosity to "hear what this babbler would say" to the poor ignorant Indians were much awakened, and some appeared to be wounded with a view of their perishing state.

Those who had lately obtained relief were filled with comfort at this season. They appeared calm and composed, and seemed to rejoice in Christ Jesus. Some of them took their distressed friends by the hand, telling them of the goodness of Christ and the comfort that is to be enjoyed in Him, and thence invited them to come and give up their hearts to Him. I could observe some of them, in the most honest and unaffected manner (without any design of being taken notice of) lifting up their eyes to heaven as if crying for mercy, while they saw the distress of the poor souls around them.

There was one remarkable instance of awakening this day that I cannot but take particular notice of here. A young Indian woman, who, I believe, never knew before she had a soul nor ever thought of any such thing, hearing that there was something strange among the Indians, came to see what was the matter. In her way to the Indians she called at my lodgings, and when I told her I designed presently to preach to the Indians, laughed, and seemed to mock; but went however to them.

I had not proceeded far in my public discourse, before she felt effectually that she had a soul. Before I had concluded my discourse, she was so convinced of her sin and misery and so distressed with concern for her soul's salvation that she seemed like one pierced through with a dart, and cried out incessantly. She could neither go nor stand, nor sit on her seat without being held up. After public service was over, she lay flat on the ground praying earnestly, and would take no notice of, nor give any answer to any that spoke to her. I hearkened to know what she said, and perceived the burden of her prayer to be, *Guttummaukalummeh wechaumeh kmeleh Ndah*, that is, "Have mercy on me, and help me to give You my heart." Thus she continued praying incessantly for many hours together. This was indeed a surprising day of God's power and seemed enough to convince an atheist of the truth, importance and power of God's Word.

August 9. Spent almost the whole day with the Indians, the former part of it in discoursing to many of them privately, especially to some who had lately received comfort, endeavoring to inquire into the grounds of it, as well as to give them some proper instructions, cautions, and directions.

In the afternoon discoursed to them publicly. There were now present about seventy persons, old and young. I opened and applied the Parable of the Sower, Matthew 13. Was enabled to discourse with much plainness, and found afterwards that this discourse was very instructive to them. There were many tears among them while I was discoursing publicly, but no considerable cry. Yet some were much affected with a few words spoken from Matthew 11:28, "Come unto me, all ye that labor," with which I concluded my discourse. But while I was discoursing near night to two or three of the awakened persons, a divine influence seemed to attend what was spoken to them in a powerful manner, causing the persons to cry out in anguish of soul, although I spoke not a word of terror. On the contrary, I set before them the fullness and all-sufficiency of Christ's merits and His willingness to save all that came to Him, and thereupon pressed them to come without delay.

The cry of these was soon heard by others, who, though scattered before, immediately gathered round. I then proceeded in the same strain of gospel invitation, till they all, except two or three, melted into tears and cries and seemed in the greatest distress to find and secure an interest in the great Redeemer. Some who had but little more than a ruffle made in their passions the day before, seemed now to be deeply affected and wounded at heart. The concern in general appeared near as prevalent as it was the day before. There was indeed a very great mourning among them, and yet everyone seemed to mourn apart. For so great was their concern, that almost everyone was praying and crying for himself, as if none had been near. *Guttummaukalummeh, guttummaukalummeh*, that is, "Have mercy upon me, have mercy upon me," was the common cry.

It was very affecting to see the poor Indians, who the other day were hallooing and yelling in their idolatrous feasts and drunken frolics, now crying to God with such importunity for an interest in His dear Son! Found two or three persons, who, I had reason to hope, had taken comfort upon good grounds since the evening before. These, with others that had obtained comfort, were together and seemed to rejoice much that God was carrying on His work with such power upon others.

August 10. Rode to the Indians and began to discourse more privately to those who had obtained comfort and satisfaction, endeavoring to instruct, direct, caution and comfort them. But others being eager of hearing every word that related to spiritual concerns, soon came together one after another. When I had discoursed to the young converts more than half an hour, they seemed much melted with divine things and earnestly desirous to be with Christ. I told them of the godly soul's perfect purity and full enjoyment of Christ immediately upon its separation from the body, and that it would be forever inconceivably more happy than they had ever been for any short space of time when Christ seemed near to them, in prayer or other duties.

That I might make way for speaking of the resurrection of the body, and thence of the complete blessedness of the man, I said, "But perhaps some of you will say, I love my body as well as my soul, and I cannot bear to think that my body should lie dead, if my soul is happy." To which they all cheerfully replied, *Muttoh, muttoh* (before I had opportunity to prosecute what I designed respecting the resurrection), "No, no." They did not regard their bodies, if their souls might be but with Christ. Then they appeared willing to be absent from the body, that they might be present with the Lord.

When I had spent some time with these, I turned to the other Indians and spoke to them from Luke 19:10, "For the Son of man is come to seek . . ." I had not discoursed long before their concern rose to a great degree, and the house was filled with cries and groans. When I insisted on the compassion and care of the Lord Jesus Christ for those that were lost, who thought themselves undone and could find no way of escape, this melted them down the more and aggravated their distress that they could not find and come to so kind a Saviour.

Sundry persons, who before had been but slightly awakened, were now deeply wounded with a sense of their sin and misery. One man in particular, who was never before awakened, was now made to feel that "the word of the Lord was quick and powerful, sharper than any two-edged sword." He seemed to be pierced at heart with distress, and his concern appeared most rational and scriptural; for he said that all the wickedness of his past life was brought fresh to his remembrance, and he saw all the vile actions he had done formerly as if done but yesterday.

Found one that had newly received comfort, after pressing distress from day to day. Could not but rejoice and admire divine goodness in what appeared this day. There seems to be some good done by every discourse; some newly awakened every day, and some comforted. It was refreshing to observe the conduct of those that had obtained comfort, while others were distressed with fear and concern; that is, lifting up their hearts to God for them.

Lord's Day, August 11. Discoursed in the forenoon from the Parable of the Prodigal Son, Luke 15. Observed no such remarkable effect of the Word upon the assembly as in days past. There were numbers of careless spectators of the white people, some Quakers, and others. In the afternoon I discoursed upon a part of Peter's sermon, Acts 2, and at the close of my discourse to the Indians made an address to the white people. Divine truths seemed then to be attended with power both to English and Indians. Several of the white heathen were awakened and could not longer be idle spectators, but found they had souls to save or lose as well as the Indians; a great concern spread through the whole assembly. This also appeared to be a day of God's power, especially towards the conclusion of it, although the influence attending the Word seemed scarce so powerful now as in some days past.

The number of the Indians, old and young, was now upwards of seventy. One or two were newly awakened this day, who never had appeared to be moved with concern for their souls before. Those who had obtained relief and comfort, and had given hopeful evidences of having passed a saving change, appeared humble and devout and behaved in an agreeable and Christian-like manner. I was refreshed to see the tenderness of conscience manifest in some of them, one instance of which I cannot but notice. Perceiving one of them very sorrowful in the morning, I inquired into the cause of her sorrow. I found the difficulty was that she had been angry with her child the evening before and was now exercised with fears lest her anger had been inordinate and sinful. This so grieved her that she waked and began to sob before daylight, and continued weeping for several hours together.

August 14. Spent the day with the Indians. There was one of them who had some time since put away his wife (as is common among them) and taken another woman. Now he has been brought under some serious impressions and is much concerned about that affair in particular. He seemed fully convinced of the wickedness of that practice and earnestly desirous to know what God would have him do in his present circumstances. When the law of God respecting marriage had been opened to them, and the cause of his leaving his wife inquired into, and when it appeared she had given him no just occasion by unchastity to desert her, and that she was willing to forgive his past misconduct and to live peaceably with him for the future, and that she moreover insisted on it as her right to enjoy him; he was then told that it was his indispensable duty to renounce the woman he had last taken and receive the other who was his proper wife, and live peaceably with her during life. With this he readily and cheerfully complied and thereupon publicly renounced the woman he had last taken and publicly promised to live with and be kind to his wife during life, she also promising the same to him. Here appeared a clear demonstration of the power of God's Word upon their hearts. I suppose a few weeks before, the whole world could not have persuaded this man to a compliance with Christian rules in this affair.

I was not without fears, lest this proceeding might be like putting "new wine into old bottles," and that some might be prejudiced against Christianity when they saw the demands made by it. But the man being much concerned about the matter, the determination of it could be deferred no longer and it seemed to have a good rather than an ill effect among the Indians, who generally owned that the laws of Christ were good and right respecting the affairs of marriage. In the afternoon I preached to them from the apostle's discourse to Cornelius, Acts 10:34. There appeared some affectionate concern among them, though not equal to what appeared in several of the former days. They still attended and heard as for their lives, and the Lord's work seemed still to be promoted and propagated among them.

August 16. Spent a considerable time in conversing privately with sundry of the Indians. Found one that had got relief and comfort, after pressing concern, and could not but hope, when I came to discourse particularly with her, that her comfort was of the right kind. In the afternoon, I preached to them from John 6:26-34. Toward the close of my discourse, divine truths were attended with considerable power upon the audience, and more especially after public service was over, when I particularly addressed sundry distressed persons.

There was a great concern for their souls spread pretty generally among them. Especially there were two persons newly awakened to a sense of their sin and misery, one of whom was lately come, and the other had all along been very attentive, and desirous of being awakened, but could never before have any lively view of her perishing state. But now her concern and spiritual distress was such that, I thought, I had never seen any more pressing.

Sundry old men were also in distress for their souls so that they could not refrain from weeping and crying aloud, and their bitter groans were the most convincing, as well as affecting evidence of the reality and depth of their inward anguish. God is powerfully at work among them! True and genuine convictions of sin are daily promoted in many instances, and some are newly awakened from time to time, although some few, who felt a commotion in their passions in days past, seem now to discover that their hearts were never duly affected.

I never saw the work of God appear so independent of means as at this time. I discoursed to the people, and spoke what, I suppose, had a proper tendency to promote convictions. But God's manner of working upon them appeared so entirely supernatural and above means that I could scarce believe He used me as an instrument, or what I spake as means of carrying on His work. It seemed, as I thought, to have no connection with, nor dependence upon means in any respect. Although I could not but continue to use the means which I thought proper for the promotion of the work, yet God seemed, as I apprehended, to work entirely without them. I seemed to do nothing, and indeed to have nothing to do, but to "stand still and see the salvation of God." I found myself obliged and delighted to say, "Not unto us," not unto instruments and means, "but to thy name be glory." God appeared to work entirely alone, and I saw no room to attribute any part of this work to any created arm.

August 17. Spent much time in private conferences with the

Indians. Found one who had newly obtained relief and comfort, after a long season of spiritual trouble and distress—he having been one of my hearers at the Forks of Delaware for more than a year, and now followed me here under deep concern for his soul—and had abundant reason to hope that his comfort was well grounded and truly divine. Afterwards discoursed publicly from Acts 8:29-39, and took occasion to treat concerning baptism, in order to their being instructed and prepared to partake of that ordinance. They were yet hungry and thirsty for the Word of God, and appeared unwearied in their attendance upon it.

Lord's Day, August 18. Preached in the forenoon to an assembly of white people, made up of Presbyterians, Baptists, and Quakers. Afterwards preached to the Indians from John 6:35-40. There was considerable concern visible among them, though not equal to what has frequently appeared of late.

August 19. Preached from Isaiah 55:1, "Ho, every one that thirsteth." Divine truths were attended with power upon those who had received comfort, and others also. The former were sweetly melted and refreshed with divine invitations, the latter much concerned for their souls, that they might obtain an interest in these glorious gospel-provisions that were set before them. There were numbers of poor impotent souls that waited at the pool for healing, and the Angel seemed, as at other times of late, to trouble the waters so that there was yet a most desirable and comfortable prospect of the spiritual recovery of diseased, perishing sinners.

August 24. Spent the forenoon in discoursing to some of the Indians, in order to their receiving the ordinance of baptism. When I had opened the nature of the ordinance, the obligations attending it, the duty of devoting ourselves to God in it, and the privilege of being in covenant with Him, sundry of them seemed to be filled with love to God, and delighted with the thoughts of giving up themselves to Him in that solemn and public manner, melted and refreshed with the hopes of enjoying the blessed Redeemer.

Afterwards I discoursed publicly from I Thessalonians 4:13–

17, "But I would not have you be ignorant." There was a solemn attention and some visible concern and affection in the time of public service, which was afterwards increased by some further exhortation given them to come to Christ and give up their hearts to Him, that they might be fitted to "ascend up and meet him in the air," when He shall "descend with a shout, and the voice of the archangel."

There were several Indians newly come, who thought their state good and themselves happy because they had sometimes lived with the white people under gospel-light, had learned to read, were civil; although they appeared utter strangers to their own hearts and altogether unacquainted with the power of religion, as well as with the doctrines of grace. With those I discoursed particularly after public worship and was surprised to see their self-righteous disposition, their strong attachment to the covenant of works for salvation, and the high value they put upon their supposed attainments. Yet after much discourse, one appeared in a measure convinced that "by the deeds of the law no flesh living can be justified," and wept bitterly, inquiring what he must do to be saved!

This was very comfortable to others who had gained some experimental acquaintance with their own hearts. For before they were grieved with the conversation and conduct of these newcomers, who boasted of their knowledge, and thought well of themselves, but evidently discovered to those that had any experience of divine truths that they knew nothing of their own hearts.

Lord's Day, August 25. Preached in the forenoon from Luke 15:3–7. There being a multitude of white people present, I made an address to them at the close of my discourse to the Indians. But I could not so much as keep them orderly; for scores of them kept walking and gazing about, and behaved more indecently than any Indians I ever addressed. A view of their abusive conduct so sunk my spirits that I could scarce go on with my work.

In the afternoon discoursed from Revelation 3:20, at which time the Indians behaved seriously, though many others were vain. Afterwards baptized twenty-five persons of the Indians, fifteen adults and ten children. Most of the adults I have comfortable reason to hope are renewed persons; and there was not one of them but what I entertained some hopes of in that respect, though the case of two or three of them appeared more doubtful.

After the crowd of spectators was gone, I called the baptized persons together and discoursed to them in particular, at the same time inviting others to attend. I minded them of the solemn obligations they were now under to live to God, warned them of the evil and dreadful consequences of careless living, especially after this public profession of Christianity; gave them directions for their future conduct, and encouraged them to watchfulness and devotion by setting before them the comfort and happy conclusion of a religious life.

This was a desirable and sweet season indeed! Their hearts were engaged and cheerful in duty, and they rejoiced that they had in a public and solemn manner dedicated themselves to God. Love seemed to reign among them! They took each other by the hand with tenderness and affection, as if their hearts were knit together, while I was discoursing to them. All their deportment toward each other was such that a serious spectator might justly be excited to cry out with admiration, "Behold how they love one another"! Sundry of the other Indians, at seeing and hearing these things, were much affected and wept bitterly, longing to be partakers of the same joy and comfort that these discovered by their very countenances as well as conduct.

August 26. Preached to my people from John 6:51–55. After I had discoursed some time, I addressed those in particular who entertained hopes that they were "passed from death to life." Opened to them the persevering nature of those consolations Christ gives His people, and which I trusted He had bestowed upon some in that assembly; showed them that such have already the "beginnings of eternal life" (v. 54), and that their heaven shall speedily be completed.

I no sooner began to discourse in this strain but the dear

Christians in the congregation began to be melted with affection to, and desire of the enjoyment of Christ and of a state of perfect purity. They wept affectionately and yet joyfully, and their tears and sobs discovered brokenness of heart, and yet were attended with real comfort and sweetness. This was a tender, affectionate, humble, delightful melting, and appeared to be the genuine effect of a Spirit of adoption, and very far from the Spirit of bondage that they not long since labored under. The influence seemed to spread from these through the whole assembly, and there quickly appeared a wonderful concern among them. Many who had not yet found Christ as an all-sufficient Saviour were surprisingly engaged in seeking after Him. It was indeed a lovely and very desirable assembly. Their number was now about ninety-five persons, old and young, and almost all affected either with joy in Christ Jesus, or with utmost concern to obtain an interest in Him.

Being fully convinced it was now my duty to take a journey far back to the Indians on Susquehannah River (it being now a proper season of the year to find them generally at home), after having spent some hours in public and private discourses with my people, I told them that I must now leave them for the present, and go to their brethren far remote and preach to them. I told them I wanted the Spirit of God should go with me, without whom nothing could be done to any good purpose among the Indians—as they themselves had opportunity to see by the barrenness of our meetings at times, when there was much pains taken to affect and awaken sinners yet to little or no purpose. I asked them if they could not be willing to spend the remainder of the day in prayer for me that God would go with me and succeed my endeavors for the conversion of those poor souls. They cheerfully complied with the motion, and soon after I left them (it being then about an hour and half before sunset) they began, and continued praying all night till break of day, or very near, never mistrusting, they tell me, till they went out and viewed the stars, and saw the morning star a considerable height, that it was later than common bedtime. Thus eager and unwearied were they in their devotions! A remarkable night it was, attended, as my interpreter tells me, with a powerful influence upon those who were yet under concern, as well as those that had received comfort.

There were, I trust, this day two distressed souls brought to the enjoyment of solid comfort in Him, in whom the weary find rest. It was likewise remarkable that this day an old Indian, who has all his days been an obstinate idolater, was brought to give up his rattles (which they use for music in their idolatrous feasts and dances) to the other Indians, who quickly destroyed them. This without any attempt of mine in the affair, I having said nothing to him about it; so that it seemed it was nothing but just the power of God's Word, without any particular application to this sin, that produced this effect. Thus God has begun, thus He has hitherto surprisingly carried on a work of grace amongst these Indians. May the glory be ascribed to Him, who is the sole Author of it!

FORKS OF DELAWARE, PENNSYLVANIA, SEPTEMBER, 1745.

Lord's Day, September 1. Preached to the Indians here from Luke 14:16–23. The Word appeared to be attended with some power, and caused some tears in the assembly. Afterwards preached to a number of white people present, and observed many of them in tears, and some who had formerly been as careless and unconcerned about religion perhaps as the Indians. Towards night, discoursed to the Indians again, and perceived a greater attention and more visible concern among them than has been usual in these parts.

September 5. Discoursed to the Indians from the Parable of the Sower, afterwards conversed particularly with sundry persons, which occasioned them to weep, and even to cry out in an affecting manner, and seized others with surprise and concern. I doubt not but that a divine power accompanied what was then spoken. Sundry of these persons had been with me to Crossweeksung, and had there seen, and some of them, I trust, felt the power of God's Word in an effectual and saving manner.

I asked one of them, who had obtained comfort and given hopeful evidences of being truly religious, why he now cried. He replied, "When I thought how Christ was slain like a lamb, and spilt His blood for sinners, I could not help crying, when I was all alone": and thereupon burst out into tears and cried again. I then asked his wife, who had likewise been abundantly comforted, wherefore she cried. She answered, "I was grieved that the Indians here would not come to Christ, as well as those at Crossweeksung." I asked her if she found a heart to pray for them and whether Christ had seemed to be near to her of late in prayer, as in time past (which is my usual method of expressing a sense of the divine presence). She replied, "Yes, He has been near to me; and at some times when I have been praying alone, my heart loved to pray so, that I could not bear to leave the place, but wanted to stay and pray longer."

Lord's Day, September 8. Discoursed to the Indians in the afternoon from John 12:44–50; in the afternoon from Acts 2:36–39. The Word of God at this time seemed to fall with weight and influence upon them. There were but few present, but most that were, were in tears, and sundry cried out under distressing concern for their souls.

There was one man considerably awakened, who never before discovered any concern for his soul. There appeared a remarkable work of the Divine Spirit among them, almost generally, not unlike what has been of late at Crossweeksung. It seemed as if the divine influence had spread from thence to this place, although something of it appeared here in the awakening of my interpreter, his wife, and some few others.

Sundry of the careless white people now present were awakened (or at least startled), seeing the power of God so prevalent among the Indians. I then made a particular address to them, which seemed to make some impression upon them and excite some affection in them.

There are sundry Indians in these parts who have always refused to hear me preach, and have been enraged against those that have attended my preaching. But of late they are more bitter than ever, scoffing at Christianity, and sometimes asking my hearers how often they have cried and whether they have not now cried enough to do the turn. So that they have already "trial of cruel mockings."

September 9. Left the Indians in the Forks of Delaware and set out on a journey towards Susquehannah River, directing my course towards the Indian town more than an hundred and twenty miles westward from the Forks. Traveled about fifteen miles, and there lodged.

September 13. After having lodged out three nights, arrived at the Indian town I aimed at on Susquehannah, called Shaumoking (one of the places, and the largest of them, that I visited in May last), and was kindly received and entertained by the Indians. But had little satisfaction by reason of the heathenish dance and revel they then held in the house where I was obliged to lodge, which I could not suppress, though I often intreated them to desist, for the sake of one of their own friends who was then sick in the house and whose disorder was much aggravated by the noise. Alas! how destitute of natural affection are these poor uncultivated pagans, although they seem somewhat kind in their own way. Of a truth, "the dark corners of the earth are full of the habitations of cruelty."

This town lies partly on the east side of the river, partly on the west, and partly on a large island in it, and contains upwards of fifty houses and, they tell me, near three hundred persons, though I never saw much more than half that number in it. There are three different tribes of Indians speaking three languages wholly unintelligible to each other. About one half of its inhabitants are Delawares, the others called Senakes, and Tutelas. The Indians of this place are counted the most drunken, mischievous, and ruffianly fellows of any in these parts. Satan seems to have his seat in this town in an eminent manner.

September 14. Visited the Delaware king (who was supposed to be at the point of death when I was here in May last, but was now recovered), and discoursed with him and others respecting Christianity, and spent the afternoon with them, and had more encouragement than I expected. The king appeared kindly disposed and willing to be instructed. This gave me some encouragement that God would open an effectual door for my preaching the gospel here, and set up His kingdom in this place. Which was a support and refreshment to me in the wilderness, and rendered my solitary circumstances comfortable and pleasant.

Lord's Day, September 15. Visited the chief of the Delawares again; was kindly received by him, and discoursed to the Indians in the afternoon. Still entertained hopes that God would open their hearts to receive the gospel, though many of them in the place were so drunk from day to day that I could get no opportunity to speak to them. Towards night discoursed with one that understood the languages of the Six Nations (as they are usually called), who discovered an inclination to hearken to Christianity; which gave me some hopes that the gospel might hereafter be sent to those nations far remote.

September 16. Spent the forenoon with the Indians, endeavoring to instruct them from house to house and to engage them, as far as I could, to be friendly to Christianity. Towards night went to one part of the town where they were sober, and got together near fifty persons of them and discoursed to them, having first obtained the king's cheerful consent. There was a surprising attention among them, and they manifested a considerable desire of being further instructed. There was also one or two that seemed to be touched with some concern for their souls, who appeared well pleased with some conversation in private, after I had concluded my public discourse to them.

My spirits were much refreshed with this appearance of things, and I could not but return with my interpreter (having no other companion in this journey) to my poor hard lodgings, rejoicing in hopes that God designed to set up His kingdom here, where Satan now reigns in the most eminent manner. Found uncommon freedom in addressing the throne of grace for the accomplishment of so great and glorious a work.

September 17. Spent the forenoon in visiting and discoursing to the Indians. About noon left Shaumoking (most of the Indians going out this day on their hunting design), and traveled down the river southwestward.

September 19. Visited an Indian town called Juneauta, situate on an island in Susquehannah. Was much discouraged with the temper and behavior of the Indians here, although they appeared friendly when I was with them the last spring, and then gave me encouragement to come and see them again. But they now seemed resolved to retain their pagan notions and persist in their idolatrous practices.

September 20. Visited the Indians again at Juneauta island, and found them almost universally very busy in making preparations for a great sacrifice and dance. Had no opportunity to get them together in order to discourse with them about Christianity, by reason of their being so much engaged about their sacrifice. My spirits were much sunk with a prospect so very discouraging, and especially seeing I had now no interpreter but a pagan, who was as much attached to idolatry as any of them (my own interpreter having left me the day before, being obliged to attend upon some important business elsewhere, and knowing that he could neither speak nor understand the language of these Indians). I was under the greatest disadvantages imaginable. However, I attempted to discourse privately with some of them, but without any appearance of success. Notwithstanding, I still tarried with them.

In the evening they met together, near a hundred of them, and danced around a large fire, having prepared ten fat deer for the sacrifice. The fat of the inwards they burnt in the fire while they were dancing, and sometimes raised the flame to a prodigious height, at the same time yelling and shouting in such a manner that they might easily have been heard two miles or more. They continued their sacred dance all night, or near the matter; after which they ate the flesh of the sacrifice, and so retired each one to his lodging.

I enjoyed little satisfaction this night, being entirely alone on the island (as to any Christian company), and in the midst of this idolatrous revel. Having walked to and fro till body and mind were pained and much oppressed, I at length crept into a little crib made for corn, and there slept on the poles.

Lord's Day, September 22. Spent the day with the Indians on the island. As soon as they were well up in the morning, I attempted to instruct them, and labored for that purpose to get them together, but quickly found they had something else to do. Near noon they gathered together all their pow-wows (or conjurers), and set about half a dozen of them to playing their juggling tricks, and acting their frantic distracted postures, in order to find out why they were then so sickly upon the island, numbers of them being at that time disordered with a fever, and bloody flux.

In this exercise they were engaged for several hours, making all the wild, ridiculous, and distracted motions imaginable; sometimes singing; sometimes howling; sometimes extending their hands to the utmost stretch, spreading all their fingers; and they seemed to push with them, as if they designed to fright something away, or at least keep it off at arm's-end; sometimes stroking their faces with their hands, then spurting water as fine as mist; sometimes sitting flat on the earth, then bowing down their faces to the ground; wringing their sides, as if in pain and anguish; twisting their faces, turning up their eyes, grunting, and puffing.

Their monstrous actions tended to excite ideas of horror, and seemed to have something in them, as I thought, peculiarly suited to raise the Devil, if he could be raised by anything odd, ridiculous, and frightful. Some of them, I could observe, were much more fervent and devout in the business than others, and seemed to chant, peep, and mutter with a great degree of warmth and vigor, as if determined to awaken and engage the powers below. I sat at a small distance, not more than thirty feet from them (though undiscovered), with my Bible in my hand, resolving, if possible, to spoil their sport, and prevent their receiving any answers from the infernal world, and there viewed the whole scene.

They continued their hideous charms and incantations for more than three hours, until they had all wearied themselves out, although they had in that space of time taken sundry intervals of rest; and at length broke up, I apprehended, without receiving any answer at all.

After they had done powwowing, I attempted to discourse with them about Christianity. But they soon scattered, and gave me no opportunity for anything of that nature. A view of these things, while I was entirely alone in the wilderness, destitute of the society of anyone that so much as "named the name of Christ," greatly sunk my spirits, gave me the most gloomy turn of mind imaginable, almost stripped me of all resolution and hope respecting further attempts for propagating the gospel, and converting the pagans, and rendered this the most burdensome and disagreeable Sabbath that ever I saw.

But nothing, I can truly say, sunk and distressed me like the loss of my hope respecting their conversion. This concern appeared so great, and seemed to be so much my own that I seemed to have nothing to do on earth, if this failed. A prospect of the greatest success in the saving conversion of souls under gospel light, would have done little or nothing towards compensating for the loss of my hope in this respect; and my spirits now were so damped and depressed that I had no heart nor power to make any further attempts among them for that purpose, and could not possibly recover my hope, resolution, and courage, by the utmost of my endeavors.

The Indians of this island can many of them understand the English language considerably well, having formerly lived in some part of Maryland among or near the white people, but are very vicious, drunken, and profane, although not so savage as those who have less acquaintance with the English. Their customs in divers respects differ from those of other Indians upon this river. They do not bury their dead in a common form, but let their flesh consume above ground in close cribs made for that purpose; and at the end of a year, or sometimes a longer space of time, they take the bones, when the flesh is all consumed, and wash and scrape them, and afterwards bury them with some ceremony.

Their method of charming or conjuring over the sick seems somewhat different from that of other Indians, though for substance the same. The whole of it, among these and others, perhaps is an imitation of what seems, by Naaman's expression, II Kings 5:11, to have been the custom of the ancient heathens. For it seems chiefly to consist in their "striking their hands over the diseased," repeatedly stroking them, "and calling upon their gods," excepting the spurting of water like a mist, and some other frantic ceremonies, common to the other conjurations I have already mentioned.

When I was in these parts in May last, I had an opportunity of learning many of the notions and customs of the Indians, as well as of observing many of their practices. I then traveled more than an hundred and thirty miles upon the river above the English settlements. Had in that journey a view of some persons of seven or eight distinct tribes, speaking so many different languages.

But of all the sights I ever saw among them, or indeed anywhere else, none appeared so frightful, or so near akin to what is usually imagined of infernal powers—none ever excited such images of terror in my mind—as the appearance of one who was a devout and zealous reformer, or rather restorer of what he supposed was the ancient religion of the Indians. He made his appearance in his pontifical garb, which was a coat of bears' skins, dressed with the hair on, and hanging down to his toes, a pair of bearskin stockings, and a great wooden face, painted the one half black, and the other tawny, about the color of an Indian's skin, with an extravagant mouth, cut very much awry. The face was fastened to a bearskin cap, which was drawn over his head. He advanced toward me with the instrument in his hand that he used for music in his idolatrous worship, which was a dry tortoise shell, with some corn in it, and the neck of it drawn on to a piece of wood, which made a very convenient handle.

As he came forward, he beat his tune with the rattle, and

danced with all his might, but did not suffer any part of his body, not so much as his fingers, to be seen; and no man would have guessed by his appearance and actions, that he could have been a human creature, if they had not had some intimation of it otherwise. When he came near me, I could not but shrink away from him, although it was then noonday, and I knew who it was, his appearance and gestures were so prodigiously frightful. He had a house consecrated to religious uses, with divers images cut out upon the several parts of it; I went in and found the ground beaten almost as hard as a rock with their frequent dancing in it.

I discoursed with him about Christianity, and some of my discourse he seemed to like, but some of it he disliked entirely. He told me that God had taught him his religion, and that he never would turn from it, but wanted to find some that would join heartily with him in it; for the Indians, he said, were grown very degenerate and corrupt. He had thoughts, he said, of leaving all his friends, and traveling abroad, in order to find some that would join with him; for he believed God had some good people somewhere that felt as he did He had not always, he said, felt as he now did, but had formerly been like the rest of the Indians, until about four or five years before that time: then, he said, his heart was very much distressed, so that he could not live among the Indians, but got away into the woods, and lived alone for some months.

At length, he says, God comforted his heart, and showed him what he should do. Since that time he had known God and tried to serve Him; he loved all men, be they who they would, so as he never did before. He treated me with uncommon courtesy, and seemed to be hearty in it. I was told by the Indians that he opposed their drinking strong liquor with all his power; and if at any time he could not dissuade them from it, by all he could say, he would leave them, and go crying into the woods. It was manifest he had a set of religious notions that he had looked into for himself, and not taken for granted upon bare tradition; and he relished or disrelished whatever was spoken of a religious nature, according as it either agreed or disagreed with his standard. And while I was discoursing he would sometimes say, "Now that I like; so God has taught me," and so on. And some of his sentiments seemed very just. Yet he utterly denied the being of a Devil, and declared there was no such creature known among the Indians of old times, whose religion he supposed he was attempting to revive.

He likewise told me that departed souls all went southward, and that the difference between the good and bad was this, that the former were admitted into a beautiful town with spiritual walls, or walls agreeable to the nature of souls; and that the latter would forever hover round those walls, and in vain attempt to get in. He seemed to be sincere, honest, and conscientious in his own way, and according to his own religious notions, which was more than I ever saw in any other pagan. I perceived he was looked upon and derided among most of the Indians as a precise zealot, that made a needless noise about religious matters; but I must say, there was something in his temper and disposition that looked more like true religion than anything I ever observed amongst other heathens.

But, alas! how deplorable is the state of the Indians upon this river! The brief representation I have here given of their notions and manners is sufficient to show that they are "led captive by Satan at his will," in the most eminent manner. Methinks they might likewise be sufficient to excite the compassion, and engage the prayers of pious souls for these their fellow men, who sit in "the regions of the shadow of death."

September 23. Made some further attempts to instruct and Christianize the Indians on this island, but all to no purpose. They live so near the white people that they are always in the way of strong liquor, as well as the ill examples of nominal Christians; which renders it so unspeakably difficult to treat with them about Christianity.

FORKS OF DELAWARE, OCTOBER, 1745.

October 1. Discoursed to the Indians here, and spent some time in private conferences with them about their souls' concerns, and afterwards invited them to accompany, or if not, to follow me down to Crossweeksung, as soon as their convenience would admit; which invitation sundry of them cheerfully accepted.

CROSSWEEKSUNG, IN NEW JERSEY, OCTOBER, 1745.

Preached to my people from John 14:1–6. The divine presence seemed to be in the assembly. Numbers were affected with divine truths, and it was a season of comfort to some in particular. Oh, what a difference is there between these and the Indians I had lately treated with upon Susquehannah! To be with those seemed like being banished from God, and all His people; to be with these like being admitted into His family, and to the enjoyment of His divine presence! How great is the change lately made upon numbers of these Indians, who not many months ago were as thoughtless and averse to Christianity as those upon Susquehannah! How astonishing is that grace which has made this change!

Lord's Day, October 6. Preached in the forenoon from John 10:7–11. There was a considerable melting among my people; the dear young Christians were refreshed, comforted, and strengthened, and one or two persons newly awakened. In the afternoon I discoursed on the story of the jailer, Acts 16, and in the evening expounded Acts 20:1–12. There was at this time a very agreeable melting spread through the whole assembly.

After public service was over I withdrew (being much tired with the labors of the day), and the Indians continued praying among themselves for near two hours together. These exercises appeared to be attended with a blessed quickening influence from on high. I could not but earnestly wish that numbers of God's people had been present at this season to see and hear these things which I am sure must refresh the heart of every true lover of Zion's interest. To see those, who very lately were savage pagans and idolaters, "having no hope, and without God in the world," now filled with a sense of divine love and grace, and worshiping the "Father in spirit and in truth," as numbers here appeared to do, was not a little affecting. Especially to see them appear so tender and humble, as well as lively, fervent, and devout in the divine service.

October 25. Discoursed to my people respecting the resurrection, from Luke 20:27–36. And when I came to mention the blessedness the godly shall enjoy at that season; their final freedom from death, sin, and sorrow; their equality to the angels in regard of their nearness to, and enjoyment of Christ (some imperfect degree of which they are favored with in the present life, from whence springs their sweetest comfort); and their being the children of God, openly acknowledged by Him as such; I say, when I mentioned these things, numbers of them were much affected, and melted with a view of this blessed state.

October 26. Being called to assist in the administration of the Lord's Supper in a neighboring congregation, I invited my people to go with me, who in general embraced the opportunity cheerfully, and attended the several discourses of that solemnity with diligence and affection, most of them now understanding something of the English language.

Lord's Day, October 27. While I was preaching to a vast assembly of people abroad, who appeared generally easy and secure enough, there was one Indian woman, a stranger, who never heard me preach before, nor ever regarded anything about religion—being now persuaded by some of her friends to come to meeting, though much against her will—was seized with pressing concern for her soul, and soon after expressed a great desire of going home, more than forty miles distant, to call her husband, that he also might be awakened to a concern for his soul. Some other of the Indians also appeared to be affected with divine truths this day.

The pious people of the English, numbers of whom I had

opportunity to converse with, seemed refreshed with seeing the Indians worship God in that devout and solemn manner with the assembly of His people. And with those mentioned in Acts 11:18, they could not but "glorify God, saying, Then hath God also to the Gentiles granted repentance unto life."

October 28. Discoursed from Matthew 22:1–13. I was enabled to open the Scripture and adapt my discourse and expressions to the capacities of my people—I know not how—in a plain, easy, and familiar manner, beyond all that I could have done by the utmost study. Yea, I did this with as much freedom as if I had been addressing a common audience, who had been instructed in the doctrine of Christianity all their days.

The Word of God at this time seemed to fall upon the assembly with a divine power and influence, especially toward the close of my discourse. There was both a sweet melting and bitter mourning in the audience. The dear Christians were refreshed and comforted, convictions revived in others, and sundry persons newly awakened who had never been with us before. So much of the divine presence appeared in the assembly that it seemed "this was no other than the house of God, and the gate of heaven." All that had any savor and relish of divine things were even constrained by the sweetness of that season to say, "Lord, it is good for us to be here!" If ever there was among my people an appearance of the New Jerusalem, "as a bride adorned for her husband," there was much of it at this time. So agreeable was the entertainment where such tokens of the divine presence were that I could scarce be willing in the evening to leave the place and repair to my lodgings. I was refreshed with a view of the continuance of this blessed work of grace among them, and its influence upon strangers of the Indians that had of late, from time to time, providentially fallen into these parts.

Lord's Day, November 3. Preached to my people from Luke 16:17, "And it is easier for heaven and earth . . ." more especially for the sake of several lately brought under deep concern for their souls. There was some apparent concern and affection in the assembly, though far less than has been usual of late.

Afterwards I baptized fourteen persons of the Indians, six adults and eight children. One of these was near fourscore years of age, and I have reason to hope God has brought her savingly home to Himself. Two of the others were men of fifty years old, who had been singular and remarkable, even among the Indians, for their wickedness. One of them had been a murderer, and both notorious drunkards, as well as excessively quarrelsome. But now I cannot but hope both are become subjects of God's special grace, especially the worst of them. I deferred their baptism for many weeks after they had given evidences of having passed a great change, that I might have more opportunities to observe the fruits of the impressions they had been under, and apprehended the way was now clear. There was not one of the adults I baptized but what had given me some comfortable grounds to hope that God had wrought a work of special grace in their hearts, although I could not have the same degree of satisfaction respecting one or two of them, as the rest.

November 4. Discoursed from John 11, briefly explaining most of the chapter. Divine truths made deep impressions upon many in the assembly. Numbers were affected with a view of the power of Christ, manifested in His raising the dead. Especially when this instance of His power was improved to show His power and ability to raise dead souls (such as many of them then felt themselves to be) to a spiritual life; as also to raise the dead at the last day, and dispense to them due rewards and punishments.

There were sundry of the persons lately come here from remote places that were now brought under deep and pressing concern for their souls. Particularly one—who not long since came half-drunk, and railed on us, and attempted by all means to disturb us while engaged in the divine worship—was now so concerned and distressed for her soul that she seemed unable to get any ease without an interest in Christ. There were many tears and affectionate sobs and groans in the assembly in general, some weeping for themselves, others for their friends. And although persons are doubtless much easier affected now than they were in the beginning of this religious concern, when tears and cries for their souls were things unheard of among them; yet I must say, their affection in general appeared genuine and unfeigned. Especially this appeared very conspicuous in those newly awakened. So that true and genuine convictions of sin seem still to be begun and promoted in many instances.

Baptized a child this day, and perceived sundry of the baptized persons affected with the administration of this ordinance, as being thereby reminded of their own solemn engagements.

I have now baptized in all forty-seven persons of the Indians, twenty-three adults and twenty-four children. Thirty-five of them belong to these parts, and the rest to the Forks of Delaware. Through rich grace, none of them as yet have been left to disgrace their profession of Christianity by any scandalous or unbecoming behavior.

## General Remarks on Part One

I might now justly make many remarks on a work of grace so very remarkable as this has been in divers respects; but shall confine myself to a few general hints only.

I. It is remarkable that God began this work among the Indians at a time when I had the least hope and, to my apprehension, the least rational prospect of seeing a work of grace propagated amongst them.

My bodily strength had been much wasted by a late tedious journey to Susquehannah, where I was necessarily exposed to hardships and fatigues among the Indians; my mind also was exceedingly depressed with a view of the unsuccessfulness of my labors. I had little reason so much as to hope that God had made me instrumental in the saving conversion of any of the Indians, except my interpreter and his wife. Whence I was ready to look upon myself as a burden to the Honourable Society that employed and supported me in this business, and began to entertain serious thoughts of giving up my mission. I almost resolved I would do so, at the conclusion of the present year, if I had then no better prospect of special success in my work than I had hitherto had.

I cannot say I entertained these thoughts because I was weary of the labors and fatigues that necessarily attended my present business, or because I had light and freedom in my own own mind to turn any other way; but purely through dejection of spirit, pressing discouragement, and an apprehension of its being unjust to spend money, consecrated to religious uses, only to civilize the Indians, and bring them to an external profession of Christianity. This was all that I could then see any prospect of having effected, while God seemed, as I thought, evidently to frown upon the design of their saving conversion by withholding the convincing and renewing influences of His blessed Spirit from attending the means I had hitherto used with them for that end.

In this frame of mind I first visited these Indians at Crossweeksung, apprehending it was my indispensable duty, seeing I had heard there was a number in these parts, to make some attempts for their conversion to God, though I cannot say I had any hope of success, my spirits being now so extremely sunk. I do not know that my hopes respecting the conversion of the Indians were ever reduced to so low an ebb since I had any special concern for them, as at this time. And yet this was the very season that God saw fittest to begin this glorious work in! And thus He "ordained strength out of weakness" by making bare His almighty arm at a time when all hopes and human probabilities most evidently appeared to fail. Whence I learn that it is good to follow the path of duty, though in the midst of darkness and discouragement.

II. It is remarkable how God providentially, and in a manner almost unaccountable, called these Indians together to be instructed in the great things that concerned their souls; how He seized their minds with the most solemn and weighty concern for their eternal salvation, as fast as they came to the place where His Word was preached.

When I first came into these parts in June, I found not one man at the place I visited, but only four women and a few children. But before I had been here many days, they gathered from all quarters, some from more than twenty miles distant. When I made them a second visit in the beginning of August, some came more than forty miles to hear me.

Many came without any intelligence of what was going on here, and consequently without any design of theirs, so much as to gratify their curiosity. So that it seemed as if God had summoned them together from all quarters for nothing else but to deliver His message to them; and that He did this, with regard to some of them, without making use of any human means, although there were pains taken by some of them to give notice to others at remote places.

Nor is it less surprising that they were one after another affected with a solemn concern for their souls, almost as soon as they came upon the spot where divine truths were taught them. I could not but think often that their coming to the place of our public worship was like Saul and his messengers coming among the prophets; they no sooner came but they prophesied. And these were almost as soon affected with a sense of their sin and misery, and with an earnest concern for deliverance, as they made their appearance in our assembly. After this work of grace began with power among them, it was common for strangers of the Indians, before they had been with us one day, to be much awakened, deeply convinced of their sin and misery, and to enquire with great solicitude, "What shall we do to be saved?"

III. It is likewise remarkable how God preserved these poor ignorant Indians from being prejudiced against me and the truths I taught them, by those means that were used with them for that purpose by ungodly people.

There were many attempts made by some ill-minded persons of the white people to prejudice them against, or fright them from, Christianity. They sometimes told them the Indians were well enough already; that there was no need of all this noise about Christianity; that if they were Christians, they would be in no better, no safer, or happier state than they were already in.

Sometimes they told them that I was a knave, a deceiver, and the like; that I daily taught them lies, and had no other design but to impose upon them. And when none of these, and such like suggestions, would avail to their purpose, they then tried another expedient and told the Indians my design was to gather together as large a body of them as I possibly could and then sell them to England for slaves. Than which nothing could be more likely to terrify the Indians, they being naturally of a jealous disposition and the most averse to a state of servitude perhaps of any people living.

But all these wicked insinuations, through divine goodness overruling, constantly turned against the authors of them, and only served to engage the affections of the Indians more firmly to me; for they being awakened to a solemn concern for their souls, could not but observe that the persons who endeavored to embitter their minds against me, were altogether unconcerned about their own souls, and not only so, but vicious and profane. Thence could not but argue that if they had no concern for their own it was not likely they should have for the souls of others.

It seems yet the more wonderful that the Indians were preserved from once hearkening to these suggestions, inasmuch as I was an utter stranger among them and could give them no assurance of my sincere affection to, and concern for, them by anything that was past. While the persons that insinuated these things were their old acquaintance who had frequent opportunities of gratifying their thirsty appetites with strong drink, and consequently, doubtless, had the greatest interest in their affections. But from this instance of their preservation from fatal prejudices, I have had occasion with admiration to say, "If God will work, who can hinder?"

IV. Nor is it less wonderful how God was pleased to provide a remedy for my want of skill and freedom in the Indian language by remarkably fitting my interpreter for, and assisting him in, the performance of his work.

It might reasonably be supposed I must needs labor under a vast disadvantage in addressing the Indians by an interpreter; and that divine truths would unavoidably lose much of the energy and pathos with which they might at first be delivered, by reason of their coming to the audience from a second hand. But although this has often, to my sorrow and discouragement, been the case in times past when my interpreter had little or no sense of divine things, yet now it was quite otherwise. I cannot think my addresses to the Indians ordinarily since the beginning of this season of grace have lost anything of their power or pungency with which they were made, unless it were sometimes for want of pertinent and pathetic terms and expressions in the Indian language; which difficulty could not have been much redressed by my personal acquaintance with their language. My interpreter had before gained some good degree of doctrinal knowledge whereby he was rendered capable of understanding and communicating, without mistakes, the intent and meaning of my discourses; and that without being confined strictly and obliged to interpret verbatim.

He had likewise, to appearance, an experimental acquaintance with divine things; and it pleased God at this season to inspire his mind with longing desires for the conversion of the Indians, and to give him admirable zeal and fervency in addressing them in order thereto. And it is remarkable, that when I was favored with any special assistance in any work and enabled to speak with more than common freedom, fervency, and power, under a lively and affecting sense of divine things, he was usually affected in the same manner almost instantly, and seemed at once quickened and enabled to speak in the same pathetic language, and under the same influence that I did. A surprising energy often accompanied the Word at such seasons; so that the face of the whole assembly would be apparently changed almost in an instant, and tears and sobs became common among them.

He also appeared to have such a clear doctrinal view of God's usual methods of dealing with souls under a preparatory work of conviction and humiliation as he never had before; so that I could, with his help, discourse freely with the distressed persons about their internal exercises, their fears, discouragements, and temptations. He likewise took pains day and night to repeat and inculcate upon the minds of the Indians the truths I taught them daily; and this he appeared to do, not from spiritual pride, and an affectation of setting himself up as a public teacher, but from a spirit of faithfulness, and an honest concern for their souls.

His conversation among the Indians has likewise, so far as I know, been savory, as becomes a Christian and a person employed in his work; and I may justly say, he has been a great comfort to me and a great instrument of promoting this good work among the Indians; so that whatever be the state of his own soul, it is apparent God has remarkably fitted him for this work. Thus God has manifested that, without bestowing on me the gift of tongues, He could find a way wherein I might be as effectually enabled to convey the truths of His glorious gospel to the minds of these poor benighted pagans.

V. It is further remarkable that God has carried on His work here by such means, and in such a manner, as tended to obviate and leave no room for those prejudices and objections that have often been raised against such a work.

When persons have been awakened to a solemn concern for their souls by hearing the more awful truths of God's Word and the terrors of the divine law insisted upon, it has usually in such cases been objected by some that such persons were only frighted with a fearful noise of hell and damnation; and that there was no evidence that their concern was the effect of a divine influence. But God has left no room for this objection in the present case, *this work of grace having been begun and carried on by almost one continued strain of gospel invitation to perishing sinners*. This may reasonably be guessed from a view of the passages of Scripture I chiefly insisted upon in my discourses from time to time; which I have for that purpose inserted in my Journal.

Nor have I ever seen so general an awakening in any assembly in my life as appeared here, while I was opening and insisting upon the Parable of the Great Supper, Luke 14. In which discourse I was enabled to set before my hearers the unsearchable riches of gospel-grace. Not that I would be understood here that I never instructed the Indians respecting their fallen state, and the sinfulness and misery of it; for this was what I at first chiefly insisted upon with them and endeavored to repeat and inculcate in almost every discourse, knowing that without this foundation I should but build upon the sand; and that it would be in vain to invite them to Christ, unless I could convince them of their need of Him, Mark 2:17.

But still, this great awakening, this surprising concern, was never excited by any harangues of terror, but always appeared most remarkable when I insisted upon the *compassions of a dying Saviour*, the *plentiful provisions of the gospel*, and the *free offers of divine grace to needy distressed sinners*. Nor would I be understood to insinuate that such a religious concern might justly be suspected as not being genuine, and from a divine influence, because produced by the preaching of terror; for this is perhaps God's more usual way of awakening sinners, and appears entirely agreeable to Scripture and sound reason. But what I meant here to observe is that God saw fit to employ and bless milder means for the effectual awakening of these Indians, and thereby obviated the forementioned objection which the world might otherwise have had a more plausible color of making.

As there has been no room for any plausible objection against this work in regard of the means, so neither in regard of the manner in which it has been carried on. It is true, persons' concern for their souls has been exceeding great, the convictions of their sin and misery have risen to a high degree and produced many tears, cries, and groans; but then they have not been attended with those disorders, either bodily or mental, that have sometimes prevailed among persons under religious impressions. There has here been no appearance of those convulsions, bodily agonies, frightful screamings, swoonings, and the like, that have been so much complained of in some places; although there have been some who, with the jailer, have been made to tremble under a sense of their sin and misery; numbers who have been made to cry out from a distressing view of their perishing state; and some that have been, for a time, in a great measure, deprived of their bodily strength, yet without any such convulsive appearances.

Nor has there been any appearance of mental disorders here, such as visions, trances, imaginations of being under prophetic inspiration, and the like; or scarce any unbecoming disposition to appear remarkably affected either with concern or joy; though I must confess, I observed one or two persons, whose concern, I thought, was in a considerable measure affected; and one whose joy appeared to be of the same kind. But these workings of spiritual pride I endeavored to crush in their first appearances and have not since observed any affection, either of joy or sorrow, but what appeared genuine and unaffected.

VI. The effects of this work have likewise been very remarkable.

I doubt not that many of these people have gained more doctrinal knowledge of divine truths, since I first visited them in June last, than could have been instilled into their minds by the most diligent use of proper and instructive means for whole years together, without such a divine influence. Their pagan notions and idolatrous practices seem to be entirely abandoned in these parts. They are regulated and appear regularly disposed in the affairs of marriage. They seem generally divorced from drunkenness, their darling vice, the "sin that easily besets them"; so that I do not know of more than two or three who have been my steady hearers, that have drunk to excess since I first visited them, although before it was common for some or other of them to be drunk almost every day. Some of them seem now to fear this sin in particular more than death itself.

A principle of honesty and justice appears in many of them, and they seem concerned to discharge their old debts, which they have neglected, and perhaps, scarce thought of for years past. Their manner of living is much more decent and comfortable than formerly, having now the benefit of that money which they used to consume upon strong drink. Love seems to reign among them, especially those who have given evidences of having passed a saving change. I never saw any appearance of bitterness or censoriousness in these, nor any disposition to "esteem themselves better than others," who had not received the like mercy.

As their sorrows under convictions have been great and pressing, so many of them have since appeared to "rejoice with joy unspeakable, and full of glory"; and yet I never saw anything ecstatic or flighty in their joy. Their consolations do not incline them to lightness; but, on the contrary, are attended with solemnity, and oftentimes with tears, and an apparent brokenness of heart, as may be seen in several passages of my Journal. In this respect some of them have been surprised at themselves, and have with concern observed to me, that "when their hearts have been glad" (which is a phrase they commonly make use of to express spiritual joy), "they could not help crying for all."

And now, upon the whole, I think I may justly say, here are all the symptoms and evidences of a remarkable work of grace among these Indians that can reasonably be desired or looked for. May the great Author of this work maintain and promote the same here and propagate it everywhere, till "the whole earth be filled with his glory!" Amen.

I have now ridden more than three thousand miles that I have kept an exact account of, since the beginning of March last. Almost the whole of it has been in my own proper business as a missionary, upon the design (either immediately or more remotely) of propagating Christian knowledge among the Indians. I have taken pains to look out for a colleague, or companion, to travel with me; and have likewise used endeavors to procure something for his support, among religious persons in New England, which cost me a journey of several hundred miles in length. But have not as yet found any person qualified and disposed for this good work, although I had some encouragement from ministers and others that it was hopeful a maintenance might be procured for one, when the man should be found.

I have likewise of late represented to the gentlemen concerned with this mission, the necessity of having an English school speedily set up among these Indians, who are now willing to be at the pains of gathering together in a body for this purpose. And in order thereto, have humbly proposed to them the collecting of money for the maintenance of a schoolmaster, and defraying of other necessary charges in the promotion of this good work; which they are now attempting in the several congregations of Christians to which they respectively belong.

The several companies of Indians I have preached to in the summer past live at great distances from each other. It is more than seventy miles from Crossweeksung in New Jersey, to the Forks of Delaware in Pennsylvania. And from thence to sundry of the Indian settlements I visited on Susquehannah is more than an hundred and twenty miles. So much of my time is necessarily consumed in journeying that I can have but little for any of my necessary studies, and consequently for the study of the Indian languages in particular. Especially seeing I am obliged to discourse so frequently to the Indians at each of these places while I am with them, in order to redeem time to visit the rest.

I am, at times, almost discouraged from attempting to gain any acquaintance with the Indian languages, they are so very numerous (some account of which I gave in my Journal of May last), and especially seeing my other labors and fatigues engross almost the whole of my time, and bear exceeding hard upon my constitution, so that my health is much impaired. However, I have taken considerable pains to learn the Delaware language, and propose still to do so, as far as my other business and bodily health will admit. I have already made some proficiency in it, though I have labored under many and great disadvantages in my attempts of that nature. And

it is but just to observe here, that all the pains I took to ac-
quaint myself with the language of the Indians I spent my
first year with, were of little or no service to me here among
the Delawares; so that my work, when I came among these
Indians, was all to begin anew.

As these poor ignorant pagans stood in need of having "line
upon line, and precept upon precept," in order to their being
instructed and grounded in the principles of Christianity; so
I preached "publicly, and taught from house to house," almost every day for whole weeks together when I was with
them. My public discourses did not then make up one-half
of my work, while there were so many constantly coming to
me with that important inquiry, "What must we do to be
saved?" and opening to me the various exercises of their
minds.

Yet I can say (to the praise of rich grace) that the apparent
success with which my labors were crowned unspeakably
more than compensated for the labor itself, and was likewise
a great means of supporting and carrying me through the
business and fatigues, which, it seems, my nature would have
sunk under without such an encouraging prospect. But although this success has afforded matter of support, comfort,
and thankfulness; yet in this season I have found great need
of assistance in my work, and have been much oppressed for
want of one to bear a part of my labors and hardships. May
the Lord of the harvest send forth other laborers into this
part of His harvest, that those who sit in darkness may see
great light, and that the whole earth may be filled with the
knowledge of Himself! Amen.

DAVID BRAINERD

Nov. 20, 1745

# THE RISE AND PROGRESS OF A REMARKABLE WORK OF GRACE

## BRAINERD'S JOURNAL, PART II

*From November 24, 1745, to June 19, 1746, at Crossweeksung and Forks of Delaware*

CROSSWEEKSUNG, NEW JERSEY, NOVEMBER, 1745

LORD'S DAY, November 24. Preached both parts of the day from the story of Zacchaeus, Luke 19:1–9. In the latter exercise, when I opened and insisted upon the salvation that comes to the sinner upon his becoming a son of Abraham, or a true believer, the Word seemed to be attended with divine power to the hearts of the hearers. Numbers were much affected with divine truths; former convictions were revived; one or two persons newly awakened; and a most affectionate engagement in divine service appeared among them universally. The impressions they were under appeared to be the genuine effect of God's Word brought home to their hearts, by the power and influence of the Divine Spirit.

November 28. Discoursed to the Indians publicly, after having used some private endeavors to instruct and excite some in the duties of Christianity. Opened and made remarks upon the sacred story of our Lord's transfiguration, Luke 9:28–36. Had a principal view, in my insisting upon this passage of Scripture, to the edification and consolation of God's people. And observed some, that I have reason to think are truly such, exceedingly affected with an account of the glory of Christ in His transfiguration; and filled with longing desires of being with Him, that they might with open face behold His glory.

After public service was over, I asked one of them, who wept and sobbed most affectionately, what she now wanted. She replied, "Oh, to be with Christ! I do not know how to stay." This was a blessed refreshing season to the religious people in general. The Lord Jesus Christ seemed to manifest His divine glory to them, as when transfigured before His disciples. And they, with the disciples, were ready universally to say, "Lord, it is good for us to be here."

The influence of God's Word was not confined to those who had given evidences of being truly gracious, though at this time I calculated my discourse for and directed it chiefly to such. But it appeared to be a season of divine power in the whole assembly so that most were, in some measure, affected. One aged man in particular, lately awakened, was now brought under a deep and pressing concern for his soul and was earnestly inquisitive how he might find Jesus Christ. God seems still to vouchsafe His divine presence and the influence of His blessed Spirit to accompany His Word, at least in some measure, in all our meetings for divine worship.

November 30. Preached near night, after having spent some hours in private conference with some of my people about their souls' concerns. Explained and insisted upon the story of the rich man and Lazarus, Luke 16:19–26. The Word made powerful impressions upon many in the assembly, especially while I discoursed of the blessedness of "Lazarus in Abraham's bosom." This, I could perceive, affected them much more than what I spoke of the rich man's misery and torments.

And thus it has been usually with them. They have almost always appeared much more affected with the comfortable than the dreadful truths of God's Word. That which has distressed many of them under conviction is, that they found they wanted, and could not obtain, the happiness of the godly. At least, they have often appeared to be more affected with this than with the terrors of hell. But whatever be the means of their awakening, it is plain, numbers are made deeply sensible of their sin and misery, the wickedness and stubbornness of their own hearts, their utter inability to help themselves or to come to Christ for help without divine assistance; and so are brought to see their perishing need of Christ to do all for them, and to lie at the foot of sovereign mercy.

Lord's Day, December 1. Discoursed to my people in the forenoon from Luke 16:27–31. There appeared an unfeigned affection in divers persons, and some seemed deeply impressed with divine truths. In the afternoon, preached to a number of white people; at which time the Indians attended with diligence, and many of them were able to understand a considerable part of the discourse.

At night discoursed to my people again, and gave them some particular cautions and directions relating to their conduct in divers respects. And pressed them to watchfulness in all their deportment, seeing they were encompassed with those that "waited for their halting," and who stood ready to draw them into temptations of every kind, and then to expose religion for their missteps.

Lord's Day, December 15. Preached to the Indians from Luke 13:24–28. Divine truths fell with weight and power upon the audience, and seemed to reach the hearts of many. Near night discoursed to them again from Matthew 25:31–46. At which season also, the Word appeared to be accompanied with a divine influence, and made powerful impressions upon the assembly in general, as well as upon divers persons in a very special and particular manner. This was an amazing season of grace! "The word of the Lord," this day, "was quick and powerful, sharper than a two-edged sword," and pierced the hearts of many. The assembly was greatly affected, and deeply wrought upon; yet without so much apparent commotion of the passions, as was usual in the beginning of this work of grace. The impressions made by the Word of God upon the audience appeared solid, rational, and deep, worthy of the solemn truths by means of which they were produced, and far from being the effects of any sudden fright, or groundless perturbation of mind.

Oh, how did the hearts of the hearers seem to bow under the weight of divine truths! And how evident did it now appear that they received and felt them, "not as the word of man, but as the word of God!" None can frame a just idea of the appearance of our assembly as at this time, but those who have seen a congregation solemnly awed and deeply impressed by the special power and influence of divine truths delivered to them in the name of God.

December 16. Discoursed to my people in the evening from Luke 11:1–13. After having insisted some time upon the ninth verse, wherein there is a command and encouragement to ask for the divine favors, I called upon them to ask for a new heart with utmost importunity, as the man, mentioned in the parable I was discoursing upon, pleaded for loaves of bread at midnight.

There was much affection and concern in the assembly; and especially one woman appeared in great distress for her soul. She was brought to such an agony in seeking after Christ that the sweat ran off her face for a considerable time together, although the evening was very cold; and her bitter cries were the most affecting indication of the inward anguish of her heart.

December 21. My people having now attained to a considerable degree of knowledge in the principles of Christianity, I thought it proper to set up a catechetical lecture among them. This evening attempted something in that form, proposing questions to them agreeable to the reverend Assembly's *Shorter Catechism*, receiving their answers, and then explaining and insisting as appeared necessary and proper upon each question. After which I endeavored to make some practical improvement of the whole. This was the method I entered upon. They were able readily and rationally to answer many important questions I proposed to them, so that, upon trial, I found their doctrinal knowledge to exceed my own expectations.

In the improvement of my discourse, when I came to infer and open the blessedness of those who have so great and glorious a God, as had before been spoken of, "for their ever-lasting friend and portion," sundry were much affected; and especially when I exhorted and endeavored to persuade them "to be reconciled to God" through His dear Son, and thus to secure an interest in His everlasting favor. So that they appeared to be not only enlightened and instructed, but affected and engaged in their souls' concern by this method of dis-coursing.

Lord's Day, December 22. Discoursed upon the story of the young man in the gospel, Matthew 19:16–22. God made it a seasonable word, I am persuaded, to some souls. There were sundry persons of the Indians newly come here, who had frequently lived among Quakers. Being more civilized and conformed to English manners than the generality of the Indians, they had imbibed some of the Quakers' errors, especially this fundamental one: That if men will but live soberly and honestly, according to the dictates of their own consciences (or the light within), there is then no danger or doubt of their salvation.

These persons I found much worse to deal with than those who are wholly under pagan darkness, who make no pretenses to knowledge in Christianity at all, nor have any self-righteous foundation to stand upon. However, they all, except one, appeared now convinced, that this sober, honest life, of itself, was not sufficient to salvation, since Christ Himself had declared it so in the case of the young man. They seemed in some measure concerned to obtain that change of heart, the necessity of which I had been laboring to show them.

This was likewise a season of comfort to some souls, and in particular to one (the same mentioned in my Journal of the sixteenth of this month), who never before obtained any settled comfort, though I have abundant reason to think she had passed a saving change some days before. She now appeared in a heavenly frame of mind, composed and delighted with the divine will. When I came to discourse particularly with her and to enquire of her how she got relief and deliverance from the spiritual distresses she had lately been under, she answered in broken English: "Me try, me try, save my-self, last my strength be all gone [meaning her ability to save herself], could not me stir bit further. Den last, me forced let Jesus Christ alone, send me hell if He please." [1] I said, "But you were not willing to go to hell, were you?" She replied: "Could not me help it. My heart he would wicked for all. Could not me make him good": [2] (meaning she saw it was right she should go to hell, because her heart was wicked, and would be so after all she could do to mend it). I asked her, "How did you get out of this case?" She answered still in the same broken language, "By by my heart be grad desper-ately." [3] I asked her why her heart was glad, and she replied: "Grad my heart Jesus Christ do what He please with me. Den me tink, grad my heart Jesus Christ send me hell. Did not me care where He put me, me lobe Him for all," etc. [4]

And she could not readily be convinced, but that she was willing to go to hell, if Christ were pleased to send her there. Though the truth evidently was, her will was so swallowed up in the divine will that she could not frame any hell in her imagination that would be dreadful or undesirable, provided it was but the will of God to send her to it. Toward night, discoursed to them again in the catechetical method I entered upon the evening before. When I came to improve the truths I had explained to them and to answer that question, "But how shall I know whether God has chosen me to everlasting life?" by pressing them to come and give up their hearts to Christ, and thereby "to make their election sure," they then appeared much affected. The persons under concern were afresh engaged in seeking after an interest in Him; while some others, who had obtained comfort before, were refreshed to

---

[1] In proper English thus: "I tried and tried to save myself, till at last my strength was all gone, and I could not stir any further. Then at last I was forced to let Jesus Christ alone, to send me to hell if He pleased."

[2] In plain English thus: "I could not help it. My heart would be wicked for all that I could do. I could not make it good."

[3] "By and by my heart was exceeding glad."

[4] "My heart was glad that Jesus Christ would do with me what He pleased. Then I thought my heart would be glad although Christ should send me to hell. I did not care where He put me, I should love Him for all; that is, do what He would with me."

find that love to God in themselves, which was an evidence of His electing love to them.

December 25. The Indians having been used upon Christmas days to drink and revel among some of the white people in these parts, I thought it proper this day to call them together and discourse to them upon divine things; which I accordingly did from the Parable of the Barren Fig Tree, Luke 13:6-9. A divine influence, I am persuaded, accompanied the Word at this season. The power of God appeared in the assembly, not by producing any remarkable cries, but by shocking and rousing at heart, as it seemed, several stupid creatures, that were scarce ever moved with any concern before. The power attending divine truths seemed to have the influence of the earthquake rather than the whirlwind upon them. Their passions were not so much alarmed as has been common here in times past, but their judgments appeared to be powerfully convinced by the masterly and conquering influence of divine truths.

The impressions made upon the assembly in general seemed not superficial, but deep and heart-affecting. Oh, how ready did they now appear universally to embrace and comply with everything they heard and were convinced was duty! God was in the midst of us of a truth, bowing and melting stubborn hearts! How many tears and sobs were then to be seen and heard among us! What liveliness and strict attention! What eagerness and intenseness of mind appeared in the whole assembly in the time of divine service! They seemed to watch and wait for the dropping of God's Word, as the thirsty earth for the "former and latter rain."

Afterwards I discoursed to them on the duty of husbands and wives, from Ephesians 5:22,23, and have reason to think this was a word in season. Spent some time further in the evening in inculcating the truths I had insisted upon in my former discourse respecting the barren fig tree, and observed a powerful influence still accompany what was spoken.

December 26. This evening I was visited by a person under great spiritual exercise; the most remarkable instance of this

kind I ever saw. She was a woman of (I believe) more than
fourscore years, and appeared to be much broken and very
childish through age, so that it seemed impossible for man to
instill into her mind any notions of divine things, much less
to give her any doctrinal instruction because she seemed incapable of being taught. She was led by the hand into my
house and appeared in extreme anguish. I asked her what
ailed her. She answered that her heart was distressed and she
feared she should never find Christ. I asked her when she
began to be concerned, with divers other questions relating to
her distress. To all of which she answered, for substance, to
this effect: That she had heard me preach many times, but
never knew anything about it, never "felt it in her heart"
till the last Sabbath; and then it came (she said) "all one as
if a needle had been thrust into her heart." Since which time,
she had no rest day nor night. She added that on the evening
before Christmas, a number of Indians being together at the
house where she was and discoursing about Christ, their talk
pricked her heart so that she could not sit up, but fell down
on her bed.

At this time she went away (as she expressed it), and felt
as if she dreamed, and yet is confident she did not dream.
When she was thus gone, she saw two paths, one appeared
very broad and crooked and that turned to the left hand. The
other appeared strait and very narrow; and that went up the
hill to the right hand. She traveled, she said, for some time
up the narrow right hand path, till at length something
seemed to obstruct her journey. She sometimes called it darkness, and then described it otherwise, and seemed to compare
it to a block or bar. She then remembered, what she had
heard me say about "striving to enter in at the strait gate"
(although she took little notice of it, at the time when she
heard me discourse upon that subject), and thought she would
climb over this bar. But just as she was thinking of this, she
came back again, as she termed it, meaning that she came to
herself; whereupon her soul was extremely distressed, ap-

prehending she had now turned back and forsaken Christ, and that there was therefore no hope of mercy for her.

As I was sensible that trances and imaginary views of things are of dangerous tendency in religion, when sought after and depended upon; so I could not but be much concerned about this exercise, especially at first; apprehending this might be a design of Satan to bring a blemish upon the work of God here by introducing visionary scenes, imaginary terrors, and all manner of mental disorders and delusions, in the room of genuine convictions of sin, and the enlightening influences of the blessed Spirit. I was almost resolved to declare that I looked upon this to be one of Satan's devices, and to caution my people against it, and the like exercises, as such.

However, I determined first to inquire into her knowledge, to see whether she had any just views of things that might be the occasion of her present distressing concern, or whether if it was a mere fright arising only from imaginary terrors. I asked her divers questions respecting man's primitive, and more especially his present state, and respecting her own heart; which she answered rationally, to my surprise. I thought it was next to impossible, if not altogether so, that a pagan who was become a child through age should in that state gain so much knowledge by any mere human instruction, without being remarkably enlightened by a divine influence.

I then proposed to her the provision made in the gospel for the salvation of sinners, and the ability and willingness of Christ "to save to the uttermost all (old as well as young) that come to him." To which she seemed to give a hearty assent. But instantly replied, "Ay, but I cannot come; my wicked heart will not come to Christ; I do not know how to come." This she spoke in anguish of spirit, striking on her breast, with tears in her eyes, and with such earnestness in her looks as was indeed piteous and affecting.

She seems to be really convinced of her sin and misery and her need of a change of heart, and her concern is abiding and constant. So that nothing appears but that this exercise may have a saving issue. Indeed it seems hopeful, seeing she is so solicitous to obtain an interest in Christ that her heart (as she expresses it) prays day and night.

How far God may make use of the imagination in awakening some persons under these, and such like circumstances, I cannot pretend to determine. Or whether this exercise be from a divine influence, I shall leave others to judge. But this I must say, that its effects hitherto bespeak it to be such. Nor can it, as I see, be accounted for, in a rational way, but from the influence of some spirit, either good or evil. For the woman I am sure, never heard divine things treated of in the manner she now viewed them in; and it would seem strange she should get such a rational notion of them from the mere working of her own fancy, without some superior, or at least foreign aid. Yet I must say, I have looked upon it as one of the glories of this work of grace among the Indians, and a special evidence of its being from a divine influence, that there has, till now, been no appearance of such things, no visionary notions, trances, and imaginations intermixed with those rational convictions of sin, and solid consolations, that numbers have been made the subjects of. And might I have had my desire, there had been no appearance of anything of this nature at all.

December 28. Discoursed to my people in the catechetical method I lately entered upon. In the improvement of my discourse, wherein I was comparing man's present with his primitive state and showing what he had fallen from, and the miseries he is now involved in, and exposed to in his natural estate; and pressing sinners to take a view of their deplorable circumstances without Christ, as also to strive that they might obtain an interest in Him; the Lord, I trust, granted a remarkable influence of His blessed Spirit to accompany what was spoken, and a great concern appeared in the assembly. Many were melted into tears and sobs, and the impressions made upon them seemed deep and heart-affecting.

In particular, there were two or three persons who appeared

to be brought to the last exercises of a preparatory work and reduced almost to extremity, being in a great measure convinced of the impossibility of their helping themselves or of mending their own hearts. They seemed to be upon the point of giving up all hope in themselves and of venturing upon Christ as naked, helpless, and undone. Yet they were in distress and anguish because they saw no safety in so doing, unless they could do something towards saving themselves. One of these persons was the very aged woman above mentioned, who now appeared "weary and heavy laden" with a sense of her sin and misery and her perishing need of an interest in Christ.

Lord's Day, December 29. Preached from John 3:1-5. A number of white people were present, as is usual upon the Sabbath. The discourse was accompanied with power, and seemed to have a silent, but deep and piercing influence upon the audience. Many wept and sobbed affectionately. There were some tears among the white people, as well as the Indians. Some could not refrain from crying out, though there were not many so exercised. But the impressions made upon their hearts appeared chiefly by the extraordinary earnestness of their attention, and their heavy sighs and tears.

After public worship was over, I went to my house, proposing to preach again after a short season of intermission. But they soon came in one after another, with tears in their eyes, to know "what they should do to be saved." The Divine Spirit in such a manner set home upon their hearts what I spoke to them that the house was soon filled with cries and groans. They all flocked together upon this occasion, and those whom I had reason to think in a Christless state were almost universally seized with concern for their souls.

It was an amazing season of power among them, and seemed as if God had "bowed the heavens, and come down." So astonishingly prevalent was the operation upon old as well as young that it seemed as if none would be left in a secure and natural state, but that God was now about to convert all the world. I was ready to think then that I should never again despair of the conversion of any man or woman living, be they who or what they would.

It is impossible to give a just and lively description of the appearance of things at this season, at least such as to convey a bright and adequate idea of the effects of this influence. A number might now be seen rejoicing that God had not taken away the powerful influence of His blessed Spirit from this place. They were refreshed to see so many "striving to enter in at the strait gate" and animated with such concern for them that they wanted "to push them forward," as some of them expressed it. At the same time numbers both of men and women, old and young, might be seen in tears and some in anguish of spirit, appearing in their very countenances like condemned malefactors bound towards the place of execution, with a heavy solicitude sitting in their faces; so that there seemed here (as I thought) a lively emblem of the solemn day of accounts, a mixture of heaven and hell, of joy and anguish inexpressible.

The concern and religious affection was such that I could not pretend to have any formal religious exercise among them; but spent the time in discoursing to one and another, as I thought most proper and seasonable for each, and sometimes addressed them all together, and finally concluded with prayer. Such were their circumstances at this season that I could scarce have half an hour's rest from speaking from about half an hour before twelve o'clock (at which time I began public worship) till past seven at night. There appeared to be four or five persons newly awakened this day and the evening before, some of whom but very lately came among us.

December 31. Spent some hours this day in visiting my people from house to house, and conversing with them about their spiritual concerns, endeavoring to press upon Christless souls the necessity of a renovation of heart. I scarce left a house without leaving some or other of its inhabitants in tears, appearing solicitously engaged to obtain an interest in Christ.

The Indians are now gathered together from all quarters to this place, and have built them little cottages, so that more than twenty families live within a quarter of a mile of me. A very convenient situation in regard both of public and private instruction.

January 1, 1746. Spent some considerable time in visiting my people again. Found scarce one but what was under some serious impressions respecting their spiritual concerns.

January 2. Visited some persons newly come among us, who had scarce ever heard anything of Christianity before, except the empty name. Endeavored to instruct them, particularly by the first principles of religion, in the most easy and familiar manner I could. There are strangers from remote parts almost continually dropping in among us, so that I have occasion repeatedly to open and inculcate the first principles of Christianity.

Lord's Day, January 5. Discoursed from Matthew 12:10–13. There appeared not so much liveliness and affection in divine service as usual. The same truths that have often produced many tears and sobs in the assembly, seemed now to have no special influence upon any in it.

Near night I proposed to have proceeded in my usual method of catechizing. But while we were engaged in the first prayer, the power of God seemed to descend upon the assembly in such a remarkable manner, and so many appeared under pressing concern for their souls, that I thought it much more expedient to insist upon the plentiful provision made by divine grace for the redemption of perishing sinners and to press them to a speedy acceptance of the great salvation, than to ask them questions about doctrinal points. What was most practical seemed most seasonable to be insisted upon, while numbers appeared so extraordinarily solicitous to obtain an interest in the great Redeemer. Baptized two persons this day, one adult (the woman particularly mentioned in my Journal of Dec. 22) and one child.

This woman has discovered a very sweet and heavenly frame of mind, from time to time, since her first reception of comfort. One morning in particular she came to see me, discovering an unusual joy and satisfaction in her countenance. When I inquired into the reason of it, she replied that God had made her feel that it was right for Him to do what He pleased with all things. . . She moreover inquired, whether I was not sent to preach to the Indians, by some good people a great way off. I replied, "Yes, by the good people in Scotland." She answered that her heart loved those good people so, the evening before, that she could scarce help praying for them all night, her heart would go to God for them, so that "the blessing of those ready to perish" is like to come upon those pious persons who have communicated of their substance to the propagation of the gospel.

January 13. Was visited by divers persons under deep concern for their souls, one of whom was newly awakened. It is a most agreeable work to treat with souls who are solicitously inquiring "what they shall do to be saved." As we are never to be "weary in well doing," so the obligation seems to be peculiarly strong when the work is so very desirable. Yet I must say, my health is so much impaired and my spirits so wasted with my labors and solitary manner of living (there being no human creature in the house with me), that their repeated and almost incessant application to me for help and direction are sometimes exceeding burdensome, and so exhaust my spirits, that I become fit for nothing at all, entirely unable to prosecute any business sometimes for days together. What contributes much toward this difficulty is that I am obliged to spend much time in communicating a little matter to them, there being oftentimes many things necessary to be premised, before I can speak directly to what I principally aim at. Which things would readily be taken for granted, where there was a competency of doctrinal knowledge.

January 14. Spent some time in private conference with my people, and found some disposed to take comfort, as I thought, upon slight grounds. They are now generally awakened, and it is become so disgraceful, as well as terrifying to the conscience, to be destitute of religion that they are in imminent danger of taking up with any appearances of grace, rather than to live under the fear and disgrace of an unregenerate state.

January 18. Prosecuted my catechetical method of discoursing. There appeared a great solemnity and some considerable affection in the assembly. This method of instructing I find very profitable. When I first entered upon it, I was exercised with fears lest my discourses would unavoidably be so doctrinal that they would tend only to enlighten the head, but not to affect the heart. But the event proves quite otherwise; for these exercises have hitherto been remarkably blessed in the latter, as well as the former respects.

Lord's Day, January 19. Discoursed to my people from Isaiah 55:7. Toward night catechized in my ordinary method. This appeared to be a powerful season of grace among us. Numbers were much affected. Convictions were powerfully revived, and divers of the Christians refreshed and strengthened. One weary, heavy-laden soul, I have abundant reason to hope, was brought to true rest and solid comfort in Christ, who afterwards gave me such an account of God's dealing with his soul as was abundantly satisfying, as well as refreshing, to me.

He told me he had often heard me say that persons must see and feel themselves utterly helpless and undone; that they must be emptied of a dependence upon themselves and of all hope of saving themselves by their own doings, in order to their coming to Christ for salvation. He had long been striving after this view of things, supposing this would be an excellent frame of mind to be thus emptied of a dependence upon his own goodness; that God would have respect to this frame, would then be well pleased with him and bestow eternal life upon him. But when he came to feel himself in this helpless undone condition, he found it quite contrary to all his thoughts and expectations; so that it was not the same frame, nor indeed anything like the frame he had been seeking after.

Instead of its being a good frame of mind, he now found

nothing but badness in himself, and saw it was forever impossible for him to make himself any better. He wondered, he said, that he had ever hoped to mend his own heart. He was amazed he had never before seen that it was utterly impossible for him, by all his contrivances and endeavors, to do anything that way, since the matter now appeared to him in so clear a light. Instead of imagining now, that God would be pleased with him for the sake of this frame of mind and this view of his undone estate, he saw clearly and felt it would be just with God to send him to eternal misery; and that there was no goodness in what he then felt; for he could not help seeing that he was naked, sinful, and miserable, and there was nothing in such a sight to deserve God's love or pity.

He saw these things in a manner so clear and convincing that it seemed to him, he said, he could convince everybody of their utter inability ever to help themselves and their unworthiness of any help from God. In this frame of mind he came to public worship this evening; and while I was inviting sinners to come to Christ naked and empty, without any goodness of their own to recommend them to His acceptance, then he thought with himself that he had often tried to come and give up his heart to Christ, and he used to hope that some time or other he should be able to do so. But now he was convinced he could not, and it seemed utterly vain for him ever to try any more; and he could not, he said, find a heart to make any further attempt, because he saw it would signify nothing at all. Nor did he now hope for a better opportunity or more ability hereafter, as he had formerly done, because he saw and was fully convinced his own strength would forever fail.

While he was musing in this manner, he saw, he said, with his heart (which is a common phrase among them) something that was unspeakably good and lovely, and what he had never seen before; and this stole away his heart whether he would or no. He did not, he said, know what it was he saw. He did not say, "This is Jesus Christ"; but it was such glory and beauty as he never saw before. He did not now give away his heart so as he had formerly intended and attempted to do, but it went away of itself after that glory he then discovered. He used to try to make a bargain with Christ, to give up his heart to Him that he might have eternal life for it. But now he thought nothing about himself or what would become of him hereafter; but was pleased and his mind wholly taken up with the unspeakable excellency of what he then beheld.

After some time he was wonderfully pleased with the way of salvation by Christ; so that it seemed unspeakably better to be saved altogether by the mere free grace of God in Christ, than to have any hand in saving himself. The consequence of this exercise is that he appears to retain a sense and relish of divine things, and to maintain a life of seriousness and true religion.

January 28. The Indians in these parts have in times past run themselves in debt by their excessive drinking. Some have taken the advantage of them and put them to trouble and charge by arresting sundry of them, whereby it was supposed their hunting lands, in great part, were much endangered and might speedily be taken from them. Being sensible that they could not subsist together in these parts, in order to there being a Christian congregation, if these lands should be taken, which was thought very likely, I thought it my duty to use my utmost endeavors to prevent so unhappy an event. Having acquainted the gentlemen concerned with this mission of the affair, according to the best information I could get of it, they thought it proper to expend the money they had been, and still were, collecting for the religious interest of the Indians (at least a part of it), for discharging their debts and securing these lands, that there might be no entanglement lying upon them to hinder the settlement and hopeful enlargement of a Christian congregation of Indians in these parts. Having received orders from them, I answered, in behalf of the Indians, "Eighty-two pounds five shillings, New Jersey currency, at eight shillings per ounce"; and so prevented the danger of difficulty in this respect.

As God has wrought a wonderful work of grace among these Indians and now inclines others from remote places to fall in among them almost continually; and as He has opened a door for the prevention of the difficulty now mentioned, which seemed greatly to threaten their religious interests, as well as worldly comfort; it is hopeful that He designs to establish a church for Himself among them and hand down true religion to their posterity.

January 31. This day the person I had made choice of and engaged for a schoolmaster among the Indians arrived among us, and was heartily welcomed by my people universally. Whereupon I distributed several dozen of primers among the children and young people.

February 1, 1746. My schoolmaster entered upon his business among the Indians. He has generally about thirty children and young persons in his school in the daytime, and about fifteen married people in his evening school. The number of the latter sort of persons being less than it would be if they could be more constant at home and spare time from their necessary employments for an attendance upon these instructions.

In the evening, catechized in my usual method. Towards the close of my discourse, a surprising power seemed to attend the Word, especially to some persons. One man considerably in years, who had been a remarkable drunkard, a conjurer, and murderer, that was awakened some months before, was now brought to great extremity under his spiritual distress, so that he trembled for hours together and apprehended himself just dropping into hell, without any power to rescue or relieve himself. Divers others appeared under great concern as well as he, and solicitous to obtain a saving change.

February 8. Spent a considerable part of the day in visiting my people from house to house, and conversing with them about their souls' concerns. Divers persons wept while I discoursed to them and appeared concerned for nothing so much as for an interest in the great Redeemer. In the evening catechized as usual. Divine truths made some impression upon the audience and were attended with an affectionate engagement of soul in some.

Lord's Day, February 9. Discoursed to my people from the story of the blind man, Matthew 10:46–52. The Word of God seemed weighty and powerful upon the assembly at this time, and made considerable impressions upon many. Divers in particular, who have generally been remarkably stupid and careless under the means of grace, were now awakened and wept affectionately. The most earnest attention, as well as tenderness and affection, appeared in the audience universally.

Baptized three persons, two adults and one child. The adults, I have reason to hope, were both truly pious. There was a considerable melting in the assembly, while I was discoursing particularly to the persons and administering the ordinance. God has been pleased to own and bless the administration of this, as well as of His other ordinances, among the Indians. There are some here that have been powerfully awakened at seeing others baptized. Some that have obtained relief and comfort, just in the season when this ordinance has been administered.

Toward night catechized. God made this a powerful season to some. There were many affected. Former convictions appeared to be powerfully revived. There was likewise one who had been a vile drunkard, remarkably awakened. He appeared to be in great anguish of soul, wept, and trembled, and continued so to do till near midnight. There was also a poor, heavy-laden soul, who had been long under spiritual distress, as constant and pressing as ever I saw, that was now brought to a comfortable calm and seemed to be bowed and reconciled to divine sovereignty. She told me she now saw and felt it was right God should do with her as He pleased, and her heart felt pleased and satisfied it should be so. Although of late she had often found her heart rise and quarrel with God because He would, if He pleased, send her to hell after all she had done or could do to save herself. She added that the heavy burden she had lain under was now removed; that she had tried to recover her concern and distress again (fearing that the Spirit of God was departing from her, and would leave her wholly careless), but that she could not recover it; that she felt she never could do anything to save herself, but must perish forever if Christ did not do all for her; that she did not deserve He should help her; and that it would be right if He should leave her to perish. But Christ could save her, though she could do nothing to save herself, and here she seemed to rest.

FORKS OF DELAWARE, IN PENNSYLVANIA, FEBRUARY, 1746.

Lord's Day, February 16. Knowing that divers of the Indians in those parts were obstinately set against Christianity, and that some of them had refused to hear me preach in times past, I thought it might be proper and beneficial to the Christian interest here to have a number of my religious people from Crossweeksung with me in order to converse with them about religious matters; hoping it might be a means to convince them of the truth and importance of Christianity to see and hear some of their own nation discoursing of divine things, and manifesting earnest desires that others might be brought out of heathenish darkness, as themselves were.

Having taken half a dozen of the most serious and knowing persons for this purpose, I this day met with them and the Indians of this place (sundry of whom probably could not have been prevailed upon to attend the meeting had it not been for these religious Indians that accompanied me here), and preached to them. Some of them who had, in times past, been extremely averse to Christianity, now behaved soberly, and some others laughed and mocked. However the Word of God fell with such weight and power that sundry seemed to be stunned, and expressed a willingness to "hear me again of these matters."

Afterwards prayed with and made an address to the white people present, and could not but observe some visible effects of the Word, such as tears and sobs, among them. After public worship, spent some time and took pains to convince those that mocked, of the truth and importance of what I had been insisting upon; and so endeavored to awaken their attention to divine truths. Had reason to think, from what I observed then and afterwards, that my endeavors took considerable effect upon one of the worst of them.

Those few Indians then present, who used to be my hearers in these parts (some having removed from hence to Cross-weeksung), seemed somewhat kindly disposed toward, and glad to see me again. They had been so much attacked by some of the opposing pagans that they were almost ashamed or afraid to manifest their friendship.

February 17. After having spent much time in discoursing to the Indians in their respective houses, I got them together and repeated and inculcated what I had before taught them. Afterwards discoursed to them from Acts 8:5-8. A divine influence seemed to attend the Word. Sundry of the Indians here appeared to be somewhat awakened, and manifested a concern of mind by their earnest attention, tears and sobs. My people from Crossweeksung continued with them day and night, repeating and inculcating the truths I had taught them; sometimes they prayed and sang psalms among them, discoursing with each other, in their hearing, of the great things God had done for them and for the Indians from whence they came. This seemed (as my people told me) to take more effect upon them than when they directed their discourses immediately to them.

February 18. Preached to an assembly of Irish people near fifteen miles distant from the Indians.

February 19. Preached to the Indians again after having spent considerable time in conversing with them more privately. There appeared a great solemnity, and some concern and affection among the Indians belonging to these parts, as well as a sweet melting among those who came with me. Divers of the Indians here seemed to have their prejudices and aversion to Christianity removed, and appeared well disposed and inclined to hear the Word of God.

February 20. Preached to a small assembly of High Dutch people who had seldom heard the gospel preached and were (some of them at least) very ignorant; but divers of them have lately been put upon an inquiry after the way of salvation, with some thoughtfulness. They gave wonderful attention, and some of them were much affected under the Word and afterwards said (as I was informed) that they never had been so much enlightened about the way of salvation in their whole lives before. They requested me to tarry with them, or come again and preach to them. It grieved me that I could not comply with their request, for I could not but be affected with their circumstances; they being as "sheep not having a shepherd," and some of them appearing under some degree of soul trouble, standing in peculiar need of the assistance of an experienced spiritual guide.

February 21. Preached to a number of people, many of them Low Dutch. Sundry of the fore-mentioned High Dutch attended the sermon, though eight or ten miles distant from their houses. Divers of the Indians also belonging to these parts, came of their own accord with my people (from Crossweeksung) to the meeting. There were two in particular, who, though the last Sabbath they opposed and ridiculed Christianity, now behaved soberly. May the present encouraging appearance continue.

February 22. Preached to the Indians. They appeared more free from prejudice and more cordial to Christianity than before. Some of them appeared affected with divine truths.

Lord's Day, February 23. Preached to the Indians from John 6:35-37. After public service, discoursed particularly with sundry of them, and invited them to go down to Crossweeksung and tarry there at least for some time, knowing they would then be free from the scoffs and temptations of the opposing pagans, as well as in the way of hearing divine truths discoursed of, both in public and private. Got a promise of some of them that they would speedily pay us a visit and attend some further instructions. They seemed to be considerably enlightened and much freed from their prejudices against Christianity. But it is much to be feared their prejudices will revive again, unless they could enjoy the means of instruction here, or be removed where they might be under such advantages and out of the way of their pagan acquaintance.

CROSSWEEKSUNG, IN NEW JERSEY, MARCH, 1746.

March 1. Catechized in my ordinary method. Was pleased and refreshed to see them answer the questions proposed to them with such remarkable readiness, discretion, and knowledge. Toward the close of my discourse, divine truths made considerable impressions upon the audience and produced tears and sobs in some under concern; and more especially a sweet and humble melting in sundry that, I have reason to hope, were truly gracious.

Lord's Day, March 2. Preached from John 15:1–6. The assembly appeared not so lively in their attention as usual, nor so much affected with divine truths in general as has been common. Some of my people, who went up to the Forks of Delaware with me, being now returned, were accompanied by two of the Indians belonging to the Forks who had promised me a speedy visit. May the Lord meet with them there. They can scarce go into a house now but they will meet with Christian conversation, whereby it is hopeful they may be both instructed and awakened.

Discoursed to the Indians again in the afternoon and observed among them some liveliness and engagement in divine service, though not equal to what has often appeared here. I know of no assembly of Christians where there seems to be so much of the presence of God, where brotherly love so much prevails, and where I should so much delight in the public worship of God, in general, as in my own congregation; although not more than nine months ago, they were worshiping devils and dumb idols under the power of pagan darkness and superstition. Amazing change this! effected by nothing less than divine power and grace! "This is the doing of the Lord, and it is justly marvelous in our eyes!"

March 5. Spent some time just at evening in prayer, singing, and discoursing to my people upon divine things. Observed some agreeable tenderness and affection among them. Their present situation is so compact and commodious that they are easily and quickly called together with only the sound of a conch shell, so that they have frequent opportunities of attending religious exercises publicly; which seems to be a great means, under God, of keeping alive the impressions of divine things in their minds.

March 8. Catechized in the evening. My people answered the questions proposed to them well. I can perceive their knowledge in religion increases daily. What is still more desirable, the divine influence that has been so remarkable among them appears still to continue in some good measure. The divine presence seemed to be in the assembly this evening. Some, who I have good reason to think are Christians indeed, were melted with a sense of the divine goodness and their own barrenness and ingratitude, and seemed to hate themselves, as one of them afterwards expressed it. Convictions also appeared to be revived in several instances; and divine truths were attended with such influence upon the assembly in general, that it might justly be called, "an evening of divine power."

### Some Results of the Work of the Spirit

Lord's Day, March 9. Preached from Luke 10:38–42. The Word of God was attended with power and energy upon the audience. Numbers were affected and concerned to obtain the one thing needful. Sundry that have given good evidences of being truly gracious were much affected with a sense of their want of spirituality, and saw the need they stood in of growing in grace. Most that had been under any impressions of divine things in times past seemed now to have those impressions revived.

In the afternoon proposed to have catechized in my usual method. But while we were engaged in the first prayer in the Indian language (as usual), a great part of the assembly was so much moved and affected with divine things that I thought it seasonable and proper to omit the proposing of questions for that time, and insist upon the most practical truths. And accordingly did so, making a further improvement of the passage of Scripture I discoursed upon in the former part of the day.

There appeared to be a powerful divine influence in the congregation. Sundry that I have reason to think are truly pious were so deeply affected with a sense of their own barrenness and their unworthy treatment of the blessed Redeemer that they looked on Him as pierced by themselves, and mourned, yea, some of them were in bitterness as for a first-born. Some poor awakened sinners also appeared to be in anguish of soul to obtain an interest in Christ. So that there was a great mourning in the assembly, many heavy groans, sobs, and tears; and one or two persons newly come among us were considerably awakened.

Methinks it would have refreshed the heart of any who truly love Zion's interest to have been in the midst of this divine influence and seen the effects of it upon saints and sinners. The place of divine worship appeared both solemn and sweet, and was so endeared by a display of the divine presence and grace that those who had any relish of divine things could not but cry, "How amiable are thy tabernacles, O Lord of hosts!" After public worship was over, numbers came to my house where we sang and discoursed of divine things; and the presence of God seemed here also to be in the midst of us.

While we were singing, there was one (the woman mentioned in my Journal of February 9) who, I may venture to say, if I may be allowed to say so much of any person I ever saw, was "filled with joy unspeakable and full of glory," and could not but burst forth in prayer and praises to God before us all, with many tears, crying sometimes in English and sometimes in Indian: "O, blessed Lord, do come, do come! Oh, do take me away, do let me die and go to Jesus Christ! I am afraid if I live I shall sin again! Oh, do let me die now! O, dear Jesus, do come! I cannot stay, I cannot stay! Oh, how can I live in this world! Do take my soul away from this sinful place! Oh, let me never sin any more! Oh, what shall I do, what shall I do! Dear Jesus, O, dear Jesus." In this ecstasy she continued some time, uttering these and such like expressions incessantly. The grand argument she used with God to take her away immediately was that "if she lived, she should sin against Him."

When she had a little recovered herself, I asked her if Christ was not now sweet to her soul. Whereupon, turning to me with tears in her eyes and with all the tokens of deep humility I ever saw in any person, she said: "I have many times heard you speak of the goodness and the sweetness of Christ, that He was better than all the world. But oh! I knew nothing what you meant, I never believed you! I never believed you! But now I know it is true!" Or words to that effect. I answered, "And do you see enough in Christ for the greatest of sinners?" She replied, "Oh! enough, enough! for all the sinners in the world if they would but come."

When I asked her if she could not tell them of the goodness of Christ, turning herself about to some poor Christless souls who stood by and were much affected, she said, "Oh! there is enough in Christ for you, if you would but come! Oh, strive, strive to give up your hearts to Him!" Upon hearing something of the glory of heaven mentioned, that there was no sin in that world, she again fell into the same ecstasy of joy and desire of Christ's coming, repeating her former expressions: "O, dear Lord, do let me go! Oh, what shall I do, what shall I do! I want to go to Christ! I cannot live! Oh, do let me die!"

She continued in this sweet frame for more than two hours before she was well able to get home. I am very sensible there may be great joys arising even to an ecstasy where there is still no substantial evidence of their being well grounded. But in the present case there seemed to be no evidence wanting in order to prove this joy to be divine, either in regard of its *preparatives*, *attendants*, or *consequents*.

Of all the persons I have seen under spiritual exercise, I scarce ever saw one appear more bowed and broken under convictions of sin and misery (or what is usually called a *preparatory work*) than this woman. Nor scarce any who seemed to have a greater acquaintance with her own heart than she had. She would frequently complain to me of the hardness and rebellion of her heart; would tell me that her heart rose and quarreled with God when she thought He would do with her as He pleased and send her to hell notwithstanding her prayers, good frames; that her heart was not willing to come to Christ for salvation, but tried everywhere else for help.

As she seemed to be remarkably sensible of her stubbornness and contrariety to God under conviction, so she appeared to be no less remarkably bowed and reconciled to divine sovereignty before she obtained any relief or comfort; something of which I have before noticed in my Journal of February 9. Since which time she has seemed constantly to breathe the spirit and temper of the new creature, crying after Christ, not through fear of hell as before, but with strong desires after Him as her only satisfying portion; and has many times wept and sobbed bitterly, because (as she apprehended) she did not and could not love Him. When I have sometimes asked her why she appeared so sorrowful and whether it was because she was afraid of hell, she would answer, "No, I be not distressed about that; but my heart is so wicked I cannot love Christ," and thereupon burst into tears. But although this has been the habitual frame of her mind for several weeks together, so that the exercise of grace appeared evident to others, yet she seemed wholly insensible of it herself, and never had any remarkable comfort and sensible satisfaction till this evening.

This sweet and surprising ecstasy appeared to spring from a true spiritual discovery of the glory, ravishing beauty, and excellency of Christ. It was not from any gross imaginary notions of His human nature, such as that of seeing Him in such a place or posture, as hanging on the cross, as bleeding, dying, as gently smiling, and the like; which delusions some have been carried away with. Nor did it rise from sordid, selfish apprehensions of her having any benefit whatsoever conferred on her; but from a view of His personal excellency and transcendent loveliness, which drew forth those vehe-

282 THE LIFE AND DIARY OF DAVID BRAINERD

ment desires of enjoying Him which she now manifested, and made her long "to be absent from the body, that she might be present with the Lord."

The *attendants* of this ravishing comfort were such as abundantly discovered its spring to be divine, and that it was truly a "joy in the Holy Ghost." Now she viewed divine truths as living realities; and could say, "I know these things are so, I feel they are true!" Now her soul was resigned to the divine will in the most tender points; so that when I said to her, "What if God should take away your husband from you (who was then very sick), how do you think you could bear that?" She replied, "He belongs to God, and not to me; He may do with him just what He pleases." Now she had the most tender sense of the evil of sin, and discovered the utmost aversion to it; longing to die that she might be delivered from it. Now she could freely trust her all with God for time and eternity.

When I questioned her how she could be willing to die, and leave her little infant; and what she thought would become of it in that case, she answered, "God will take care of it. It belongs to Him; He will take care of it." Now she appeared to have the most humbling sense of her own meanness and unworthiness, her weakness and inability to preserve herself from sin, and to persevere in the way of holiness, crying, "If I live, I shall sin." I then thought I had never seen such an appearance of ecstasy and humility meeting in any one person in all my life before.

The *consequents* of this joy are no less desirable and satisfactory than its attendants. She since appears to be a most tender, broken-hearted, affectionate, devout, and humble Christian, as exemplary in life and conversation as any person in my congregation. May she still "grow in grace, and in the knowledge of Christ."

March 15. In the evening catechized. My people answered the questions put to them with surprising readiness and judgment. There appeared some warmth and feeling sense of divine things among those, who, I have reason to hope, are real

Christians, while I was discoursing upon "peace of conscience, and joy in the Holy Ghost." These seemed quickened and enlivened in divine service, though there was not so much appearance of concern among those I have reason to think in a Christless state.

Lord's Day, March 16. Preached to my congregation from Hebrews 2:1–3. Divine truths seemed to have some considerable influence upon many of the hearers; and produced many tears, as well as heavy sighs and sobs among both those who have given evidences of being real Christians, and others also. The impressions made upon the audience appeared in general deep and heart affecting, not superficial, noisy, and affected.

Toward night discoursed again on the great salvation. The Word was again attended with some power upon the audience. Numbers wept affectionately, and, to appearance, unfeignedly; so that the Spirit of God seemed to be moving upon the face of the assembly. Baptized the woman particularly mentioned in my Journal of last Lord's Day, who now, as well as then, appeared to be in a devout, humble, and excellent frame of mind.

My house being thronged with my people in the evening, I spent the time in religious exercises with them, till my nature was almost spent. They are so unwearied in religious exercises, and insatiable in their thirsting after Christian knowledge, that I can sometimes scarce avoid laboring so as greatly to exhaust my strength and spirits.

March 19. Sundry of the persons that went with me to the Forks of Delaware in February last, having been detained there by the dangerous illness of one of their company, returned home but this day. Whereupon my people generally met together of their own accord, in order to spend some time in religious exercises; and especially to give thanks to God for His preserving goodness to those who had been absent from them for several weeks, and recovering mercy to him who had been sick; and that He had now returned them all in safety. I being then absent, they desired my schoolmaster to assist them in carrying on their religious solemnity; who tells me they appeared engaged and affectionate in repeated prayer and singing.

Lord's Day, March 23. There being about fifteen strangers, adult persons, come among us in the week past—divers of whom had never been in any religious meeting till now—I thought it proper to discourse this day in a manner peculiarly suited to their circumstances and capacities; and accordingly attempted it from Hosea 13:9, "O Israel, thou hast destroyed thyself . . ." In the forenoon, I opened in the plainest manner I could man's apostasy and ruined state, after having spoken some things respecting the being and perfections of God, and His creation of man in a state of uprightness and happiness. In the afternoon, endeavored to open the glorious provision God has made for the redemption of apostate creatures, by giving His own dear Son to suffer for them and satisfy divine justice on their behalf. There was not that affection and concern in the assembly that has been common among us, although there was a desirable attention appearing in general, and even in most of the strangers.

Near sunset I felt an uncommon concern upon my mind, especially for the poor strangers, that God had so much withheld His presence, and the powerful influence of His Spirit, from the assembly in the exercises of the day; and thereby denied them of that degree of conviction which I hoped they might have had. In this frame I visited sundry houses and discoursed with some concern and affection to divers persons particularly, but without much appearance of success, till I came to a house where divers of the strangers were. There the solemn truths I discoursed of appeared to take effect, first upon some children, then upon divers adult persons that had been somewhat awakened before, and afterwards upon several of the pagan strangers.

I continued my discourse, with some fervency, till almost every one in the house was melted into tears; and divers wept aloud and appeared earnestly concerned to obtain an interest in Christ. Upon this, numbers soon gathered from all the houses round about and so thronged the place that we were

obliged to remove to the house where we usually meet for
public worship. The congregation gathering immediately,
and many appeared remarkably affected. I discoursed some
time from Luke 19:10, "For the Son of man is come to seek
and to save that which was lost"; endeavoring to open the
mercy, compassion, and concern of Christ for lost, helpless,
and undone sinners.

There was much visible concern and affection in the assembly; and I doubt not but that a divine influence accompanied what was spoken to the hearts of many. There were
five or six of the strangers, men and women, who appeared
to be considerably awakened. And in particular one very
rugged young man, who seemed as if nothing would move
him, was now brought to tremble like the jailer, and weep
for a long time.

The pagans that were awakened seemed at once to put off
their savage roughness and pagan manners, and became sociable, orderly, and humane in their carriage. When they first
came, I exhorted my religious people to take pains with them
(as they had done with other strangers from time to time) to
instruct them in Christianity. But when some of them attempted something of that nature, the strangers would soon
rise up and walk to other houses, in order to avoid the hearing of such discourses. Whereupon some of the serious persons
agreed to disperse themselves into the several parts of the
settlement. So that wherever the strangers went, they met
with some instructive discourse and warm addresses respecting their souls' concern.

But now there was no need of using policy in order to get
an opportunity of conversing with some of them about their
spiritual concerns; for they were so far touched with a sense
of their perishing state, as made them tamely yield to the
closest addresses that were made them respecting their sin
and misery, their need of an acquaintance with, and interest
in, the great Redeemer.

March 24. Numbered the Indians to see how many souls
God had gathered together here since my coming into these

parts, and found there were now about an hundred and thirty persons together, old and young. Sundry of those that are my stated hearers, perhaps to the number of fifteen or twenty, were absent at this season. So that if all had been together, the number would now have been very considerable; especially considering how few were together at my first coming into these parts, the whole number not amounting to ten persons at that time.

My people went out this day upon the design of clearing some of their land, above fifteen miles distant from this settlement, in order to their settling there in a compact form; where they might be under advantages of attending the public worship of God, of having their children taught in a school; and at the same time have a conveniency for planting, their land in the place of our present residence being of little or no value for that purpose. The design of their settling thus in a body, and cultivating their lands (which they have done very little in their pagan state), being of such necessity and importance to their religious interest, as well as worldly comfort, I thought it proper to call them together, and show them the duty of laboring with faithfulness and industry; and that they must not now "be slothful in business" as they had ever been in their pagan state.

I endeavored to press the importance of their being laborious, diligent, and vigorous in the prosecution of their business, especially at the present juncture (the season of planting being now near), in order to their being in a capacity of living together, and enjoying the means of grace and instruction. Having given them directions for their work, which they very much wanted, as well as for their behavior in divers respects, I explained, sang, and endeavored to inculcate upon them Psalm 127, common meter, Dr. Watts' version. Having recommended them, and the design of their going forth, to God, by prayer with them, I dismissed them to their business.

In the evening, read and expounded to those of my people who were yet at home, and the strangers newly come, the substance of the third chapter of Acts. Numbers seemed to melt under the Word, especially while I was discoursing upon verse 19, "Repent ye therefore, and be converted . . ." Sundry of the strangers also were affected. When I asked them afterwards whether they did not now feel that their hearts were wicked, as I had taught them, one replied, "Yes, I feel it now." Although before she came here—upon hearing that I taught the Indians their hearts were all bad by nature and needed to be changed and made good by the power of God— she had said, "My heart was not wicked, and I have never done anything that was bad in my life." This indeed seems to be the case with them, I think, universally in their pagan state. They seem to have no consciousness of sin and guilt, unless they can charge themselves with some gross acts of sin contrary to the commands of the second table.

March 27. Discoursed to a number of my people in one of their houses in a more private manner. Inquired particularly into their spiritual states in order to see what impressions of a religious nature they were under. Laid before them the marks and tokens of a regenerate, as well as unregenerate state; and endeavored to suit and direct my discourse to them severally, according as I apprehended their states to be. There was a considerable number gathered together before I finished my discourse; and divers seemed much affected while I was urging the necessity and infinite importance of getting into a renewed state. I find particular and close dealing with souls in private is often very successful.

March 29. In the evening catechized as usual upon Saturday. Treated upon the "benefits which believers receive from Christ at death." The questions were answered with great readiness and propriety. Those who, I have reason to think, are the dear people of God, were sweetly melted almost in general. There appeared such a liveliness and vigor in their attendance upon the Word of God, and such eagerness to be made partakers of the benefits then mentioned, that they seemed to be not only "looking for, but hasting to the coming of the day of God." Divine truths seemed to distill upon the audience with a gentle, but melting efficacy, as the refreshing "showers upon the new-mown grass."

The assembly in general, as well as those who appear truly religious, were affected with some brief account of the blessedness of the godly at death; and most then discovered an affectionate inclination to cry, "Let me die the death of the righteous," although many were not duly engaged to obtain the change of heart that is necessary in order to that blessed end.

March 31. Called my people together, as I had done the Monday morning before, and discoursed to them again on the necessity and importance of their laboring industriously, in order to their living together and enjoying the means of grace. Having engaged in solemn prayer to God among them, for a blessing upon their attempts, I dismissed them to their work. Numbers of them, both men and women, seemed to offer themselves willingly to this service; and some appeared affectionately concerned that God might go with them, and begin their little town for them; that by His blessing it might be a place comfortable for them and theirs, in regard both of procuring the necessaries of life, and of attending the worship of God.

Lord's Day, April 6. Preached from Matthew 7:21–23, "Not every one that saith unto me . . ." There were considerable effects of the Word visible in the audience, and such as were very desirable: an earnest attention, a great solemnity, many tears and heavy sighs, which were modestly suppressed in a considerable measure, and appeared unaffected, and without any indecent commotion of the passions. Divers of the religious people were put upon serious and close examination of their spiritual states by hearing that "not every one that saith to Christ, Lord, Lord, shall enter into his kingdom." Some of them expressed fears lest they had deceived themselves, and taken up a false hope, because they found they had done so little of the "will of his Father who is in heaven."

There was one man brought under very great and pressing

concern for his soul; which appeared more especially after his retirement from public worship. That which he says gave him his great uneasiness was not so much any particular sin as that he had never done the will of God at all, but had sinned continually, and so had no claim to the kingdom of heaven.

In the afternoon I opened to them the discipline of Christ in His Church, and the method in which offenders are to be dealt with. At which time the religious people were much affected, especially when they heard that the offender, continuing obstinate, must finally be esteemed and treated "as an heathen man," as a pagan, that has no part nor lot among God's visible people. Of this they seemed to have the most awful apprehensions; a state of heathenism, out of which they were so lately brought, appearing very dreadful to them. After public worship I visited sundry houses to see how they spent the remainder of the Sabbath, and to treat with them solemnly on the great concerns of their souls. The Lord seemed to smile upon my private endeavors, and to make these particular and personal addresses more effectual upon some than my public discourses.

April 7. Discoursed to my people in the evening from I Corinthians 11:23–26, "For I have received of the Lord . . ." Endeavored to open to them the institution, nature, and ends of the Lord's Supper, as well as the qualifications and preparations necessary to the right participation of that ordinance. Sundry persons appeared much affected with the love of Christ manifested in His making this provision for the comfort of His people, at a season when Himself was just entering upon His sharpest sufferings.

Lord's Day, April 20. Discoursed both forenoon and afternoon from Luke 24, explaining most of the chapter, and making remarks upon it. There was a desirable attention in the audience, though there was not so much appearance of affection and tenderness among them as has been usual. Our meeting was very full, there being sundry strangers present who had never been with us before.

In the evening catechized. My people answered the questions proposed to them readily and distinctly; and I could perceive they advanced in their knowledge of the principles of Christianity. There appeared an affectionate melting in the assembly at this time. Sundry who, I trust, are truly religious, were refreshed and quickened, and seemed, by their discourse and behavior after public worship, to have their "hearts knit together in love." This was a sweet and blessed season, like many others, that my poor people have been favored with in months past. God has caused this little fleece to be repeatedly wet with the blessed dews of His divine grace, while all the earth around has been comparatively dry.

April 25. Of late I apprehended that a number of persons in my congregation were proper subjects of the ordinance of the Lord's Supper, and that it might be seasonable speedily to administer it to them. Having taken advice of some of the reverend correspondents in this solemn affair, I accordingly proposed and appointed the next Lord's Day, with leave of divine Providence, for the administration of this ordinance, and this day, as preparatory thereto, was set apart for solemn fasting and prayer.

The design of this preparatory solemnity was to implore the blessing of God upon our renewing covenant with Him and with one another to walk together in the fear of God, in love and Christian fellowship, and to intreat that His presence might be with us in our designed approach to His Table; as well as to humble ourselves before God on account of the apparent withdrawment (at least in a measure) of that blessed influence which has been so prevalent upon persons of all ages among us; as also on account of the rising appearance of carelessness, vanity, and vice among some who, sometime since, appeared to be touched and affected with divine truths, and brought to some sensibility of their miserable and perishing state by nature. Also, that we might importunately pray for the peaceable settlement of the Indians together in a body, that they might be a commodious congregation for the worship of God; and that God would blast and defeat all the attempts that were or might be made against that pious design.[5]

The solemnity was observed and seriously attended, not only by those who proposed to communicate at the Lord's Table, but by the whole congregation universally. In the former part of the day, I endeavored to open to my people the nature and design of a fast, as I had attempted more briefly to do before, and to instruct them in the duties of such a solemnity. In the afternoon, I insisted upon the special reasons there were for our engaging in these solemn exercises at this time; both in regard of the need we stood in of divine assistance, in order to a due preparation for that sacred ordinance some of us were proposing, with leave of divine Providence, speedily to attend upon; and also in respect of the manifest decline of God's work here, as to the effectual conviction and conversion of sinners, there having been few of late deeply awakened out of a state of security. The worship of God was attended with great solemnity and reverence, with much tenderness and many tears, by those who appear to be truly religious. There was some appearance of divine power upon those who had been awakened sometime before, and who were still under concern.

After repeated prayer and attendance upon the Word of God, I proposed to the religious people, with as much brevity and plainness as I could, the substance of the doctrine of the Christian faith, as I had formerly done previous to their baptism, and had their renewed cheerful assent to it. I then led them to a solemn renewal of their baptismal covenant, wherein they had explicitly and publicly given up themselves to God the Father, Son, and Holy Ghost, avouching Him to be their God; and at the same time renouncing their heathen-

---

[5] There being at this time a terrible clamor raised against the Indians in various places in the country, and insinuations as though I were training them up to cut people's throats. Numbers wishing to have them banished out of these parts, and some giving out great words, in order to fright and deter them from settling upon the best and most convenient tract of their own lands, threatening to molest and trouble them in the law, pretending a claim to these lands themselves, although never purchased of the Indians.

ish vanities, their idolatrous and superstitious practices, and
solemnly engaging to take the Word of God, so far as it was
or might be made known to them, for the rule of their lives,
promising to walk together in love, to watch over themselves,
and one another; to lead lives of seriousness and devotion,
and to discharge the relative duties incumbent upon them
respectively.

This solemn transaction was attended with much gravity
and seriousness, and at the same time with utmost readiness,
freedom, and cheerfulness. A religious union and harmony of
soul seemed to crown the whole solemnity. I could not but
think in the evening that there had been manifest tokens of
the divine presence with us in all the several services of the
day; though it was also manifest there was not that concern
among Christless souls that has often appeared here.

April 26. Toward noon prayed with a dying child and gave
a word of exhortation to the bystanders to prepare for death,
which seemed to take effect upon some. In the afternoon discoursed to my people from Matthew 26:26–30 of the *author*,
the *nature*, and *design* of the Lord's Supper; and endeavored to
point out the *worthy* receivers of that ordinance.

The religious people were affected, and even melted with
divine truths, with a view of the dying love of Christ. Sundry
others who had been for some months under convictions of
their perishing state, appeared now to be much moved with
concern and afresh engaged in seeking after an interest in
Christ; although I cannot say the Word of God appeared so
quick and powerful, so sharp and piercing to the assembly,
as it had sometimes formerly done. Baptized two adult persons, both serious and exemplary in their lives, and, I hope,
truly religious. One of them was the man particularly mentioned in my Journal on April 6. Although he was then
greatly distressed because "he had never done the will of
God," he has since, it is hoped, obtained spiritual comfort
upon good grounds.

In the evening I catechized those that were designed to
partake of the Lord's Supper the next day, upon the institu-

tion, nature, and end of that ordinance. Had abundant satisfaction respecting their doctrinal knowledge and fitness in
that respect for an attendance upon it. They likewise appeared, in general, to have an affecting sense of the solemnity
of this sacred ordinance, and to be humbled under a sense of
their own unworthiness to approach to God in it; and to be
earnestly concerned that they might be duly prepared for an
attendance upon it. Their hearts were full of love one toward
another, and that was the frame of mind they seemed much
concerned to maintain, and bring to the Lord's Table with
them. In the singing and prayer, after catechizing, there appeared an agreeable tenderness and melting among them and
such tokens of brotherly love and affection that would even
constrain one to say, "Lord, it is good to be here"; it is good
to dwell where such a heavenly influence distills.

Lord's Day, April 27. Preached from Titus 2:14, "Who gave
himself for us, that he might redeem us from all iniquity, and
purify unto himself a peculiar people, zealous of good works."
The Word of God at this time was attended with some appearance of divine power upon the assembly; so that the attention and gravity of the audience was remarkable; and especially towards the conclusion of the exercise, divers persons
were much affected.

Administered the sacrament of the Lord's Supper to twenty-
three persons of the Indians (the number of men and women
being near equal), divers others, to the number of five or six,
being now absent at the Forks of Delaware, who would
otherwise have communicated with us. The ordinance was
attended with great solemnity, and with a most desirable
tenderness and affection. It was remarkable that in the season
of the performance of the sacramental actions, especially in
the distribution of the bread, they seemed to be affected in a
most lively manner, as if Christ had been really crucified
before them. The words of the institution, when repeated and
enlarged upon in the season of the administration, seemed to
meet with the same reception, to be entertained with the
same full and firm belief and affectionate engagement of soul,

as if the Lord Jesus Christ Himself had been present and had personally spoken to them. The affections of the communicants, although considerably raised, were notwithstanding agreeably regulated and kept within proper bounds. So that there was a sweet, gentle, and affectionate melting, without any indecent or boisterous commotion of the passions.

Having rested some time after the administration of the sacrament (being extremely tired with the necessary prolixity of the work), I walked from house to house, and conversed particularly with most of the communicants, and found they had been almost universally refreshed at the Lord's Table, as with new wine. Never did I see such an appearance of Christian love among any people in all my life. It was so remarkable that one might well have cried with an agreeable surprise, "Behold, how they love one another!" I think there could be no greater tokens of mutual affection among the people of God in the early days of Christianity than what now appeared here. The sight was so desirable, and so well becoming the gospel, that nothing less could be said of it than that it was "the doing of the Lord," the genuine operations of Him who is love!

Toward night discoursed again on the forementioned Titus 2:14, and insisted on the immediate end and design of Christ's death, namely, "That he might redeem his people from all iniquity." This appeared to be a season of divine power among us. The religious people were much refreshed and seemed remarkably tender and affectionate, full of love, joy, peace, and desirous of being completely "redeemed from all iniquity"; so that some of them afterwards told me they had never felt the like before. Convictions also appeared to be revived in many instances; and divers persons were awakened whom I had never observed under any religious impressions before.

Such was the influence that attended our assembly, and so unspeakably desirable the frame of mind that many enjoyed in the divine service, that it seemed almost grievous to conclude the public worship. The congregation when dismissed,

although it was then almost dark, appeared loath to leave
the place and employments that had been rendered so dear
to them by the benefits enjoyed, while a blessed quickening
influence distilled upon them. On the whole, I must say, I
had great satisfaction relative to the administration of this
ordinance in divers respects. I have abundant reason to think
that those who came to the Lord's Table had a good degree
of doctrinal knowledge of the nature and design of the ordinance, and that they acted with understanding in what they
did.

In the preparatory services I found, I may justly say, uncommon freedom in opening to their understandings and capacities the covenant of grace, and in showing them the nature of this ordinance as a seal of that covenant. Many of
them knew of no such thing as a seal before my coming among
them, or at least of the use and design of it in the common
affairs of life. They were likewise thoroughly sensible that it
was no more than a seal or sign, and not the real body and
blood of Christ; that it was designed for the refreshment and
edification of the soul, and not for the feasting of the body.
They were also acquainted with the end of the ordinance,
that they were therein called to commemorate the dying love
of Christ.

This competency of doctrinal knowledge, together with
their grave and decent attendance upon the ordinance, their
affectionate melting under it, and the sweet and Christian
frame of mind they discovered consequent upon it, gave me
great satisfaction respecting my administration of it to them.
And oh, what a sweet and blessed season was this! God Himself, I am persuaded, was in the midst of His people attending
His own ordinances. I doubt not but many in the conclusion
of the day could say with their whole hearts, "Verily, a day
thus spent in God's house is better than a thousand elsewhere." There seemed to be but one heart among the pious
people. The sweet union, harmony, and endearing love and
tenderness subsisting among them was, I thought, the most
lively emblem of the heavenly world I had ever seen.

April 28. Concluded the sacramental solemnity with a discourse upon John 14:15, "If ye love me, keep my commandments." At which time there appeared a very agreeable tenderness in the audience in general, but especially in the communicants. Oh, how free, how engaged and affectionate did these appear in the service of God! They seemed willing to have their "ears bored to the doorposts of God's house," and to be His servants forever.

Observing numbers in this excellent frame and the assembly in general affected, and that by a divine influence, I thought it proper to improve this advantageous season, as Hezekiah did the desirable season of his great Passover (II Chron. 31), in order to promote the blessed reformation begun among them; and to engage those that appeared serious and religious to persevere therein. Accordingly proposed to them that they should renewedly enter into covenant before God, that they would watch over themselves and one another, lest they should dishonor the name of Christ by falling into sinful and unbecoming practices.

I especially urged that they would watch against the sin of drunkenness (the sin that easily besets them), and the temptations leading thereto; as well as the appearance of evil in that respect. They cheerfully complied with the proposal and explicitly joined in that covenant. Whereupon I proceeded in the most solemn manner I was capable of, to call God to witness respecting their sacred engagement, and minded them of the greatness of the guilt they would contract to themselves in the violation of it. I also observed to them that God would be a terrible witness against those who should presume to do so in the "great and notable day of the Lord."

It was a season of amazing solemnity! A divine awe appeared upon the face of the whole assembly in this transaction! Affectionate sobs, sighs, and tears were now frequent in the audience, and I doubt not but that many silent cries were then sent up to the fountain of grace for supplies of grace sufficient for the fulfillment of these solemn engagements. Baptized six children this day.

Lord's Day, May 4. My people were now removed to their lands, mentioned in my Journal of March 24, where they have since made provision for a compact settlement, in order to their more convenient enjoyment of the gospel and other means of instruction, as well as the comforts of life. Therefore, I this day visited them, being now obliged to board with an English family at some distance from them, and preached to them in the forenoon from Mark 4:5, "And some fell on stony ground." Endeavored to show them the reason there was to fear lest many promising appearances and hopeful beginnings in religion might prove abortive, like the "seed dropped upon stony places."

In the afternoon discoursed upon Romans 8:9, "Now if any man have not the Spirit of Christ, he is none of his." I have reason to think this discourse was peculiarly seasonable and that it had a good effect upon some of the hearers. Spent some hours afterwards in private conferences with my people, and labored to regulate some things I apprehended amiss among some of them.

May 5. Visited my people again and took care of their worldly concerns, giving them directions relating to their business. I daily discover more and more of what importance it is like to be to their religious interests that they become laborious and industrious, acquainted with the affairs of husbandry and able, in a good measure, to raise the necessaries and comforts of life within themselves; for their present method of living greatly exposes them to temptations of various kinds.

## THE CONVERSION OF A CONJURER

May 9. Preached from John 5:40, "And ye will not come to me . . . ," in the open wilderness, the Indians having as yet no house for public worship in this place, nor scarce any shelters for themselves. Divine truths made considerable impressions upon the audience, and it was a season of solemnity, tenderness, and affection.

Baptized one man this day (the conjurer and murderer mentioned in my Journal of August 8, 1745, and February 1, 1746) who appears to be such a remarkable instance of divine grace that I cannot omit some brief account of him here. He lived near and sometimes attended my meeting in the Forks of Delaware for more than a year together; but was, like many others of them, extremely attached to strong drink and seemed to be no ways reformed by the means I used with them for their instruction and conversion. At this time he likewise murdered a likely young Indian; which threw him into some kind of horror and desperation so that he kept at a distance from me and refused to hear me preach for several months together, till I had an opportunity of conversing freely with him, and giving him encouragement, that his sin might be forgiven for Christ's sake. After which he again attended my meeting sometimes.

But that which was the worst of all his conduct was his conjuration. He was one of them who are sometimes called powwows among the Indians; and notwithstanding his frequent attendance upon my preaching, he still followed his old charms and juggling tricks, "giving out that himself was some great one, and to him they gave heed," supposing him to be possessed of a great power. So that when I have instructed them respecting the miracles wrought by Christ in healing the sick, and mentioned them as evidences of His divine mission and the truth of His doctrines, they have quickly observed the wonders of that kind which this man had performed by his magic charms. Whence they had a high opinion of him and his superstitious notions, which seemed to be a fatal obstruction to some of them in regard of their receiving the gospel.

I have often thought it would be a great favor to the design of gospelizing these Indians if God would take that wretch out of the world, for I had scarce any hope of his ever coming to good. But God "whose thoughts are not as man's thoughts" has been pleased to take a much more desirable method with him; a method agreeable to His own interest among the Indians, as well as effectual to the salvation of this poor soul. To God be the glory of it.

The first genuine concern for his soul that ever appeared in him was excited by seeing my interpreter and his wife baptized at the Forks of Delaware, July 21, 1745. Which so prevailed upon him that, with the invitation of an Indian who was a friend to Christianity, he followed me down to Crossweeksung in the beginning of August following, in order to hear me preach, and there continued for several weeks in the season of the most remarkable and powerful awakening among the Indians. At this time he was more effectually awakened and brought under great concern for his soul. Then, upon his "feeling the word of God in his heart," as he expresses it, his spirit of conjuration left him entirely, and he had no more power of that nature since than any other man living. He declares that he does not now so much as know how he used to charm and conjure and that he could not do anything of that nature if he was never so desirous of it.

He continued under convictions of his sinful and perishing state, and a considerable degree of concern for his soul, all the fall and former part of the winter past, but was not so deeply exercised till sometime in January. Then the Word of God took such hold upon him that he was brought into great distress and knew not what to do, nor where to turn himself. He then told me that, when he used to hear me preach from time to time in the fall of the year, my preaching pricked his heart and made him very uneasy, but did not bring him to so great distress because he still hoped he could do something for his own relief. But now, he said, I drove him up into "such a sharp corner" that he had no way to turn and could not avoid being in distress.

He continued constantly under the heavy burden and pressure of a wounded spirit till at length he was brought into the acute anguish and utmost agony of soul (mentioned in my Journal of February 1) which continued that night and part of the next day. After this, he was brought to the utmost calmness and composure of mind, his trembling and heavy burden was removed, and he appeared perfectly sedate; although he had, to his apprehensions, scarce any hope of salvation.

I observed him to appear remarkably composed and thereupon asked him how he did. He replied, "It is done, it is done, it is all done now." I asked him what he meant. He answered, "I can never do any more to save myself; it is all done forever. I can do no more." I queried with him whether he could not do a little more rather than to go to hell. He replied, "My heart is dead, I can never help myself." I asked him what he thought would become of him then and he answered, "I must go to hell." I asked him if he thought it was right that God should send him to hell. He replied, "Oh, it is right. The Devil has been in me ever since I was born." I asked him if he felt this when he was in such great distress the evening before. He answered, "No, I did not then think it was right. I thought God would send me to hell and that I was then dropping into it. But my heart quarreled with God and would not say it was right He should send me there. But now I know it is right, for I have always served the Devil, and my heart has no goodness in it now, but is as bad as ever it was." I thought I had scarce ever seen any person more effectually brought off from a dependence upon his own contrivances and endeavors for salvation, or more apparently to lie at the foot of sovereign mercy, than this man now did under these views of things.

In this frame of mind he continued for several days, passing sentence for condemnation upon himself and constantly owning that it would be right he should be damned, and that he expected this would be his portion for the greatness of his sins. Yet it was plain he had a secret hope of mercy, though imperceptible to himself, which kept him not only from despair but from any pressing distress; so that instead of being sad and dejected, his very countenance appeared pleasant and agreeable.

While he was in this frame he sundry times asked me when I would preach again, and seemed desirous to hear the Word of God every day. I asked him why he wanted to hear me preach, seeing "his heart was dead, and all was done," that "he could never help himself and expected that he must go to hell." He replied, "I love to hear you speak about Christ for all." I added, "But what good will that do you if you must go to hell at last?"—using now his own language with him; having before, from time to time, labored in the best manner I could to represent to him the excellency of Christ, His all-sufficiency and willingness to save lost sinners and persons just in his case; although to no purpose as to yielding him any special comfort. He answered, "I would have others come to Christ, if I must go to hell myself."

It was remarkable that he seemed to have a great love to the people of God, and nothing affected him so much as the thoughts of being separated from them. This seemed to be a very dreadful part of the hell to which he thought himself doomed. It was likewise remarkable that in this season he was most diligent in the use of all means for his soul's salvation; although he had the clearest view of the insufficiency of means to afford him help. He would frequently say that all he did "signified nothing at all"; and yet was never more constant in doing, attending secret and family prayer daily, and surprisingly diligent and attentive in hearing the Word of God; so that he neither despaired of mercy, nor yet presumed to hope upon his own doings, but used means because appointed of God in order to salvation; and because he would wait upon God in his own way.

After he had continued in this frame of mind more than a week, while I was discoursing publicly he seemed to have a lively, soul-refreshing view of the excellency of Christ, and the way of salvation by Him, which melted him into tears and filled him with admiration, comfort, satisfaction, and praise to God. Since then he has appeared to be a humble, devout, and affectionate Christian; serious and exemplary in his conversation and behavior, frequently complaining of his barrenness, his want of spiritual warmth, life, and activity, and yet frequently favored with quickening and refreshing influences. In all respects, so far as I am capable to judge, he bears the marks and characters of one "created anew in Christ Jesus to good works."

His zeal for the cause of God was pleasing to me when he was with me at the Forks of Delaware in February last. There was an old Indian at the place where I preached who threatened to bewitch me and my religious people who accompanied me there. This man presently challenged him to do his worst, telling him that himself had been as great a conjurer as he, and that notwithstanding as soon as he felt that Word in his heart which these people loved (meaning the Word of God), his power of conjuring immediately left him. "And so it would you," said he, "if you did but once feel it in your heart; and you have no power to hurt them, nor so much as to touch one of them." So that I may conclude my account of him by observing (in allusion to what was said of Paul), that he now zealously defends and practically "preaches the faith which he once destroyed," or at least was instrumental of obstructing. May God have the glory of the amazing change He has wrought in him!

Lord's Day, May 18. Discoursed both parts of the day from Revelation 3:20, "Behold I stand at the door . . ." There appeared some affectionate melting towards the conclusion of the forenoon exercise, and one or two instances of fresh awakening. In the intermission of public worship, I took occasion to discourse to numbers in a more private way on the kindness and patience of the blessed Redeemer in standing and knocking, in continuing His gracious calls to sinners who had long neglected and abused His grace; which seemed to take some effect upon sundry.

In the afternoon, divine truths were attended with solemnity, and with some tears, although there was not that powerful awakening and quickening influence which in times past has been common in our assemblies. The appearance of the audience under divine truths was comparatively discouraging; and I was ready to fear that God was about to withdraw the blessed influence of His Spirit from us.

May 19. Visited and preached to my people from Acts 20:18, 19, "And when they were come to him, he said unto them, Ye know, from the first day . . . ," and endeavored to rectify their notions about religious affections. I showed them, on the one hand, the desirableness of religious affection, tenderness, and fervent engagement in the worship and service of God, when such affection flows from a true spiritual discovery of divine glories, from a justly affecting sense of the transcendent excellency and perfections of the blessed God, a view of the glory and loveliness of the great Redeemer; and that such views of divine things will naturally excite us to "serve the Lord with many tears," with much affection and fervency, and yet "with all humility of mind."

On the other hand, observed the sinfulness of seeking after high affections immediately and for their own sakes, that is, of making them the object that our eye and heart is nextly and principally set upon when the glory of God ought to be so. Showed them that if the heart be directly and chiefly fixed on God and the soul engaged to glorify Him, some degree of religious affection will be the effect and attendant of it. But to seek after affection directly and chiefly, to have the heart principally set upon that, is to place it in the room of God and His glory. If it be sought that others may take notice and admire us for our spirituality and forwardness in religion, it is then abominable pride. If for the sake of feeling the pleasure of being affected, it is then idolatry and self-gratification. Labored also to expose the disagreeableness of those affections that are sometimes wrought up in persons by the power of fancy and their own attempts for that purpose, while I still endeavored to recommend to them that religious affection, fervency, and devotion which ought to attend all our religious exercises, and without which religion will be but an empty name and lifeless carcass.

This appeared to be a seasonable discourse, and proved very satisfactory to some of the religious people who before were exercised with some difficulties relating to this point. Afterwards took care of, and gave my people directions about, their worldly affairs.

May 24. Visited the Indians and took care of their secular business, which they are not able to manage themselves without the constant care and advice of others. Afterwards discoursed to some particularly about their spiritual concerns.

Lord's Day, June 1, 1746. Preached both forenoon and afternoon from Matthew 11:27, 28. The presence of God seemed to be in the assembly, and numbers were considerably melted and affected under divine truths. There was a desirable appearance in the congregation in general, an earnest attention and agreeable tenderness, and it seemed as if God designed to visit us with further showers of divine grace. I then baptized ten persons, five adults and five children, and was not a little refreshed with this addition made to the church of such as, I hope, shall be saved.

I have reason to hope that God has lately (at and since our celebration of the Lord's Supper) brought home to Himself sundry souls who had long been under spiritual trouble and concern; although there have been few instances of persons lately awakened out of a state of security. Those comforted of late seem to be brought in, in a more silent way, neither their concern nor consolation being so powerful and remarkable as appeared among those more suddenly wrought upon in the beginning of this work of grace.

June 6. Discoursed to my people from part of Isaiah 53. The divine presence appeared to be among us in some measure. Divers persons were much melted and refreshed. One man in particular who had long been under concern for his soul was now brought to see and feel, in a very lively manner, the impossibility of his doing anything to help himself, or to bring him into the favor of God by his tears, prayers, and other religious performances; and found himself undone as to any power or goodness of his own, and that there was no way left him but to leave himself with God to be disposed of as He pleased.

June 7. [I was] desired by the Rev. William Tennent to be his assistant in the administration of the Lord's Supper; my people also being invited to attend the sacramental solemnity, they cheerfully embraced the opportunity, and this day attended the preparatory services with me.

Lord's Day, June 8. Most of my people who had been communicants at the Lord's Table before, being present at this sacramental occasion, communicated with others in this holy ordinance. [This was] at the desire, and I trust, to the satisfaction and comfort of numbers of God's people who had longed to see this day and whose hearts had rejoiced in this work of grace among the Indians, which prepared the way for what appeared so agreeable at this time. Those of my people who communicated seemed in general agreeably affected at the Lord's Table, and some of them considerably melted with the love of Christ; although they were not so remarkably refreshed and feasted at this time, as when I administered this ordinance to them in our own congregation only.

Some of the bystanders were affected with seeing these who had been "aliens from the commonwealth of Israel and strangers to the covenant of promise," who of all men had lived "without hope, and without God in the world," now brought near to God as His professing people, and sealing covenant with Him, by a solemn and devout attendance upon this sacred ordinance. As numbers of God's people were refreshed with this sight and thereby excited to bless God for the enlargement of His kingdom in the world, so some others, I was told, were awakened by it, apprehending the danger they were in of being themselves finally cast out, while they saw others "from the east and west" preparing and hopefully prepared in some good measure to "sit down in the kingdom of God."

At this season others of my people also who were not communicants were considerably affected; convictions were revived in divers instances. One (the man particularly mentioned in my Journal of April sixth) obtained comfort and satisfaction and has since given me such an account of his spiritual exercises and the manner in which he obtained relief, as appears very hopeful. It seems as if he "who commanded the light to shine out of darkness" had now "shined in his heart and given him the light of" and experimental "knowledge of the glory of God in the face of Jesus Christ."

June 9. A considerable number of my people met together early in the day in a retired place in the woods and prayed, sang, and conversed of divine things, and were seen by some religious persons of the white people to be affected and engaged, and divers of them in tears in these religious exercises.

Afterwards they attended the concluding exercises of the sacramental solemnity, and then returned home, divers of them "rejoicing for all the goodness of God" they had seen and felt; so that this appeared to be a profitable, as well as a comfortable season to numbers of my congregation. Their being present at this occasion, and a number of them communicating at the Lord's Table with others of God's people, was, I trust, for the honor of God and the interest of religion in these parts, as numbers, I have reason to think, were quickened by means of it.

June 13. Preached to my people upon the new creature, from II Corinthians 5:17, "If any man be in Christ . . ." The presence of God appeared to be in the assembly. It was a sweet and agreeable meeting, wherein the people of God were refreshed and strengthened, beholding their faces in the glass of God's Word and finding in themselves the marks and lineaments of the new creature. Some sinners under concern were also renewedly affected and afresh engaged for the securing of their eternal interests.

Baptized five persons at this time, three adults and two children. One of these was the very aged woman of whose exercise I gave an account in my Journal of December 26. She now gave me a very punctual, rational, and satisfactory account of the remarkable change she experienced some months after the beginning of her concern, which, I must say, appeared to be the genuine operations of the Divine Spirit, so far as I am capable of judging. Although she was become so childish through old age that I could do nothing in a way of questioning with her, nor scarce make her understand any that I asked her; yet when I let her alone to go on with her own story, she could give a very distinct and particular relation of the many and various exercises of soul she had experienced; so deep were the impressions left upon her mind by that influence, and that exercise she had been under! And I have great reason to hope she is born anew in her old age, she being, I presume, upwards of fourscore. I had good hopes of the other adults and trust they are such as God will own "in the day when he makes up his jewels."

June 19 (1746). Visited my people with two of the reverend correspondents.[6] Spent some time in conversation with some of them upon spiritual things; and took some care of their worldly concerns.

This day makes up a complete year from the first time of my preaching to these Indians in New Jersey. What amazing things has God wrought in this space of time for these poor people! What a surprising change appears in their tempers and behavior! How are morose and savage pagans in this short space of time transformed into agreeable, affectionate, and humble Christians, and their drunken and pagan howlings turned into devout and fervent prayers and praises to God! They "who were sometimes darkness are now become light in the Lord." May they walk as children of the light and of the day. And now to Him that is of power to stablish them according to the gospel, and the preaching of Christ—to God only wise, be glory, through Jesus Christ, for ever and ever. Amen.

---

[6] Representatives in America of the Society (in Scotland) for Propagating Christian Knowledge, which supported and directed Mr. Brainerd in his work among the Indians.—H.

*Editor's Note*

This is the end of the section taken from "Brainerd's Journal," written especially for the Society (in Scotland) for Propagating Christian Knowledge, and covering the period from June 19, 1745, to June 19, 1746. From this point on, the remainder of the record is taken from "Brainerd's Life and Diary" and follows in chronological order. The period is from June 29, 1746, to October 9, 1747.

—P. E. H., Jr.

# DAVID BRAINERD'S
# LIFE AND DIARY

## PART VII–VIII

# PART VII

## From the Close of His Journal to His Return from the Susquehannah

### *June–September, 1746*

LORD'S DAY, June 29, 1746. Preached, both parts of the day, from John 14:19, "Yet a little while, and the world seeth me no more." God was pleased to assist me, to afford me both freedom and power, especially towards the close of my discourses, both forenoon and afternoon. God's power appeared in the assembly in both exercises. Numbers of God's people were refreshed and melted with divine things; one or two comforted, who had been long under distress. Convictions, in divers instances, were powerfully revived; and one man in years much awakened, who had not long frequented our meeting and appeared before as stupid as a stock. God amazingly renewed and lengthened out my strength. I was so spent at noon that I could scarce walk, and all my joints trembled so that I could not sit, nor so much as hold my hand still. And yet God strengthened me to preach with power in the afternoon, although I had given out word to my people that I did not expect to be able to do it.

Spent some time afterwards in conversing, particularly, with several persons about their spiritual state; and had some satisfaction concerning one or two. Prayed afterwards with a sick child, and gave a word of exhortation. Was assisted in all my work. Blessed be God! Returned home with more health than I went out with; although my linen was wringing wet upon me, from a little after ten in the morning till past five in the afternoon. My spirits also were considerably refreshed and my soul rejoiced in hope that I had through grace done something for God. In the evening, walked out and enjoyed a sweet season in secret prayer and praise. But oh, I found the truth of the Psalmist's words, "My goodness extendeth not to thee!" I could not make any returns to God; I longed to live only to Him and to be in tune for His praise and service forever. Oh, for spirituality and holy fervency that I might spend and be spent for God to my latest moment!

Monday, June 30. Spent the day in writing, but under much weakness and disorder. Felt the labors of the preceding day, although my spirits were so refreshed the evening before that I was not then sensible of my being spent.

Tuesday, July 1. In the afternoon, visited and preached to my people from Hebrews 9:27, "And as it is appointed unto men once to die, . . ." on occasion of some persons lying at the point of death, in my congregation. God gave me some assistance, and His Word made some impressions on the audience in general. This was an agreeable and comfortable evening to my soul. My spirits were somewhat refreshed, with a small degree of freedom and help enjoyed in my work.

Lord's Day, July 6. (At Elisabeth Town.) Enjoyed some composure and serenity of mind in the morning; heard Mr. Dickinson preach in the forenoon and was refreshed with his discourse; was in a melting frame some part of the time of sermon; partook of the Lord's Supper and enjoyed some sense of divine things in that ordinance. In the afternoon, I preached from Ezekiel 33:11, "As I live, saith the Lord God . . ." God favored me with freedom and fervency and helped me to plead His cause beyond my own power.

Monday, July 7. My spirits were considerably refreshed and raised, in the morning. There is no comfort, I find, in any enjoyment without enjoying God and being engaged in His service. In the evening, had the most agreeable conversation that ever I remember in all my life, upon God's being all in all, and all enjoyments being just that to us which God makes them and no more. It is good to begin and end with God. Oh, how does a sweet solemnity lay a foundation for true pleasure and happiness!

Tuesday, July 8. Rode home, and enjoyed some agreeable meditations by the way.

Wednesday, July 9. Spent the day in writing, enjoyed some comfort and refreshment of spirit in my evening retirement.

Thursday, July 10. Spent most of the day in writing. Towards night rode to Mr. Tennent's; enjoyed some agreeable conversation. Went home in the evening in a solemn, sweet frame of mind; was refreshed in secret duties, longed to live wholly and only for God, and saw plainly there was nothing in the world worthy of my affection; so that my heart was dead to all below; yet not through dejection, as at some times, but from views of a better inheritance.

Friday, July 11. Was in a calm, composed frame, in the morning, especially in the season of my secret retirement. I think I was well pleased with the will of God, whatever it was, or should be, in all respects I had then any thought of. Intending to administer the Lord's Supper the next Lord's Day, I looked to God for His presence and assistance upon that occasion; but felt a disposition to say, "The will of the Lord be done," whether it be to give me assistance or not. Spent some little time in writing; visited the Indians and spent some time in serious conversation with them, thinking it not best to preach, many of them being absent.

Saturday, July 12. This day was spent in fasting and prayer by my congregation, as preparatory to the sacrament. I discoursed, both parts of the day, from Romans 4:25, "Who was delivered for our offenses . . ." God gave me some assistance in my discourses and something of divine power attended the Word, so that this was an agreeable season. Afterwards led them to a solemn renewal of their covenant and fresh dedication of themselves to God. This was a season both of solemnity and sweetness, and God seemed to be in the midst of us. Returned to my lodgings, in the evening, in a comfortable frame of mind.

Lord's Day, July 13. In the forenoon, discoursed on the Bread of life, from John 6:35. God gave me some assistance, in part of my discourse especially, and there appeared some tender affection in the assembly under divine truths. My soul also was somewhat refreshed. Administered the sacrament of the Lord's Supper to thirty-one persons of the Indians. God seemed to be present in this ordinance, and the communicants were sweetly melted and refreshed, most of them. Oh, how they melted, even when the elements were first uncovered! There was scarcely a dry eye among them when I took off the linen and showed them the symbols of Christ's broken body.

Having rested a little, after the administration of the sacrament, I visited the communicants and found them generally in a sweet loving frame. In the afternoon, discoursed upon coming to Christ, and the satisfaction of those who do so, from the same verse I insisted on in the forenoon. This was likewise an agreeable season, a season of much tenderness, affection, and enlargement in divine service. God, I am persuaded, crowned our assembly with His divine presence. I returned home much spent, yet rejoicing in the goodness of God.

Monday, July 14. Went to my people, and discoursed to them from Psalm 119:106, "I have sworn, and I will perform it." Observed: 1) That all God's judgments or commandments are righteous; 2) That God's people have sworn to keep them, and this they do especially at the Lord's Table. There appeared to be a powerful divine influence on the assembly and considerable melting under the Word. Afterwards, I led them to a renewal of their covenant before God (as I did on April 28), that they would watch over themselves and one another, lest they should fall into sin and dishonor the name of Christ. This transaction was attended with great solemnity, and God seemed to own it by exciting in them a fear and jealousy of themselves lest they should sin against God; so that the presence of God seemed to be among us in this conclusion of the sacramental solemnity.

> The next day he set out on a journey towards Philadelphia, from whence he did not return till Saturday. He went his journey and spent the week under a great degree of illness of body and dejection of mind.—J. E.

Lord's Day, July 20. Preached twice to my people from John 17:24, "Father, I will that they also, whom thou hast given me, be with me where I am, that they may behold my glory, which thou hast given me." Was helped to discourse with great clearness and plainness in the forenoon. In the afternoon, enjoyed some tenderness and spake with some influence. Divers were in tears; and some, to appearance, in distress.

Monday, July 21. Preached to the Indians, chiefly for the sake of some strangers. Then proposed my design of taking a journey speedily to Susquehannah; exhorted my people to pray for me that God would be with me in that journey. Then chose divers persons of the congregation to travel with me. Afterwards, spent some time in discoursing to the strangers, and was somewhat encouraged with them. Took care of my people's secular business and was not a little exercised with it. Had some degree of composure and comfort in secret retirement.

Tuesday, July 22. Was in a dejected frame, most of the day; wanted to wear out life and have it at an end, but had some desires of living to God and wearing out life *for Him*. Oh, that I could indeed do so!

> The next day he went to Elisabeth Town, to a meeting of the Presbytery; and spent this, and Thursday, and the former part of Friday, under a very great degree of melancholy and exceeding gloominess of mind; not through any fear of future punishment, but as being distressed with a senselessness of all good, so that the whole world appeared empty and gloomy to him. But in the latter part of Friday, he was greatly relieved and comforted.—J. E.

Saturday, July 26. Was comfortable in the morning; my countenance and heart were not sad as in days past; enjoyed some sweetness in lifting up my heart to God. Rode home to my people and was in a comfortable, pleasant frame by the way. My spirits were much relieved of their burden, and I felt free to go through all difficulties and labors in my Master's service.

Lord's Day, July 27. Discoursed to my people, in the forenoon, from Luke 12:37, on the duty and benefit of *watching*. God helped me in the latter part of my discourse, and the power of God appeared in the assembly. In the afternoon, discoursed from Luke 13:25, "When once the master of the house is risen up . . ." Here also I enjoyed some assistance, and the Spirit of God seemed to attend what was spoken so that there was a great solemnity and some tears among Indians and others.

Monday, July 28. Was very weak and scarce able to perform any business at all, but enjoyed sweetness and comfort in prayer, both morning and evening. Was composed and comfortable through the day; my mind was intense and my heart fervent, at least in some degree, in secret duties. I longed to *spend and be spent for God.*

Tuesday, July 29. My mind was cheerful and free from those melancholy damps that I am often exercised with; had freedom in looking up to God, at sundry times in the day. In the evening, I enjoyed a comfortable season in secret prayer; was helped to plead with God for my own dear people that He would carry on His own blessed work among them. Was assisted also in praying for the divine presence to attend me in my intended journey to Susquehannah, and was helped to remember dear brethren and friends in New England. I scarce knew how to leave the throne of grace, and it grieved me that I was obliged to go to bed. I longed to do something for God, but knew not how. Blessed be God for this freedom from dejection.

Wednesday, July 30. Was uncommonly comfortable, both in body and mind, in the forenoon especially. My mind was solemn, I was assisted in my work, and God seemed to be near to me so that the day was as comfortable as most I have enjoyed for some time. In the evening, was favored with assistance in secret prayer and felt much as I did the evening before. Blessed be God for that freedom I then enjoyed at the throne of grace, for myself, my people, and my dear friends. It is good for me to draw near to God.

Friday, August 1. In the evening, enjoyed a sweet season in secret prayer; clouds of darkness and perplexing care were sweetly scattered, and nothing anxious remained. Oh, how serene was my mind at this season! How free from that distracting concern I have often felt! "Thy will be done" was a petition sweet to my soul, and if God had bidden me choose for myself in any affair, I should have chosen rather to have referred the choice to Him; for I saw He was infinitely wise and could not do anything amiss, as I was in danger of doing. Was assisted in prayer for my dear flock that God would promote His own work among them, and that God would go with me in my intended journey to Susquehannah; was helped to remember dear friends in New England and my dear brethren in the ministry. I found enough in the sweet duty of prayer to have engaged me to continue in it the whole night, would my bodily state have admitted of it. Oh, how sweet it is to be enabled heartily to say, *Lord not my will, but thine be done!*

Saturday, August 2. Near night, preached from Matthew 11:29, "Take my yoke upon you." Was considerably helped, and the presence of God seemed to be somewhat remarkably in the assembly. Divine truths made powerful impressions, both upon saints and sinners. Blessed be God for such a revival among us. In the evening, was very weary, but found my spirits supported and refreshed.

Lord's Day, August 3. Discoursed to my people, in the forenoon, from Colossians 3:4, and observed that Christ is the believer's life. God helped me and gave me His presence in this discourse. It was a season of considerable power in the assembly. In the afternoon, preached from Luke 19:41, 42, "And when he was come near, he beheld the city . . ." I enjoyed some assistance, though not so much as in the forenoon. In the evening, I enjoyed freedom and sweetness in secret prayer. God enlarged my heart, freed me from melancholy damps, and gave me satisfaction in drawing near to Himself. Oh, that my soul could magnify the Lord, for these seasons of composure and resignation to His will!

Tuesday, August 5. Towards night, preached at the funeral of one of my Christians, from Isaiah 57:2, "He shall enter into peace." I was oppressed with the nervous headache and considerably dejected; however, had a little freedom some part of the time I was discoursing. Was extremely weary in the evening; but notwithstanding, enjoyed some liberty and cheerfulness of mind in prayer; and found the dejection that I feared much removed, and my spirits considerably refreshed.

Thursday, August 7. Rode to my house where I spent the last winter, in order to bring some things I needed for my Susquehannah journey. Was refreshed to see that place which God so marvelously visited with the showers of His grace. Oh, how amazing did the power of God often appear there! "Bless the Lord, O my soul, and forget not all his benefits."

Saturday, August 9. In the afternoon, visited my people. Set their affairs in order, as much as possible, and contrived for them the management of their worldly business; discoursed to them in a solemn manner, and concluded with prayer. Was composed and comfortable in the evening, and somewhat fervent in secret prayer. Had some sense and view of the eternal world and found a serenity of mind. Oh, that I could magnify the Lord for any freedom He affords me in prayer!

Lord's Day, August 10. Discoursed to my people, both parts of the day, from Acts 3:19, "Repent ye, therefore . . ." In discoursing of repentance in the forenoon, God helped me so that my discourse was searching. Some were in tears, both of the Indians and white people, and the Word of God was attended with some power. In the intermission, I was engaged in discoursing to some in order to their baptism, as well as with one who had then lately met with some comfort after spiritual trouble and distress. In the afternoon, was somewhat assisted again, though weak and weary. Afterwards baptized six persons, three adults and three children. Was in a comfortable frame in the evening and enjoyed some satisfaction in secret prayer. I scarce ever in my life felt myself so full of tenderness, as this day.

Monday, August 11. Being about to set out on a journey

to Susquehannah the next day, with leave of Providence, I spent some time this day in prayer with my people that God would bless and succeed my intended journey; that He would send forth His blessed Spirit with His Word, and set up His kingdom among the poor Indians in the wilderness.

While I was opening and applying part of Psalm 110 and Psalm 2, the power of God seemed to descend on the assembly in some measure. While I was making the first prayer, numbers were melted, and I found some affectionate enlargement of soul myself. Preached from Acts 4:31, "And when they had prayed, the place was shaken." God helped me, and my interpreter also. There was a shaking and melting among us, and divers, I doubt not, were in some measure "filled with the Holy Ghost." Afterwards, Mr. Macknight prayed; I then opened the two last stanzas of the Seventy-second Psalm; at which time God was present with us, especially while I insisted upon the promise of *all nations blessing* the great Redeemer.

My soul was refreshed to think that this day, this blessed glorious season, should surely come; and, I trust, numbers of my dear people were also refreshed. Afterwards prayed; had some freedom, but was almost spent; then walked out and left my people to carry on religious exercises among themselves. They prayed repeatedly and sang, while I rested and refreshed myself. Afterwards, went to the meeting; prayed with, and dismissed the assembly. Blessed be God, this has been a day of grace. There were many tears and affectionate sobs among us this day. In the evening, my soul was refreshed in prayer. Enjoyed liberty at the throne of grace in praying for my people and friends, and the Church of God in general. "Bless the Lord, O my soul."

> The next day, he set out on his journey towards Susquehannah, and six of his Christian Indians with him, whom he had chosen out of his congregation as those that he judged most fit to assist him in the business he was going upon. He took his way through Philadelphia; intending to go to Susquehannah River, far down, where it is settled by the white

people, below the country inhabited by the Indians; and so to travel up the river to the Indian habitations. For although this was much farther about, yet hereby he avoided the huge mountains and hideous wilderness that must be crossed in the nearer way; which in time past he found to be extremely difficult and fatiguing. He rode this week as far as Charlestown, a place of that name about thirty miles westward of Philadelphia, where he arrived on Friday. In his way hither he was for the most part, in a composed, comfortable state of mind.—J. E.

Saturday, August 16. (At Charlestown.) It being a day kept by the people of the place where I now was, as preparatory to the celebration of the Lord's Supper, I tarried; heard Mr. Treat preach; and then preached myself. God gave me some good degree of freedom, and helped me to discourse with warmth and application to the conscience. Afterwards, I was refreshed in spirit, though much tired; and spent the evening agreeably, having some freedom in prayer, as well as Christian conversation.

Lord's Day, August 17. Enjoyed liberty, composure, and satisfaction, in the secret duties of the morning; had my heart somewhat enlarged in prayer for dear friends, as well as for myself. In the forenoon, attended Mr. Treat's preaching, partook of the Lord's Supper, five of my people also communicating in this holy ordinance. I enjoyed some enlargement and outgoing of soul in this season. In the afternoon, preached from Ezekiel 33:11, "Say unto them, as I live, saith the Lord God . . ." Enjoyed not so much sensible assistance as the day before; however, was helped to some fervency in addressing immortal souls. Was somewhat confounded in the evening because I thought I had done little or nothing for God; yet enjoyed some refreshment of spirit in Christian conversation and prayer. Spent the evening, till near midnight, in religious exercises and found my bodily strength, which was much spent when I came from the public worship, something renewed before I went to bed.

Monday, August 18. Rode on my way towards Paxton, upon Susquehannah River. Felt my spirits sink, towards night, so that I had little comfort.

Tuesday, August 19. Rode forward still and at night lodged by the side of Susquehannah. Was weak and disordered both this and the preceding day, and found my spirits considerably damped, meeting with none that I thought godly people.

Wednesday, August 20. Having lain in a cold sweat all night, I coughed much bloody matter this morning, and was under great disorder of body, and not a little melancholy. But what gave me some encouragement was [that] I had a secret hope that I might speedily get a dismission from earth and all its toils and sorrows. Rode this day to one Chambers', upon Susquehannah, and there lodged. Was much afflicted, in the evening, with an ungodly crew, drinking and swearing. Oh, what a hell would it be to be numbered with the ungodly! Enjoyed some agreeable conversation with a traveler, who seemed to have some relish of true religion.

Thursday, August 21. Rode up the river about fifteen miles and there lodged in a family that appeared quite destitute of God. Labored to discourse with the man about the life of religion, but found him very artful in evading such conversation. Oh, what a death it is to some, to hear of the things of God! Was not so dejected as at some times.

Friday, August 22. Continued my course up the river; my people [were] now with me who before were parted from me; traveled above all the English settlements; at night lodged in the open woods and slept with more comfort than while among an ungodly company of white people. Enjoyed some liberty in secret prayer this evening; and was helped to remember dear friends, as well as my dear flock, and the Church of God in general.

Saturday, August 23. Arrived at the Indian town, called Shaumoking, near night. Was not so dejected as formerly; but yet somewhat exercised. Felt somewhat composed in the evening; enjoyed some freedom in leaving my all with God.

Through the great goodness of God, I enjoyed some liberty of mind and was not distressed with a despondency, as frequently heretofore.

Lord's Day, August 24. Towards noon, visited some of the Delawares and discoursed with them about Christianity. In the afternoon, discoursed to the [Indian] king, and others, upon divine things; who seemed disposed to hear. Spent most of the day in these exercises. In the evening, enjoyed some comfort and satisfaction and especially had some sweetness in secret prayer. This duty was made so agreeable to me that I loved to walk abroad and repeatedly engage in it. Oh, how comfortable is a little glimpse of God!

Monday, August 25. Spent most of the day in writing. Sent out my people that were with me to talk with the Indians, and contract a friendship and familiarity with them, that I might have a better opportunity of treating with them about Christianity. Some good seemed to be done by their visit this day, divers appeared willing to hearken to Christianity. My spirits were a little refreshed this evening, and I found some liberty and satisfaction in prayer.

Tuesday, August 26. About noon, discoursed to a considerable number of Indians and God helped me, I am persuaded. I was enabled to speak with much plainness, and some warmth and power. The discourse had impression upon some and made them appear very serious. I thought things now appeared as encouraging, as they did at Crossweeks. At the time of my first visit to those Indians, I was a little encouraged. I pressed things with all my might and called out my people, who were then present, to give in their testimony for God. Towards night, was refreshed; felt a heart to pray for the setting up of God's kingdom here, as well as for my dear congregation below and my dear friends elsewhere.

Wednesday, August 27. There having been a thick smoke in the house where I lodged all night before, whereby I was almost choked, I was this morning distressed with pains in my head and neck, and could have no rest. In the morning the smoke was still the same, and a cold easterly storm gathering.

I could neither live within doors nor without any long time together. I was pierced with the rawness of the air abroad, and in the house distressed with the smoke. I was this day very vapory, and lived in great distress, and had not health enough to do anything to any purpose.

Thursday, August 28. In the forenoon, I was under great concern of mind about my work. Was visited by some who desired to hear me preach; discoursed to them, in the afternoon, with some fervency and labored to persuade them to turn to God. Was full of concern for the kingdom of Christ, and found some enlargement of soul in prayer, both in secret and in my family. Scarce ever saw more clearly, than this day, that it is God's work to convert souls, and especially poor heathens. I knew I could not touch them; I saw I could only speak to dry bones, but could give them no sense of what I said. My eyes were up to God for help. I could say the work was His, and if done, the glory would be His.

Friday, August 29. Felt the same concern of mind, as the day before. Enjoyed some freedom in prayer and a satisfaction to leave all with God. Traveled to the Delawares, found few at home; felt poorly, but was able to spend some time alone in reading God's Word and in prayer, and enjoyed some sweetness in these exercises. In the evening, was assisted repeatedly in prayer and found some comfort in coming to the throne of grace.

Saturday, August 30. Spent the forenoon in visiting a trader that came down the river sick and who appeared as ignorant as any Indian. In the afternoon, spent some time in writing, reading, and prayer.

Lord's Day, August 31. Spent much time, in the morning, in secret duties; found a weight upon my spirits, and could not but cry to God with concern and engagement of soul. Spent some time also in reading and expounding God's Word to my dear family that was with me, as well as in singing and prayer with them. Afterwards, spake the Word of God to some few of the Susquehannah Indians. In the afternoon, felt very weak and feeble. Near night, was something refreshed in mind with some views of things relating to my great work. Oh, how heavy is my work when faith cannot take hold of an almighty arm for the performance of it! Many times have I been ready to sink in this case. Blessed be God, that I may repair to a full fountain.

Monday, September 1. Set out on a journey towards a place called The Great Island, about fifty miles distant from Shaumoking, in the northwestern branch of Susquehannah. Traveled some part of the way, and at night lodged in the woods. Was exceeding feeble this day, and sweat much the night following.

Tuesday, September 2. Rode forward, but no faster than my people went on foot. Was very weak, on this as well as the preceding days. I was so feeble and faint that I feared it would kill me to lie out in the open air. Some of our company being parted from us so that we had now no axe with us, I had no way but to climb into a young pine tree, and with my knife to lop the branches and make a shelter from the dew. But the evening being cloudy, and very likely for rain, I was still under fears of being extremely exposed; sweat much in the night, so that my linen was almost wringing wet all night. I scarce ever was more weak and weary than this evening, when I was able to sit up at all. This was a melancholy situation I was in; but I endeavored to quiet myself with considerations of the possibility of my being in much worse circumstances among enemies.

Wednesday, September 3. Rode to the Delaware-town; found divers drinking and drunken. Discoursed with some of the Indians about Christianity; observed my interpreter much engaged and assisted in his work; some few persons seemed to hear with great earnestness and engagement of soul. About noon, rode to a small town of Shauwaunoes, about eight miles distant; spent an hour or two there, and returned to the Delaware-town and lodged there. Was scarce ever more confounded with a sense of my own unfruitfulness and unfitness for my work than now. Oh, what a dead, heartless, barren, unprofitable wretch did I see myself to be! My spirits were so low, and my bodily strength so wasted, that I could do nothing at all. At length, being much overdone, lay down on a buffalo skin; but sweat much the whole night.

Thursday, September 4. Discoursed with the Indians, in the morning, about Christianity. My interpreter afterwards carried on the discourse to a considerable length. Some few appeared well disposed and somewhat affected. Left this place and returned towards Shaumoking, and at night lodged in the place where I lodged the Monday night before. Was in very uncomfortable circumstances in the evening, my people being belated and not coming to me till past ten at night. I had no fire to dress any victuals or to keep me warm, or keep off wild beasts; and I was scarce ever more weak and worn out in all my life. However, I lay down and slept before my people came up, expecting nothing else but to spend the whole night alone and without fire.

Friday, September 5. Was exceeding weak so that I could scarcely ride; it seemed sometimes as if I must fall off from my horse and lie in the open woods; however, got to Shaumoking towards night; felt something of a spirit of thankfulness that God had so far returned me. Was refreshed to see one of my Christians whom I left here in my late excursion.

Saturday, September 6. Spent the day in a very weak state; coughing and spitting blood and having little appetite to any food I had with me; was able to do very little except discourse a while of divine things to my own people and to some few I met with. Had, by this time, very little life or heart to speak for God, through feebleness of body and flatness of spirits. Was scarcely ever more ashamed and confounded in myself, than now. I was sensible that there were numbers of God's people who knew I was then out upon a design (or at least the pretense) of doing something for God, and in His cause, among the poor Indians; and they were ready to suppose that I was "fervent in spirit."

But oh, the heartless frame of mind that I felt filled me with confusion! Oh (methought) if God's people knew me, as God knows, they would not think so highly of my zeal and resolution for God, as perhaps now they do! I could not but desire they should see how heartless and irresolute I was, that they might be undeceived and "not think of me above what they ought to think." And yet, I thought, if they saw the utmost of my flatness and unfaithfulness, the smallness of my courage and resolution for God, they would be ready to shut me out of their doors as unworthy of the company or friendship of Christians.

Lord's Day, September 7. Was much in the same weak state of body and afflicted frame of mind as in the preceding day. My soul was grieved and mourned that I could do nothing for God. Read and expounded some part of God's Word to my own dear family, and spent some time in prayer with them; discoursed also a little to the pagans; but spent the Sabbath with a little comfort.

Monday, September 8. Spent the forenoon among the Indians; in the afternoon, left Shaumoking and returned down the river a few miles. Had proposed to have tarried a considerable time longer among the Indians upon Susquehannah; but was hindered from pursuing my purpose by the sickness that prevailed there, the weakly circumstances of my own people that were with me, and especially my own extraordinary weakness, having been exercised with great nocturnal sweats and a coughing up of blood in almost the whole of the journey. I was a great part of the time so feeble and faint that it seemed as though I never should be able to reach home, and at the same time was very destitute of the comforts, and even necessaries of life; at least, what was necessary for one in so weak a state.

In this journey I sometimes was enabled to speak the Word of God with some power, and divine truths made some impressions on divers that heard me; so that several, both men and women, old and young, seemed to cleave to us and be well disposed towards Christianity. But others mocked and shouted, which damped those who before seemed friendly, at least some of them. Yet God at times was evidently present, assisting me, my interpreter, and other dear friends who were with me. God gave, sometimes, a good degree of freedom in prayer for the ingathering of souls there.

I could not but entertain a strong hope that the journey should not be wholly fruitless. Whether the issue of it would be the setting up of Christ's kingdom there, or only the drawing of some few persons down to my congregation in New Jersey; or whether they were now only being prepared for some further attempts that might be made among them, I did not determine; but I was persuaded the journey would not be lost. Blessed be God, that I had any encouragement and hope.

Tuesday, September 9. Rode down the river near thirty miles. Was extremely weak, much fatigued, and wet with a thunderstorm. Discoursed with some warmth and closeness to some poor ignorant souls on the life and power of religion; what were, and what were not, the evidences of it. They seemed much astonished when they saw my Indians ask a blessing and give thanks at dinner; concluding that a very high evidence of grace in them; but were astonished when I insisted that neither that, nor yet secret prayer, was any sure evidence of grace. Oh, the ignorance of the world! How are some empty outward forms, that may all be entirely selfish, mistaken for true religion, infallible evidences of it! The Lord pity a deluded world!

Wednesday, September 10. Rode near twenty miles homeward. Was much solicited to preach, but was utterly unable, through bodily weakness. Was extremely overdone with heat and showers this day, and coughed up a considerable quantity of blood.

Thursday, September 11. Rode homeward, but was very weak and sometimes scarce able to ride. Had a very importunate invitation to preach at a meeting house I came by, the people being then gathering; but could not, by reason of weakness. Was resigned and composed under my weakness, but was much exercised with concern for my companions in travel, whom I had left with much regret, some lame, and some sick.

Friday, September 12. Rode about fifty miles and came just

at night to a Christian friend's house, about twenty-five miles westward from Philadelphia. Was courteously received, and kindly entertained, and found myself much refreshed in the midst of my weakness and fatigues.

Saturday, September 13. Was still agreeably entertained with Christian friendship and all things necessary for my weak circumstances. In the afternoon, heard Mr. Treat preach and was refreshed in conversation with him, in the evening.

Lord's Day, September 14. At the desire of Mr. Treat and the people, I preached both parts of the day (but short) from Luke 14:23, "And the Lord said unto the servant, Go out . . ." God gave me some freedom and warmth in my discourse; and I trust, helped me in some measure to labor in singleness of heart. Was much tired in the evening, but was comforted with the most tender treatment I ever met with in my life. My mind, through the whole of this day, was exceeding calm. I could ask for nothing in prayer, with any encouragement of soul, but that "the will of God might be done."

Monday, September 15. Spent the whole day, in concert with Mr. Treat, in endeavors to compose a difference subsisting between certain persons in the congregation where we now were; and there seemed to be a blessing on our endeavors. In the evening, baptized a child; was in a calm, composed frame, and enjoyed, I trust, a spiritual sense of divine things while administering the ordinance. Afterwards, spent the time in religious conversation till late in the night. This was indeed a pleasant agreeable evening.

Tuesday, September 16. Continued still at my friend's house, about twenty-five miles westward of Philadelphia. Was very weak, unable to perform any business, and scarcely able to sit up.

Wednesday, September 17. Rode into Philadelphia. Still very weak, and my cough and spitting of blood continued. Enjoyed some agreeable conversation with friends, but wanted more spirituality.

Thursday, September 18. Went from Philadelphia to Mr.

Treat's; was agreeably entertained on the road; and was in a sweet, composed frame in the evening.

Friday, September 19. Rode from Mr. Treat's to Mr. Stockston's at Prince-Town; was extremely weak, but kindly received and entertained. Spent the evening with some degree of satisfaction.

Saturday, September 20. Arrived among my own people, just at night. Found them praying together and went in and gave them some account of God's dealings with me and my companions in the journey; which seemed affecting to them. I then prayed with them, and thought the divine presence was among us. Divers were melted into tears and seemed to have a sense of divine things. Being very weak, I was obliged soon to repair to my lodgings, and felt much worn out, in the evening. Thus God has carried me through the fatigues and perils of another journey to Susquehannah and returned me again in safety, though under a great degree of bodily indisposition. Oh, that my soul were truly thankful for renewed instances of mercy! Many hardships and distresses I endured in this journey! But the Lord supported me under them all.

# PART VIII

AFTER HIS RETURN FROM HIS LAST JOURNEY TO SUSQUEHAN-
NAH, UNTIL HIS DEATH

*1746, 1747*

Hitherto Mr. Brainerd had kept a constant diary, giving an account of what passed from day to day, with very little interruption; but henceforward his diary is very much interrupted by his illness; under which he was often brought so low as either not to be capable of writing, or not well able to bear the burden of a care so constant, as was requisite to recollect, every evening, what had passed in the day, and digest it and set down an orderly account of it in writing. However, his diary was not wholly neglected; but he took care, from time to time, to take some notice in it of the most material things concerning himself and the state of his mind, even till within a few days of his death; as the reader will see afterwards.[1]—J. E.

LORD'S DAY, September 21, 1746. I was so weak I could not preach, nor pretend to ride over to my people in the forenoon. In the afternoon, rode out, sat in my chair, and

---

[1] Mr. Shepard, in his *Select Cases Resolved*, under the first case says as follows: "I have lately known one very able, wise and godly, put upon the rack by him that, envying God's people's peace, knows how to change himself into an angel of light; for it being his usual course, in the time of his health to make a diary of his hourly life, and finding much benefit by it, he was in conscience pressed by the power and delusion of Satan to make and take the same daily survey of his life in the time of his sickness; by means of which he spent his enfeebled spirits, cast on fuel to fire his sickness. Had not a friend of his convinced him of his erroneous conscience misleading him at that time, he had murdered his body out of conscience to save his soul and to preserve his grace. And do you think these were the motions of God's Spirit, which like those locusts, Revelation 9:10, had faces like men, but had tails like scorpions, and stings in their tails?"

discoursed to my people from Romans 14:7, 8, "For none of us liveth to himself." I was strengthened and helped in my discourse, and there appeared something agreeable in the assembly. I returned to my lodgings extremely tired; but thankful that I had been enabled to speak a word to my poor people I had been so long absent from. Was able to sleep very little this night, through weariness and pain. Oh, how blessed should I be, if the little I do were all done with right views! Oh, that, whether I live, I might live to the Lord; or whether I die, I might die unto the Lord; that, whether living or dying, I might be the Lord's!

Saturday, September 27. Spent this day, as well as the whole week past, under a great degree of bodily weakness, exercised with a violent cough and a considerable fever. I had no appetite to any kind of food; and frequently brought up what I ate, as soon as it was down. Oftentimes had little rest in my bed, by reason of pains in my breast and back. I was able, however, to ride over to my people, about two miles, every day and take some care of those who were then at work upon a small house for me to reside in amongst the Indians.[2]

I was sometimes scarce able to walk, and never able to sit up the whole day, through the week. Was calm and composed and but little exercised with melancholy damps, as in former seasons of weakness. Whether I should ever recover or no, seemed very doubtful; but this was many times a comfort to me, that life and death did not depend upon my choice. I was pleased to think that He who is infinitely wise had the determination of this matter; and that I had no trouble to consider and weigh things upon all sides, in order to make the choice whether I should live or die. Thus my time was consumed; I had little strength to pray, none to write or read, and scarce any to meditate; but through divine goodness, I could with great composure look death in the face, and frequently with sensible joy. Oh, how blessed it is, to be habitu-

---

[2] This was the fourth house he built for his residence among the Indians. Besides that at Kaunaumeek, and that at the Forks of Delaware, and another at Crossweeksung, he built one now at Cranbury.

ally prepared for death! The Lord grant that I may be actually ready also!

Lord's Day, September 28. Rode to my people; and, though under much weakness, attempted to preach from II Corinthians 13:5, "Examine yourselves." Discoursed about half an hour, at which season divine power seemed to attend the Word; but, being extremely weak, I was obliged to desist. After a turn of faintness, with much difficulty I rode to my lodgings, where betaking myself to my bed, I lay in a burning fever, and almost delirious, for several hours; till towards morning, my fever went off with a violent sweat. I have often been feverish and unable to rest quietly after preaching; but this was the most severe distressing turn that ever preaching brought upon me. Yet I felt perfectly at rest in my own mind because I had made my utmost attempts to speak for God, and knew I could do no more.

Tuesday, September 30. Yesterday and today, was in the same weak state, or rather weaker than in days past; was scarce able to sit up half the day. Was in a composed frame of mind, remarkably free from dejection and melancholy damps. God has been pleased, in a great measure, to deliver me from these unhappy glooms, in the general course of my present weakness hitherto, and also from a peevish, froward spirit. And oh, how great a mercy is this! Oh, that I might always be perfectly quiet in seasons of greatest weakness, although nature should sink and fail! Oh, that I may always be able with utmost sincerity to say, "Lord, not my will, but thine be done!" This, through grace, I can say at present with regard to life or death, "The Lord do with me as seems good in his sight"; that whether I live or die, I may glorify Him, who is "worthy to receive blessing, and honor, and dominion forever. Amen."

Saturday, October 4. Spent the former part of this week under a great degree of infirmity and disorder, as I had done several weeks before. Was able, however, to ride a little every day, although unable to sit up half the day till Thursday. Took some care daily of some persons at work upon my house. On Friday afternoon, found myself wonderfully revived and strengthened. Having some time before given notice to my people, and to those at the Forks of Delaware in particular, that I designed, with leave of Providence, to administer the sacrament of the Lord's Supper upon the first Sabbath in October, in the afternoon I preached from II Corinthians 13:5, finishing what I had proposed to offer upon the subject the Sabbath before. The sermon was blessed of God to the stirring up religious affection and a spirit of devotion in the people of God, and to the great affecting of one who had backslidden from God, which caused him to judge and condemn himself. I was surprisingly strengthened in my work while I was speaking, but was obliged immediately after to repair to bed, being now removed into my own house among the Indians. This gave me such speedy relief and refreshment, as I could not well have lived without.

Spent some time on Friday night in conversing with my people about divine things, as I lay upon my bed. Found my soul refreshed, though my body was weak. This being Saturday, I discoursed particularly with divers of the communicants; and this afternoon preached from Zechariah 12:10, "And I will pour on the house of David . . ." There seemed to be a tender melting and hearty mourning for sin in numbers in the congregation. My soul was in a comfortable frame, and I enjoyed freedom and assistance in public service; was myself, as well as most of the congregation, much affected with the humble confession and apparent broken-heartedness of the forementioned backslider; and could not but rejoice that God had given him such a sense of his sin and unworthiness. Was extremely tired in the evening, but lay on my bed and discoursed to my people.

Lord's Day, October 5. Was still very weak. In the morning, considerably afraid I should not be able to go through the work of the day and I had much to do, both in private and public. Discoursed before the administration of the sacrament from John 1:29, "Behold the Lamb of God, that taketh away the sin of the world." Where I considered:

I. In what respects Christ is called the Lamb of God, and observed that He is so called (1) from the purity and innocency of His nature; (2) from His meekness and patience under sufferings; (3) from His being that atonement which was pointed out in the sacrifice of lambs, and in particular by the paschal lamb.

II. How and in what sense He "takes away the sin of the world: not because all the world shall actually be redeemed from sin by Him, but because (1) He has done and suffered sufficient to answer for the sins of the world, and so to redeem all mankind; (2) He actually does take away the sins of the elect world.

III. How we are to behold Him in order to have our sins taken away: (1) not with our bodily eyes; nor (2) by imagining Him on the cross; but (3) by a spiritual view of His glory and goodness, engaging the soul to rely on Him.

The divine presence attended this discourse, and the assembly was considerably melted with divine truths. After sermon baptized two persons. Then administered the Lord's Supper to near forty communicants of the Indians, besides divers dear Christians of the white people. It seemed to be a season of divine power and grace, and numbers seemed to rejoice in God. Oh, the sweet union and harmony then appearing among the religious people! My soul was refreshed, and my religious friends of the white people with me. After the sacrament, could scarcely get home, though it was not more than twenty rods; but was supported and led by my friends, and laid on my bed, where I lay in pain till some time in the evening; and then was able to sit up and discourse with friends. Oh, how was this day spent in prayers and praises among my dear people! One might hear them all the morning before public worship, and in the evening till near midnight, praying and singing praises to God in one or another of their houses. My soul was refreshed, though my body was weak.

Saturday, October 11. Towards night was seized with an ague, which was followed with a hard fever and considerable pain. Was treated with great kindness and was ashamed to see so much concern about so unworthy a creature as I knew myself to be. Was in a comfortable frame of mind, wholly submissive with regard to life or death. It was indeed a peculiar satisfaction to me to think that it was not my concern or business to determine whether I should live or die. I likewise felt peculiarly satisfied while under this uncommon degree of disorder; being now fully convinced of my being really weak and unable to perform my work. Whereas at other times my mind was perplexed with fears that I was a misimprover of time, by conceiting [imagining] I was sick when I was not in reality so. Oh, how precious is time! And how guilty it makes me feel when I think I have trifled away and misimproved it, or neglected to fill up each part of it with duty to the utmost of my ability and capacity!

Lord's Day, October 12. Was scarce able to sit up, in the forenoon; in the afternoon, attended public worship and was in a composed comfortable frame.

Lord's Day, October 19. Was scarcely able to do anything at all in the week past, except that on Thursday I rode out about four miles; at which time I took cold. As I was able to do little or nothing, so I enjoyed not much spirituality, or lively religious affection; though at some times I longed much to be more fruitful and full of heavenly affection. Was grieved to see the hours slide away, while I could do nothing for God. Was able this week to attend public worship. Was composed and comfortable, willing either to die or live; but found it hard to be reconciled to the thoughts of living useless. Oh, that I might never live to be a burden to God's creation, but that I might be allowed to repair home when my sojourning work is done!

> This week, he went back to his Indians at Cranbury, to take some care of their spiritual and temporal concerns; and was much spent with riding, though he rode but a little way in a day.—J. E.

Thursday, October 23. Went to my own house and set things in order. Was very weak and somewhat melancholy;

labored to do something, but had no strength and was forced to lie down on my bed, very solitary.

Friday, October 24. Spent the day in overseeing and directing my people about mending their fence and securing their wheat. Found that all their concerns of a secular nature depended upon me. Was somewhat refreshed in the evening, having been able to do something valuable in the daytime. Oh, how it pains me to see time pass away when I can do nothing to any purpose!

Saturday, October 25. Visited some of my people; spent some time in writing and felt much better in body than usual. When it was near night, I felt so well that I had thoughts of expounding; but in the evening was much disordered again and spent the night in coughing and spitting blood.

Lord's Day, October 26. In the morning, was exceeding weak; spent the day, till near night, in pain to see my poor people wandering as sheep not having a shepherd, waiting and hoping to see me able to preach to them before night. It could not but distress me to see them in this case, and to find myself unable to attempt anything for their spiritual benefit. But towards night, finding myself a little better, I called them together to my house and sat down and read and expounded Matthew 5:1-16. This discourse, though delivered in much weakness, was attended with power to many of the hearers; especially what was spoken upon the last of these verses; where I insisted on the infinite wrong done to religion, by having our *light* become *darkness*, instead of *shining before men*. Many in the congregation were now deeply affected with a sense of their deficiency in regard of a spiritual conversation that might recommend religion to others, and a spirit of concern and watchfulness seemed to be excited in them.

There was one, in particular, who had fallen into the sin of drunkenness some time before, now deeply convinced of his sin and the great dishonor done to religion by his misconduct, and he discovered a great degree of grief and concern on that account. My soul was refreshed to see this. Though I had no strength to speak so much as I would have done, but was obliged to lie down on the bed; yet I rejoiced to see such an humble melting in the congregation; and that divine truths, though faintly delivered, were attended with so much efficacy upon the auditory.

Monday, October 27. Spent the day in overseeing and directing the Indians, about mending the fence round their wheat; was able to walk with them and contrive their business all the forenoon. In the afternoon, was visited by two dear friends and spent some time in conversation with them. Towards night, I was able to walk out and take care of the Indians again. In the evening, enjoyed a very peaceful frame.

Tuesday, October 28. Rode to Prince-Town in a very weak state; had such a violent fever by the way that I was forced to alight at a friend's house and lie down for some time. Near night, was visited by Mr. Treat, Mr. Beaty, and his wife, and another friend. My spirits were refreshed to see them, but I was surprised, and even ashamed, that they had taken so much pains as to ride thirty or forty miles to see me. Was able to sit up most of the evening; and spent the time in a very comfortable manner with my friends.

Wednesday, October 29. Rode about ten miles with my friends that came yesterday to see me; and then parted with them all but one, who stayed on purpose to keep me company and cheer my spirits. Was extremely weak and very feverish, especially towards night; but enjoyed some comfort.

Thursday, October 30. Rode three or four miles to visit Mr. Wales; spent some time, in an agreeable manner, in conversation; and though extremely weak, enjoyed a comfortable, composed frame of mind.

Friday, October 31. Spent the day among friends, in a comfortable frame of mind, though exceeding weak and under a considerable fever.

Saturday, November 1. Took leave of friends after having spent the forenoon with them and returned home to my own house. Was much disordered in the evening and oppressed with my cough; which has now been constant for a long time with a hard pain in my breast, and fever.

Lord's Day, November 2. Was unable to preach, and scarcely able to sit up the whole day. Was grieved and almost sunk to see my poor people destitute of the means of grace. Especially considering they could not read, and so were under great disadvantages for spending the Sabbath comfortably. Oh, methought, I could be contented to be sick if my poor flock had a faithful pastor to feed them with spiritual knowledge! A view of their want of this was more afflictive to me than all my bodily illness.

Monday, November 3. Being now in so weak and low a state that I was utterly incapable of performing my work, and having little hope of recovery, unless by much riding, I thought it my duty to take a long journey into New England and to divert myself among my friends, whom I had not now seen for a long time. And accordingly took leave of my congregation this day. Before I left my people, I visited them all in their respective houses and discoursed to each one, as I thought most proper and suitable for their circumstances, and found great freedom and assistance in so doing. I scarcely left one house but some were in tears; and many were not only affected with my being about to leave them, but with the solemn addresses I made them upon divine things; for I was helped to be fervent in spirit, while I discoursed to them.

When I had thus gone through my congregation (which took me most of the day), and had taken leave of them and of the school, I left home and rode about two miles to the house where I lived in the summer past, and there lodged. Was refreshed this evening in that I had left my congregation so well-disposed and affected, and that I had been so much assisted in making my farewell addresses to them.

Tuesday, November 4. Rode to Woodbridge, and lodged with Mr. Pierson; continuing still in a very weak state.

## His Illness at Elisabeth Town

Wednesday, November 5. Rode to Elisabeth Town; intending, as soon as possible, to prosecute my journey into New England. But was in an hour or two taken much worse.

After this, for near a week, I was confined to my chamber and most of the time to my bed; and then so far revived as to be able to walk about the house; but was still confined within doors.

In the beginning of this extraordinary turn of disorder after my coming to Elisabeth Town, I was enabled through mercy to maintain a calm, composed, and patient spirit, as I had been before from the beginning of my weakness. After I had been in Elisabeth Town about a fortnight, and had so far recovered that I was able to walk about the house, upon a day of thanksgiving kept in this place I was enabled to recall and recount over the mercies of God in such a manner as greatly affected me, and filled me with thankfulness and praise.

Especially my soul praised God for His work of grace among the Indians, and the enlargement of His dear kingdom. My soul blessed God for what He is in Himself and adored Him that He ever would display Himself to creatures. I rejoiced that He was God and longed that all should know it, and feel it, and rejoice in it. "Lord, glorify Thyself," was the desire and cry of my soul. Oh, that *all people* might love and praise the blessed God; that He might have all possible honor and glory from the intelligent world!

After this comfortable thanksgiving season, I frequently enjoyed freedom, enlargement, and engagedness of soul in prayer, and was enabled to intercede with God for my dear congregation, very often for every family, and every person, in particular. It was often a great comfort to me that I could pray heartily to God for those to whom I could not speak and whom I was not allowed to see. But at other times, my spirits were so flat and low, and my bodily vigor so much wasted, that I had scarce any affections at all.

In December, I had revived so far as to be able to walk abroad and visit friends, and seemed to be on the gaining hand with regard to my health, in the main, until Lord's Day, December 21. At which time I went to the public worship; and it being sacrament day, I labored much at the Lord's Table to bring forth a certain corruption and have it slain, as being an enemy to God and my own soul. Could not but hope that I had gained some strength against this, as well as other corruptions; and felt some brokenness of heart for my sin.

After this, having perhaps taken some cold, I began to decline as to bodily health; and continued to do so, till the latter end of January, 1747. Having a violent cough, a considerable fever, an asthmatic disorder, and no appetite for any manner of food, nor any power of digestion, I was reduced to so low a state that my friends, I believe, generally despaired of my life. Some of them for some time together thought I could scarce live a day. At this time I could think of nothing with any application of mind, and seemed to be in a great measure void of all affection, and was exercised with great temptations; but yet was not, ordinarily, afraid of death.

Lord's Day, February 1. Though in a very weak and low state, I enjoyed a considerable deal of comfort and sweetness in divine things; and was enabled to plead and use arguments with God in prayer, I think, with a childlike spirit. That passage of Scripture occurred to my mind and gave me great assistance: "If ye, being evil, know how to give good gifts to your children, how much more will your heavenly Father give the Holy Spirit to them that ask him?" This text I was helped to plead and insist upon; and saw the divine faithfulness engaged for dealing with me better than any earthly parent can do with his child. This season so refreshed my soul that my body seemed also to be a gainer by it. And from this time, I began gradually to amend.

As I recovered some strength, vigor, and spirit, I found at times some freedom and life in the exercises of devotion, and some longings after spirituality and a life of usefulness to the interests of the great Redeemer. At other times, I was awfully barren and lifeless, and out of frame for the things of God; so that I was ready often to cry out, "Oh, that it were with me as in months past!" Oh, that God had taken me away in the midst of my usefulness, with a sudden stroke, that I might not have been under a necessity of trifling away time in diversions! Oh, that I had never lived to spend so much precious time in so poor a manner and to so little purpose! Thus I often reflected, was grieved, ashamed, and even confounded, sunk and discouraged.

Tuesday, February 24. I was able to ride as far as Newark (having been confined within Elisabeth Town almost four months), and the next day returned to Elisabeth Town. My spirits were somewhat refreshed with the ride, though my body was weary.

Saturday, February 28. Was visited by an Indian of my own congregation, who brought me letters and good news of the sober and good behavior of my people in general. This refreshed my soul; I could not but soon retire and bless God for His goodness; and found, I trust, a truly thankful frame of spirit, that God seemed to be building up that congregation for Himself.

Wednesday, March 4. I met with reproof from a friend, which, although I thought I did not deserve it from him, yet was, I trust, blessed of God to make me more tenderly afraid of sin, more jealous over myself, and more concerned to keep both heart and life pure and unblamable. It likewise caused me to reflect on my past deadness and want of spirituality, and to abhor myself, and look on myself as most unworthy. This frame of mind continued the next day; and for several days after, I grieved to think that in my necessary diversions I had not maintained more seriousness, solemnity, heavenly affection and conversation. Thus my spirits were often depressed and sunk; and yet, I trust, that reproof was made to be beneficial to me.

Wednesday, March 11, being kept in Elisabeth Town as a day of fasting and prayer, I was able to attend public worship; which was the first time I was able so to do after December 21. Oh, how much weakness and distress did God carry me through in this space of time! But having obtained help from Him, I yet live. Oh, that I could live more to His glory!

Lord's Day, March 15. Was able again to attend the public worship and felt some earnest desires of being restored to the ministerial work; felt, I think, some spirit and life to speak for God.

Wednesday, March 18. Rode out with a design to visit my people and the next day arrived among them, but was under great dejection in my journey.

On Friday morning, I rose early, walked about among my people, and inquired into their state and concerns; and found an additional weight and burden on my spirits upon hearing some things disagreeable. I endeavored to go to God with my distresses and made some kind of lamentable complaint; and in a broken manner spread my difficulties before God; but notwithstanding, my mind continued very gloomy. About ten o'clock, I called my people together, and after having explained and sung a psalm, I prayed with them. There was a considerable deal of affection among them; I doubt not, in some instances, that which was more than merely natural.

> This was the last interview that he ever had with his people. About eleven o'clock the same day, he left them; and the next day came to Elisabeth Town, his melancholy remaining still. He continued for a considerable time under a great degree of dejection through vapory disorders.—J. E.

Saturday, March 28. Was taken this morning with violent griping pains. These pains were extreme, and constant, for several hours; so that it seemed impossible for me, without a miracle, to live twenty-four hours in such distress. I lay confined to my bed the whole day, and in distressing pain all the former part of it; but it pleased God to bless means for the abatement of my distress. Was exceedingly weakened by this pain and continued so for several days following, being exercised with a fever, cough, and nocturnal sweats. In this distressed case, so long as my head was free of vapory confusions, death appeared agreeable to me. I looked on it as the end of toils and an entrance into a place "where the weary are at rest." I think I had some relish of the entertainments of the heavenly state, so that by these I was allured and drawn, as

THE LIFE AND DIARY OF DAVID BRAINERD

well as driven by the fatigues of life. Oh, how happy it is to be drawn by desires of a state of perfect holiness!

Saturday, April 4. Was sunk and dejected, very restless and uneasy, by reason of the misimprovement of time; and yet knew not what to do. I longed to spend time in fasting and prayer that I might be delivered from indolence and coldness in the things of God; but, alas, I had not bodily strength for these exercises! Oh, how blessed a thing is it to enjoy peace of conscience! But how dreadful is a want of inward peace and composure of soul! It is impossible, I find, to enjoy this happiness without redeeming time and maintaining a spiritual frame of mind.

Lord's Day, April 5. It grieved me to find myself so inconceivably barren. My soul thirsted for grace; but, alas, how far was I from obtaining what appeared to me so exceeding excellent! I was ready to despair of ever being a holy creature, and yet my soul was desirous of following hard after God; but never did I see myself so far from having apprehended, or being already perfect, as at this time.

The Lord's Supper being this day administered, I attended the ordinance; and though I saw in myself a dreadful emptiness and want of grace, and saw myself as it were at an infinite distance from that purity which becomes the gospel; yet at the communion, especially the distribution of the bread, I enjoyed some warmth of affection and felt a tender love to the brethren and, I think, to the glorious Redeemer, the First-born among them. I endeavored then to bring forth mine and His enemies, and slay them before Him; and found great freedom in begging deliverance from this spiritual death, as well as in asking divine favors for my friends, and congregation, and the Church of Christ in general.

Tuesday, April 7. In the afternoon rode to Newark, in order to marry the Reverend Mr. Dickinson;[3] and in the evening,

---

[3] The late learned and very excellent Mr. Jonathan Dickinson, pastor of a church in Elisabeth Town, president of the college of New Jersey, and one of the correspondents of the Honourable Society in Scotland for Propagating Christian Knowledge. He had a great esteem for Mr. Brainerd and kindly entertained him in his house during his sickness in the winter past; and after a short illness, he died the next ensuing October, two days before Mr. Brainerd.

performed that work. Afterwards, rode home to Elisabeth
Town, in a pleasant frame, full of composure and sweetness.

Thursday, April 9. Attended the ordination of Mr. Tucker,[4]
and afterwards the examination of Mr. Smith. Was in a comfortable frame of mind this day, and felt my heart, I think,
sometimes in a spiritual frame.

Friday, April 10. Spent the forenoon in Presbyterial business; in the afternoon, rode to Elisabeth Town; found my
brother John there.[5] Spent some time in conversation with
him; but was extremely weak and outdone, my spirits considerably sunk, and my mind dejected.

Monday, April 13. Assisted in examining my brother. In
the evening, was in a solemn devout frame, but was much
overdone and oppressed with a violent headache.

Tuesday, April 14. Was able to do little or nothing; spent
some time with Mr. Byram and other friends. This day my
brother went to my people.

Wednesday, April 15. Found some freedom at the throne
of grace, several times this day. In the afternoon, was very
weak and spent the time to very little purpose; and yet in the
evening, had, I thought, some religious warmth and spiritual
desires in prayer. My soul seemed to go forth after God and
take complacence in His divine perfections. But, alas! afterwards awfully let down my watch and grew careless and secure.

Thursday, April 16. Was in bitter anguish of soul, in the
morning, such as I have scarce ever felt, with a sense of sin
and guilt. I continued in distress the whole day, attempting
to pray wherever I went; and indeed could not help so doing,
but looked upon myself so vile, I dared not look anybody in

[4] A worthy, pious young gentleman who lived in the ministry but a very short time.
He died at Stratfield in Connecticut the December following his ordination, being a
little while after Mr. Brainerd's death at Northampton. He was taken ill on a journey,
returning from a visit to his friends at Milton (in Mass.), which, as I take it, was his
native place, and Harvard College the place of his education.

[5] This brother of his had been sent for by the correspondents to take care of, and
instruct Mr. Brainerd's congregation of Indians; he being obliged by his illness to be
absent from them. And he continued to take care of them till Mr. Brainerd's death;
and since his death, has been ordained his successor in his mission, and to the charge
of his congregation; which continues much to flourish under his pastoral care.

the face. Was even grieved that anybody should show me any respect, or at least, that they should be so deceived as to think I deserved it.

Friday, April 17. In the evening, could not but think that God helped me to "draw near to the throne of grace," though most unworthy, and gave me a sense of His favor; which gave me inexpressible support and encouragement. Though I scarcely dared to hope the mercy was real, it appeared so great; yet could not but rejoice that ever God should discover His reconciled face to such a vile sinner. Shame and confusion, at times, covered me; and then hope, and joy, and admiration of divine goodness gained the ascendant. Sometimes I could not but admire the divine goodness, that the Lord had not let me fall into all the grossest, vilest acts of sins and open scandal that could be thought of; and felt myself so necessitated to praise God that this was ready for a little while to swallow up my shame and pressure of spirit on account of my sins.

Monday, April 20. Was in a very disordered state and kept my bed most of the day. I enjoyed a little more comfort than in several of the preceding days. This day I arrived at the age of twenty-nine years.

Tuesday, April 21. I set out on my journey for New England, in order (if it might be the will of God) to recover my health by riding; traveled to New York, and there lodged.

### His Return to New England

This proved his final departure from New Jersey. He traveled slowly, and arrived among his friends at East Haddam [Conn.], about the beginning of May. There is very little account in his diary of the time that passed from his setting out on this journey to May 10. He speaks of his sometimes finding his heart rejoicing in the glorious perfections of God, and longing to live to Him; but complains of the unfixedness of his thoughts, and their being easily diverted from divine subjects, and cries out of his leanness, as testifying against him, in the loudest manner. And concerning those diversions he was obliged to use for his health, he says that he sometimes found he could use diversions with "singleness of heart," aiming at the glory of God; but that he also found there was a necessity of great care and watchfulness lest he should lose that spiritual temper of mind in his diversions, and lest they should degenerate into what was merely selfish, without any supreme aim at the glory of God in them.—J. E.

Lord's Day, May 10. (At Had Lime). I could not but feel some measure of gratitude to God at this time (wherein I was much exercised) that He had always disposed me, in my ministry, to insist on the great doctrines of *regeneration*, the *new creature, faith in Christ, progressive sanctification, supreme love to God, living entirely to the glory of God, being not our own*, and the like. God thus helped me to see, in the surest manner, from time to time, that these and the like doctrines necessarily connected with them are the *only foundation* of safety and salvation for perishing sinners; and that those divine dispositions, which are consonant hereto, are that *holiness* "without which no man shall see the Lord." The exercise of these Godlike tempers—wherein the soul acts in a kind of concert with God, and would be and do everything that is pleasing to Him—I saw, would stand by the soul in a dying hour; for God must, I think, deny Himself if He cast away His own image, even the soul that is one in desires with Himself.

Lord's Day, May 17. (At Millington). Spent the forenoon at home, being unable to attend the public worship. At this time, God gave me some affecting sense of my own vileness and the exceeding sinfulness of my heart; that there seemed to be nothing but sin and corruption within me. "Innumerable evils compassed me about": my want of spirituality and holy living, my neglect of God, and living to myself. All the abominations of my heart and life seemed to be open to my view; and I had nothing to say, but, "God be merciful to me a sinner." Towards noon, I saw that the grace of God in Christ is infinitely free towards sinners and such sinners as I was. I also saw that God is the supreme good, that in His presence is life. I began to long to die that I might be with

Him in a state of freedom from all sin. Oh, how a small glimpse of His excellency refreshed my soul! Oh, how worthy is the blessed God to be loved, adored, and delighted in, for Himself, for His own divine excellencies!

Though I felt much dullness and want of a spirit of prayer, this week, yet I had some glimpses of the excellency of divine things. Especially one morning, in secret meditation and prayer, the excellency and beauty of holiness, as a likeness to the glorious God, was so discovered to me that I began to long earnestly to be in that world where holiness dwells in perfection. I seemed to long for this perfect holiness, not so much for the sake of my own happiness (although I saw clearly that this was the greatest, yea, the only happiness of the soul), as that I might please God, live entirely to Him, and glorify Him to the utmost stretch of my rational powers and capacities.

Lord's Day, May 24. (At Long Meadow in Springfield). Could not but think, as I have often remarked to others, that much more of true religion consists in deep humility, brokenness of heart, and an abasing sense of barrenness and want of grace and holiness than most who are called Christians imagine; especially those who have been esteemed the converts of the late day. Many seem to know of no other religion but elevated joys and affections, arising only from some flights of imagination, or some suggestion made to their mind, of Christ being theirs, God loving them, and the like.

> Thursday, May 28. He came from Long Meadow to Northampton; appearing vastly better than, by his account, he had been in the winter; indeed so well, that he was able to ride twenty-five miles in a day, and to walk half a mile; and appeared cheerful and free from melancholy, but yet undoubtedly at that time in a confirmed, incurable consumption.
>
> I had much opportunity, before this, of particular information concerning him, from many who were well acquainted with him. And had myself once an opportunity of considerable conversation and some acquaintance with him

at New Haven, near four years before, at the time of the commencement when he offered that confession to the rector of the college, which has been already mentioned in this history; I being one he was pleased then several times to consult on that affair. Now I had opportunity for a more full acquaintance with him. I found him remarkably sociable, pleasant, and entertaining in his conversation; yet solid, savory, spiritual, and very profitable. He appeared meek, modest, and humble; far from any stiffness, moroseness, superstitious demureness, or affected singularly in speech or behavior, and seeming to dislike all such things.

We enjoyed not only the benefit of his conversation, but had the comfort and advantage of hearing him pray in the family, from time to time. His manner of praying was very agreeable; most becoming a worm of the dust, and a disciple of Christ, addressing an infinitely great and holy God, and Father or mercies; not with florid expressions, or a studied eloquence; not with any intemperate vehemence, or indecent boldness. It was at the greatest distance from any appearance of ostentation, and from everything that might look as though he meant to recommend himself to those that were about him, or set himself off to their acceptance. It was free also from vain repetitions, without impertinent excursions, or needless multiplying of words. He expressed himself with the strictest propriety, with weight, and pungency; and yet what his lips uttered seemed to flow from the fullness of his heart, as deeply impressed with a great and solemn sense of our necessities, unworthiness, and dependence, and of God's infinite greatness, excellency, and sufficiency, rather than merely from a warm and fruitful brain, pouring out good expressions.

And I know not that ever I heard him so much as ask a blessing or return thanks at table but there was something remarkable to be observed both in the matter and manner of the performance. In his prayers, he insisted much on the prosperity of Zion, the advancement of Christ's kingdom in the world, and the flourishing and propagation of religion among the Indians. And he generally made it one petition in his prayer, "that we might not outlive our usefulness."—J. E.

Lord's Day, May 31. (At Northampton). I had little inward sweetness in religion, most of the week past; not realizing and beholding spiritually the glory of God and the blessed Redeemer, from whence always arise my comforts and joys in religion, if I have any at all. And if I cannot so behold the excellencies and perfections of God as to cause me to rejoice in Him for what He is in Himself, I have no solid foundation for joy. To rejoice only because I apprehend I have an interest in Christ, and shall be finally saved, is a poor mean business indeed.

> This week, he consulted Dr. Mather, at my house, concerning his illness; who plainly told him, that there were great evidences of his being in a confirmed consumption, and that he could give him no encouragement that he should ever recover. But it seemed not to occasion the least discomposure in him, nor to make any manner of alteration as to the cheerfulness and serenity of his mind, or the freedom or pleasantness of his conversation.—J. E.

Lord's Day, June 7. My attention was greatly engaged, and my soul so drawn forth, this day, by what I heard of the "exceeding preciousness of the saving grace of God's Spirit," that it almost overcame my body, in my weak state. I saw that true grace is exceeding precious indeed; that it is very rare; and that there is but a very small degree of it, even where the reality of it is to be found; at least, I saw this to be my case.

In the preceding week, I enjoyed some comfortable seasons of meditation. One morning, the cause of God appeared exceeding precious to me; the Redeemer's kingdom is all that is valuable in the earth, and I could not but long for the promotion of it in the world. I saw also, that this cause is God's, that He has an infinitely greater regard and concern for it than I could possibly have; that if I have any true love to this blessed interest, it is only a drop derived from that ocean. Hence I was ready to "lift up my head with joy" and conclude, "Well, if God's cause be so dear and precious to Him, He will promote it." And thus I did as it were rest on God, that surely He would promote that which was so agreeable to His own will; though the time when must still be left to His sovereign pleasure.

> He was advised by physicians still to continue riding as what would tend, above any other means, to prolong his life. He was at a loss, for some time, which way to bend his course next; but finally determined to ride from hence to Boston; we having concluded that one of this family should go with him, and be helpful to him in his weak and low state.—J. E.

## His Stay in Boston

Tuesday, June 9. I set out on a journey from Northampton to Boston. Traveled slowly, and got some acquaintance with divers ministers on the road.

Having now continued to ride for some considerable time together, I felt myself much better than I had formerly done; and found that in proportion to the prospect I had of being restored to a state of usefulness, so I desired the continuance of life; but death appeared inconceivably more desirable to me than a useful life. Yet blessed be God, I found my heart at times fully resigned and reconciled to this greatest of afflictions, if God saw fit thus to deal with me.

Friday, June 12. I arrived in Boston this day, somewhat fatigued with my journey. Observed that there is no rest but in God; fatigues of body and anxieties of mind attend us, both in town and country; no place is exempted.

Lord's Day, June 14. I enjoyed some enlargement and sweetness in family prayer, as well as in secret exercises. God appeared excellent, His ways full of pleasure and peace, and all I wanted was a spirit of holy fervency to live to Him.

Wednesday, June 17. This and the two preceding days I spent mainly in visiting the ministers of the town, and was treated with great respect by them.

Thursday, June 18. I was taken exceeding ill, and brought to the gates of death, by the breaking of small ulcers in my lungs, as my physician supposed. In this extreme weak state I continued for several weeks, and was frequently reduced so low as to be utterly speechless, and not able so much as to whisper a word. Even after I had so far revived as to walk about the house, and to step out of doors, I was exercised every day with a faint turn, which continued usually four or five hours; at which times, though I was not so utterly speechless but that I could say Yes or No, yet I could not converse at all, nor speak one sentence, without making stops for breath. Divers times in this season, my friends gathered round my bed to see me breathe my last, which they looked for every moment as I myself also did.

How I was, the first day or two of my illness, with regard to the exercise of reason, I scarcely know; I believe I was somewhat shattered with the violence of the fever, at times. But the third day of my illness, and constantly afterwards for four or five weeks together, I enjoyed as much serenity of mind, and clearness of thought, as perhaps I ever did in my life. I think my mind never penetrated with so much ease and freedom into divine things, as at this time. I never felt so capable of demonstrating the truth of many important doctrines of the gospel as now. And as I saw clearly the truth of those great doctrines, which are justly styled the doctrines of grace; so I saw with no less clearness, that the *essence of religion* consisted in the soul's *conformity to God*, and acting above all selfish views, for *His glory*, longing to be *for Him*, to live *to Him*, and please and honor Him in all things. And this from a clear view of His infinite excellency and worthiness in Himself to be loved, adored, worshiped, and served by all intelligent creatures.

Thus I saw, that when a soul loves God with a supreme love, he therein acts like the blessed God Himself, who most justly loves Himself in that manner. So when God's interest and his are become one, and he longs that God should be glorified and rejoices to think that He is unchangeably possessed of the highest glory and blessedness, herein also he acts in conformity to God. In like manner, when the soul is fully *resigned to*, and rests satisfied and contented *with*, the divine will, here it is also *conformed to* God.

I saw further that as this divine temper, whereby the soul exalts God and treads self in the dust, is wrought in the soul by God's discovering His own glorious perfections in the face of Jesus Christ to it, as His own work; and as it is His image in the soul, He cannot but take delight in it. Then I saw again that if God should slight and reject His own moral image, He must needs deny Himself; which He cannot do. And thus I saw the stability and infallibility of this religion; and that those who are truly possessed of it have the most complete and satisfying evidence of their being interested in all the benefits of Christ's redemption, having their hearts conformed to Him. And that these, these only, are qualified for the employments and entertainments of God's kingdom of glory; as none but these have any relish for the business of heaven, which is to ascribe glory to God, and not to themselves; and that God (though I would speak it with great reverence of His name and perfection) cannot, without denying Himself, finally cast such away.

The next thing I had then to do was to inquire whether this was my religion. Here God was pleased to help me to the most easy remembrance and critical view of what had passed in course of a religious nature through several of the latter years of my life. Although I could discover much corruption attending my best duties, many selfish views and carnal ends, much spiritual pride and self-exaltation, and innumerable other evils which compassed me about; yet God was pleased, as I was reviewing quickly to put this question out of doubt, by showing me that I had from time to time acted above the utmost influence of mere self-love; that I had longed to please and glorify Him as my highest happiness.

This review was through grace attended with a present feeling of the same divine temper of mind. I felt now pleased to think of the glory of God and longed for heaven as a state where I might glorify God perfectly, rather than a place of happiness for myself. This feeling of the love of God in my heart, which I trust the Spirit of God excited in me afresh, was sufficient to give me full satisfaction and make me long, as I had many times before done, to be with Christ. . . .

As God was pleased to afford me clearness of thought and composure of mind almost continually for several weeks together under my great weakness, so He enabled me, in some measure, to improve my time, as I hope, to valuable purposes. I was enabled to write a number of important letters to friends in remote places. Sometimes I wrote when I was speechless, that is, unable to maintain conversation with anybody, though perhaps I was able to speak a word or two so as to be heard.

At this season also, while I was confined at Boston, I read with care and attention some papers of old Mr. Shepard's lately come to light and designed for the press; and as I was desired, and greatly urged, made some corrections where the sense was left dark for want of a word or two. Besides this, I had many visitants with whom, when I was able to speak, I always conversed of the things of religion. Was peculiarly disposed and assisted in distinguishing between the true and false religion of the times. There was scarce any subject that has been matter of debate in the late day but what I was at one time or other brought to a sort of necessity to discourse upon and show my opinion, and that frequently before numbers of people.

Especially, I discoursed repeatedly on the nature and necessity of that humiliation, self-emptiness, or full conviction of a person's being utterly undone in himself, which is necessary in order to a saving faith, and the extreme difficulty of being brought to this; and the great danger there is of persons taking up with some self-righteous appearances of it. The danger of this I especially dwelt upon, being persuaded that multitudes perish in this hidden way; and because so little is said from most pulpits to discover any danger here; so that persons being never effectually brought to die in themselves are never truly united to Christ, and so perish.

I also discoursed much on what I take to be the essence of

true religion, endeavoring plainly to describe that Godlike temper and disposition of soul and that holy conversation and behavior that may justly claim the honor of having God for its original and patron. I have reason to hope God blessed my way of discoursing and distinguishing to some, both ministers and people; so that my time was not wholly lost.

Mr. Brainerd's restoration from his extremely low state in Boston, so as to go abroad again and to travel, was very unexpected to him and his friends. My daughter, who was with him, writes thus concerning him in a letter dated June 23: "On Thursday, he was very ill with a violent fever and extreme pain in his head and breast, and, at turns, delirious. So he remained till Saturday evening, when he seemed to be in the agonies of death; the family was up with him till one or two o'clock, expecting every hour would be his last. On Sabbath Day he was a little revived, his head was better, but very full of pain and exceeding sore at his breast, much put to it for breath. Yesterday he was better upon all accounts. Last night he slept but little. This morning he is much worse. Dr. Pynchon says he has no hopes of his life; nor does he think it likely he will ever come out of the chamber, though he says he may be able to come to Northampton . . ."

In another letter dated June 29, she says as follows: "Mr. Brainerd has not so much pain nor fever, since I last wrote, as before. Yet he is extremely weak and low, and very faint, expecting every day will be his last. He says it is impossible for him to live, for he has hardly vigor enough to draw his breath. I went this morning into town and when I came home, Mr. Bromfield said he never expected I should see him alive; for he lay two hours, as they thought, dying. One could scarcely tell whether he was alive or not. He was not able to speak for some time, but now is much as he was before. The doctor thinks he will drop away in such a turn. Mr. Brainerd says he never felt anything so much like dissolution as what he felt today; and says he never had any conception of its being possible for any creature to be alive and yet so weak as he is from day to day. Dr. Pynchon says he should not be surprised if he should so recover as to live half a year; nor would it surprise him if he should die in half a day. Since I began to write, he is not so well, having had a faint turn again; yet patient and resigned, having no distressing fears, but the contrary."

But so it was ordered in divine providence that the strength of nature held out through this great conflict, so as just to escape the grave at that turn. Then he revived, to the astonishment of all that knew his case. After he began to revive, he was visited by his youngest brother, Mr. Israel Brainerd, a student at Yale College; who having heard of his extreme illness, went from thence to Boston, in order to see him, if he might find him alive, which he but little expected.

This visit was attended with a mixture of joy and sorrow to Mr. Brainerd. He greatly rejoiced to see his brother, especially because he had desired an opportunity of some religious conversation with him before he died. But this meeting was attended with sorrow as his brother brought to him the sorrowful tidings of his sister Spencer's death at Haddam; a sister with whom had long subsisted a peculiarly dear affection and much intimacy in spiritual matters, and whose house he used to make his home when he went to Haddam, his native place. He had heard nothing of her sickness till this report of her death. But he had these comforts, together with the tidings, namely, a confidence of her being gone to heaven and an expectation of his soon meeting her there. His brother continued with him till he left the town, and came with him from thence to Northampton. Concerning the last Sabbath Mr. Brainerd spent in Boston, he writes in his diary as follows.—J. E.

Lord's Day, July 19. I was just able to attend public worship, being carried to the house of God in a chaise. Heard Dr. Sewall preach in the forenoon and partook of the Lord's Supper at this time. In this sacrament I saw astonishing divine wisdom displayed, such wisdom as I saw required the tongues of angels and glorified saints to celebrate. It seemed to me I never should do anything at adoring the infinite wisdom of God, discovered in the contrivance of man's redemption, until I arrived at a world of perfection. Yet I could not help striving to call upon my soul, and all within me, to bless the name of God. In the afternoon, heard Mr. Prince preach. I saw more of God in the wisdom discovered in the plan of man's redemption than I saw of any other of His perfections, through the whole day.

Saturday, July 25, I arrived here, at Northampton; having set out from Boston on Monday, about four o'clock in the afternoon. In this journey, I rode about sixteen miles a day, one day with another. Was sometimes extremely tired and faint on the road so that it seemed impossible for me to proceed any further. At other times I was considerably better and felt some freedom both of body and mind.

Lord's Day, July 26. This day, I saw clearly that I should never be happy, yea, that God Himself could not make me happy, unless I could be in a capacity to "please and glorify Him forever." Take away this and admit me into all the fine havens that can be conceived of by men or angels, and I should still be miserable forever.

### His Last Days

On Wednesday morning the week after he came to Northampton, he took leave of his brother Israel, never expecting to see him again in this world; he now setting out from hence on his journey to New Haven.

When Mr. Brainerd came hither, he had so much strength as to be able, from day to day, to ride out two or three miles and to return; and sometimes to pray in the family. But from this time he gradually decayed, becoming weaker and weaker.

While he was here, his conversation from first to last was much on the same subjects as when in Boston. He spoke much of the nature of true religion in heart and practice, as distinguished from its various counterfeits; expressing his great concern that the latter so much prevailed in many places. He often manifested his great abhorrence of all such doctrines and principles in religion as had any tendencey to Antinomianism; of all such notions as seemed to diminish the necessity of holiness of life, or to abate men's regard to the commands of God and a strict, diligent, and universal practice of virtue and piety, under a pretense of depreciating our works and magnifying God's free grace. He spoke often, with much detestation, of such experiences and pretended discoveries and joys as have nothing of the nature of sanctification in them, as do not tend to strictness, tenderness, and diligence in religion, to meekness and benevolence towards mankind, and an humble behavior.

He also declared that he looked on such pretended humility as worthy of no regard which was not manifested by modesty of conduct and conversation. He spake often, with abhorrence, of the spirit and practice that appears among the greater part of Separatists at this day in the land, particularly those in the eastern parts of Connecticut; in their condemning and separating from the standing ministry and churches, their crying down learning and a learned ministry, their notion of an immediate call to the work of the ministry, and the forwardness of laymen to set up themselves as public teachers. He had been much conversant in the eastern part of Connecticut (it being near his native place) when the same principles, notion, and spirit began to operate, which have since prevailed to a greater height; and had acquaintance with some of those persons who are become heads and leaders of the Separatists.

He had also been conversant with persons of the same way elsewhere; and I heard him say, once and again, he knew by his acquaintance with this sort of people that what was chiefly and most generally in repute among them as the power of godliness was an entirely different thing from that true vital piety recommended in the Scriptures, and had nothing in it of that nature.

He manifested a great dislike of a disposition in persons to much noise and show in religion, and affecting to be abundant in proclaiming and publishing their own experiences. Though at the same time he did not condemn, but approved of Christians speaking of their own experiences on some occasions, and to some persons, with due modesty and discretion. He himself sometimes, while at my house, spake of his own experiences; but it was always with apparent reserve and in the exercise of care and judgment with respect to occasions, persons, and circumstances. He mentioned some remarkable things of his own religious experience to two young gentlemen, candidates for the ministry, who watched with him, each at a different time, when he was very low and not far from his end; but he desired both of them not to speak of what he had told them till after his death.

After he came hither, as long as he lived, he spoke much of that future prosperity of Zion which is so often foretold and promised in the Scripture. It was a theme he delighted to dwell upon; and his mind seemed to be carried forth with earnest concern about it and intense desires that religion might speedily and abundantly revive and flourish. Though he had not the least expectation of recovery, yea, the nearer death advanced, and the more the symptoms of its approach increased, still more did his mind seem to be taken up with this subject. He told me when near his end that "he never in all his life had his mind so led forth in desires and earnest prayers for the flourishing of Christ's kingdom on earth as since he was brought so exceeding low at Boston." He seemed much to wonder that there appeared no more of a disposition in ministers and people to pray for the flourishing of religion through the world; that so little a part of their prayers was generally taken up about it, in their families and elsewhere.

Particularly, he several times expressed his wonder that there appeared no more forwardness to comply with the proposal lately made, in a memorial from a number of ministers in Scotland and sent over into America, for united extraordinary prayer among Christ's ministers and people, for the coming of Christ's kingdom. He sent it as his dying advice to his own congregation that they should practice agreeably to that proposal.[6]

Though he was constantly exceeding weak, yet there ap-

---

[6] His congregation, since this, have with great cheerfulness and unanimity fallen in with this advice, and have practiced agreeably to the proposal from Scotland. They have at times appeared with uncommon engagedness and fervency of spirit in their meetings and united devotions, pursuant to that proposal. Also the Presbyteries of New York and New Brunswick, since this, have with one consent fallen in with the proposal, as likewise some others of God's people in those parts.

peared in him a continual care well to improve time, and
fill it up with something that might be profitable and in
some respect for the glory of God or the good of men;
either profitable conversation, or writing letters to absent
friends, or noting something in his diary, or looking over
his former writings, correcting them, and preparing them
to be left in the hands of others at his death, or giving some
directions concerning the future management of his people,
or employment in secret devotions. He seemed never to be
easy, however ill, if he was not doing something for God, or
in His service. After he came hither, he wrote a preface to a
diary of the famous Mr. Shepard's (in those papers before
mentioned) having been much urged to it by those gentlemen in Boston who had the care of the publications; which
diary, with his preface, has since been published.

In his diary for Lord's Day, August 9, he speaks of longing desires after death, through a sense of the excellency of a
state of perfection. In his diary for Lord's Day, August 16,
he speaks of his having so much refreshment of soul in the
house of God that it seemed also to refresh his body. This
is not only noted in his diary but was very observable to
others. It was very apparent not only that his mind was exhilarated with inward consolation but also that his animal
spirits and bodily strength seemed to be remarkably restored, as though he had forgot his illness. But this was the
last time that ever he attended public worship on the Sabbath.

On Tuesday morning that week (I being absent on a journey) he prayed with my family, but not without much
difficulty, for want of bodily strength; and this was the last
family prayer that ever he made. He had been wont, till
now, frequently to ride out two or three miles; but this
week, on Thursday, was the last time he ever did so.—J. E.

Lord's Day, August 23. This morning I was considerably refreshed with the thought, yea, the hope and expectation of
the enlargement of Christ's kingdom. I could not but hope
the time was at hand when Babylon the great would fall and
rise no more. This led me to some spiritual meditations that
were very refreshing to me. I was unable to attend public

worship either part of the day; but God was pleased to afford
me fixedness and satisfaction in divine thoughts. Nothing so
refreshes my soul as when I can go to God, yea, to God my
exceeding joy. When He is so, sensibly, to my soul, oh, how
unspeakably delightful is this!

In the week past, I had divers turns of inward refreshing;
though my body was inexpressibly weak, followed continually with agues and fevers. Sometimes my soul centered in
God as my only portion, and I felt that I should be forever
unhappy if He did not reign. I saw the sweetness and happiness of being His subject, at His disposal. This made all my
difficulties quickly vanish.

From this Lord's Day, I was troubled very much with
vapory disorders and could neither write nor read and could
scarcely live. Although, through mercy, was not so much
oppressed with heavy melancholy and gloominess as at many
other times.

> Till this week, he had been wont to lodge in a room above
> stairs; but he now grew so weak that he was no longer able
> to go upstairs and down. Friday, August 28, was the last
> time he ever went above stairs, henceforward he betook
> himself to a lower room.
>
> Wednesday, September 2, being the day of our public lec-
> ture, he seemed to be refreshed with seeing the neighboring
> ministers that came hither to the lecture and expressed a
> great desire once more to go to the house of God on that
> day. Accordingly he rode to the meeting and attended divine
> service, while the Reverend Mr. Woodbridge of Hatfield
> preached. He signified that he supposed it to be the last time
> that ever he should attend the public worship. Indeed it was
> the last time that ever he went out at our gate alive.
>
> On the Saturday evening next following, he was un-
> expectedly visited by his brother, Mr. John Brainerd, who
> came to see him from New Jersey. He was much refreshed
> by this unexpected visit, this brother being peculiarly dear
> to him. He seemed to rejoice in a devout and solemn manner
> to see him and to hear the comfortable tidings he brought
> concerning the state of his dear congregation of Christian

Indians. A circumstance of this visit of which he was exceeding glad was that his brother brought him some of his private writings from New Jersey, and particularly his diary that he had kept for many years past.—J. E.

Lord's Day, September 6. I began to read some of my private writings, which my brother brought me; and was considerably refreshed with what I met with in them.

Monday, September 7. I proceeded further in reading my old private writings and found they had the same effect upon me as before. I could not but rejoice and bless God for what passed long ago, which without writing had been entirely lost.

This evening, when I was in great distress of body, my soul longed that God should be glorified; I saw there was no heaven but this. I could not but speak to the bystanders then of the only happiness, namely, pleasing God. Oh, that I could forever live to God! The day, I trust, is at hand, the perfect day. Oh, the day of deliverance from all sin!

Lord's Day, September 13. I was much refreshed and engaged in meditation and writing and found a heart to act for God. My spirits were refreshed and my soul delighted to do something for God.

On the evening following that Lord's Day, his feet began to appear sensibly swelled; which thenceforward swelled more and more. A symptom of his dissolution coming on. The next day, his brother John left him, being obliged to return to New Jersey on some business of great importance and necessity; intending to return again with all possible speed, hoping to see his brother yet once more in the land of the living.

Mr. Brainerd having now with much deliberation considered of the important affair beforementioned, which was referred to him by the honorable commissioners in Boston, of the Corporation in London for the Propagation of the Gospel in New England and parts adjacent, namely, the fixing upon and recommending of two persons proper to be employed as missionaries to the Six Nations, he about this time wrote a letter recommending two young gentlemen of his acquaintance to those commissioners—Mr. Elihu Spencer of East Haddam and Mr. Job Strong of Northampton. The commissioners, on the receipt of this letter, cheerfully and unanimously agreed to accept of and employ the persons he had recommended. They accordingly have since waited on the commissioners to receive their instructions, and pursuant to these have applied themselves to a preparation for the business of their mission. One of them, Mr. Spencer, has been solemnly ordained to that work by several of the ministers of Boston, in the presence of an ecclesiastical council convened for that purpose; and is now gone forth to the nation of Oneidas, about a hundred and seventy miles beyond Albany.

He also this week wrote a letter to a particular gentleman in Boston (one of those charitable persons beforementioned who appeared so forward to contribute of their substance for promoting Christianity among the Indians) relating to the growth of the Indian school and the need of another schoolmaster, or some person to assist the schoolmaster in instructing the Indian children. These gentlemen, on the receipt of this letter, had a meeting and agreed with great cheerfulness to give two hundred pounds (in bills of the old tenor) for the support of another schoolmaster; and desired the Reverend Mr. Pemberton of New York (who was then at Boston and was also, at their desire, present at their meeting) as soon as possible to procure a suitable person for that service. They also agreed to allow seventy-five pounds to defray some special charges that were requisite to encourage the mission to the Six Nations (besides the salary allowed by the commissioners), which was also done on some intimation given by Mr. Brainerd.

Mr. Brainerd spent himself much in writing those letters, being exceeding weak: but it seemed to be much to his satisfaction that he had been enabled to do it, hoping that it was something done for God, and which might be for the advancement of Christ's kingdom and glory. In writing the last of these letters, he was obliged to use the hand of another, not being able to write himself.

On the Thursday of this week (Sept. 17) was the last time

that ever he went out of his lodging room. That day, he was again visited by his brother Israel, who continued with him thenceforward till his death. On that evening [there was] another sign of his approaching death, whereupon he expressed himself thus: "Oh, the glorious time is now coming! I have longed to serve God perfectly. Now God will gratify those desires!" From time to time, at the several steps and new symptoms of the sensible approach of his dissolution, he was so far from being sunk or damped that he seemed to be animated and made more cheerful, as being glad at the appearance of death's approach. He often used the epithet, "glorious," when speaking of the day of his death, calling it "that glorious day." And as he saw his dissolution gradually approaching, he talked much about it; and with perfect calmness, he spoke of a future state.

He also settled all his affairs, giving directions very particularly and minutely concerning what he would have done in one respect and another after his decease. And the nearer death approached, the more desirous he seemed to be of it. He several times spoke of the different kinds of willingness to die; and represented it as an ignoble, mean kind, to be willing to leave the body, only to get rid of pain; or to go to heaven, only to get honor and advancement there.

—J. E.

Saturday, September 19. Near night, while I attempted to walk a little, my thoughts turned thus, "How infinitely sweet it is to love God and be all for Him!" Upon which it was suggested to me, "You are not an angel, not lively and active." To which my whole soul immediately replied, "I as sincerely desire to love and glorify God, as any angel in heaven." Upon which it was suggested again, "But you are filthy, not fit for heaven." Hereupon instantly appeared the blessed robes of Christ's righteousness which I could not but exult and triumph in. I viewed the infinite excellency of God, and my soul even broke with longings that God should be glorified. I thought of dignity in heaven, but instantly the thought returned, "I do not go to heaven to get honor, but to give all possible glory and praise." Oh, how I longed that God should be glorified on earth also! Oh, I was made for eternity, if God might be glorified! Bodily pains I cared not for; though I was then in extremity, I never felt easier. I felt willing to glorify God in that state of bodily distress, as long as He pleased I should continue in it. The grave appeared really sweet, and I longed to lodge my weary bones in it.

But oh, that God might be glorified! this was the burden of all my cry. Oh, I knew, I should be active, as an angel, in heaven; and that I should be stripped of my filthy garments, so that there was no objection. But, oh, to love and praise God more, to please Him forever! This my soul panted after and even now pants for while I write. Oh, that God might be glorified in the whole earth! "Lord, let thy kingdom come." I longed for a spirit of preaching to descend and rest on ministers that they might address the consciences of men with closeness and power. I saw God "had the residue of the Spirit," and my soul longed it should be "poured from on high." I could not but plead with God for my dear congregation that He would preserve it and not suffer His great name to lose its glory in that work, my soul still longing that God might be glorified.

The extraordinary frame he was in that evening could not be hid. "His mouth spake out of the abundance of his heart," expressing in a very affecting manner much the same things as are written in his diary. Among very many other extraordinary expressions, which he then uttered, were such as these: "My heaven is to please God, and glorify Him, and to give all to Him, and to be wholly devoted to His glory. That is the heaven I long for; that is my religion, and that is my happiness, and always was ever since I suppose I had any true religion. All those that are of that religion shall meet me in heaven. I do not go to heaven to be advanced, but to give honor to God. It is no matter where I shall be stationed in heaven, whether I have a high or low seat there; but to love, and please, and glorify God is all. Had I a thousand souls, if they were worth anything,

I would give them all to God; but I have nothing to give, when all is done.

"It is impossible for any rational creature to be happy without acting all for God. God Himself could not make him happy any other way. I long to be in heaven, praising and glorifying God with the holy angels. All my desire is to glorify God. My heart goes out to the burying place; it seems to me a desirable place. But oh, to glorify God! that is it; that is above all. It is a great comfort to me to think that I have done a little for God in the world. Oh! it is but a very small matter; yet I have done a little. I lament it that I have not done more for Him.

"There is nothing in the world worth living for but doing good and finishing God's work, doing the work that Christ did. I see nothing else in the world that can yield any satisfaction besides living to God, pleasing Him, and doing His whole will. My greatest joy and comfort has been to do something for promoting the interest of religion, and the souls of particular persons. And now, in my illness, while I am full of pain and distress from day to day, all the comfort I have is in being able to do some little char (or small piece of work) for God; either by something that I say, or by writing, or some other way."

He intermingled with these and other like expressions, many pathetical counsels to those who were about him: particularly to my children and servants. He applied himself to some of my younger children at this time, calling them to him and speaking to them one by one; setting before them, in a very plain manner, the nature and essence of true piety and its great importance and necessity; earnestly warning them not to rest in anything short of a true and thorough change of heart and a life devoted to God.

He counseled them not to be slack in the great business of religion, nor in the least to delay it; enforcing his counsels with this, that his words were the words of a dying man. Said he: "I shall die here, and here I shall be buried, and here you will see my grave, and do you remember what I have said to you. I am going into eternity and it is sweet to me to think of eternity; the endlessness of it makes it sweet. But oh, what shall I say to the eternity of the wicked! I cannot mention it, nor think of it; the thought is too dreadful. When you see my grave, then remember what I said to you while I was alive; then think with yourself, how the man who lies in that grave counseled and warned me to prepare for death."

His body seemed to be marvelously strengthened through the inward vigor and refreshment of his mind; so that, although before he was so weak that he could hardly utter a sentence, yet now he continued his most affecting and profitable discourse to us for more than an hour, with scarce any intermission; and said of it, when he had done, "It was the last sermon that ever he should preach." This extraordinary frame of mind continued the next day; of which he says in his diary as follows.—J. E.

Lord's Day, September 20. Was still in a sweet and comfortable frame; and was again melted with desires that God might be glorified, and with longings to love and live to Him. Longed for the influences of the Divine Spirit to descend on ministers in a special manner. And oh, I longed to be with God, to behold His glory and to bow in His presence!

It appears by what is noted in his diary, both of this day and the evening preceding, that his mind at this time was much impressed with a sense of the importance of the work of the ministry, and the need of the grace of God and His special spiritual assistance in this work. It also appeared in what he expressed in conversation, particularly in his discourse to his brother Israel, who was then a member of Yale College at New Haven, prosecuting his studies for the work of the ministry.[7] He now, and from time to time in this his dying state, recommended to his brother a life of self-denial, of weanedness from the world and devotedness to God, and an earnest endeavor to obtain much of the grace of God's Spirit, and God's gracious influences

---

[7] This young gentleman was an ingenious, serious, studious, and hopefully truly pious person; there appeared in him many qualities giving hope of his being a great blessing in his day. But it has pleased God, since the death of his brother, to take him away also. He died that winter, at New Haven on January 6, 1748, of a nervous fever, after about a fortnight's illness.

on his heart; representing the great need which ministers have of them, and the unspeakable benefit of them from his own experience. Among many other expressions he said thus: "When ministers feel these special gracious influences on their hearts, it wonderfully assists them to come at the consciences of men, and as it were to handle them. Whereas, without them, whatever reason and oratory we make use of, we do but make use of stumps, instead of hands."—J. E.

Monday, September 21. I began to correct a little volume of my private writings. God, I believe, remarkably helped me in it. My strength was surprisingly lengthened out, my thoughts were quick and lively, and my soul refreshed, hoping it might be a work for God. Oh, how good, how sweet it is, to labor for God!

Tuesday, September 22. Was again employed in reading and correcting and had the same success as the day before. I was exceeding weak; but it seemed to refresh my soul thus to spend time.

Wednesday, September 23. I finished my corrections of the little piece before mentioned, and felt uncommonly peaceful; it seemed as if I had now done all my work in this world and stood ready for my call to a better. As long as I see anything to be done for God, life is worth having; but oh, how vain and unworthy it is to live for any lower end! This day I indited a letter, I think of great importance, to the Reverend Mr. Byram in New Jersey. Oh, that God would bless and succeed that letter, which was written for the benefit of His Church! [8] Oh, that God would purify the sons of Levi that His glory may be advanced! This night, I endured a dreadful turn, wherein my life was expected [to last] scarce an hour or minute together. But, blessed be God, I have enjoyed considerable sweetness in divine things this week, both by night and day.

Thursday, September 24. My strength began to fail exceedingly; which looked further as if I had done all my work;

---

[8] It was concerning the qualifications of ministers, and the examination and licensing of candidates for the work of the ministry.

however, I had strength to fold and superscribe my letter. About two I went to bed, being weak and much disordered, and lay in a burning fever till night, without any proper rest. In the evening, I got up, having lain down in some of my clothes; but was in the greatest distress that ever I endured, having an uncommon kind of hiccough, which either strangled me or threw me into a straining to vomit; and at the same time was distressed with griping pains. Oh, the distress of this evening! I had little expectation of my living the night through, nor indeed had any about me, and I longed for the finishing moment! I was obliged to repair to bed by six o'clock, and through mercy enjoyed some rest. But was grievously distressed at turns with the hiccough. My soul breathed after God, "When shall I come to God, even to God, my exceeding joy?" Oh, for His blessed likeness!

Friday, September 25. This day, I was unspeakably weak and little better than speechless all the day. However, I was able to write a little and felt comfortably in some part of the day. Oh, it refreshed my soul to think of former things, of desires to glorify God, of the pleasures of living to Him! Oh, my dear God, I am speedily coming to Thee, I hope. Oh, come, Lord Jesus, come quickly. Amen.[9]

Saturday, September 26. I felt the sweetness of divine things, this forenoon; and had the consolation of a consciousness that I was doing something for God.

Lord's Day, September 27. This was a very comfortable day to my soul; I think I awoke with God. I was enabled to lift up my soul to God early this morning, and while I had little bodily strength, I found freedom to lift up my heart to God for myself and others. Afterwards, was pleased with the thoughts of speedily entering into the unseen world.

Early this morning, as one of the family came into the room, he expressed himself thus: "I have had more pleasure this morning than all the drunkards in the world enjoy."

[9] This was the last time that ever he wrote in his diary with his own hand, though it is continued a little farther, in a broken manner; written by his brother Israel, but indited by his mouth in this his weak and dying state.

So much did he esteem the joy of faith above the pleasures of sin. He felt that morning an unusual appetite to food, with which his mind seemed to be exhilarated, looking on it as a sign of the very near approach of death. At this time he also said: "I was born on a Sabbath Day; and I have reason to think I was newborn on a Sabbath Day; and I hope I shall die on this Sabbath Day. I shall look upon it as a favor, if it may be the will of God that it should be so; I long for the time. Oh, why is His chariot so long in coming? Why tarry the wheels of His chariot? I am very willing to part with all. I am willing to part with my dear brother John, and never to see him again, to go to be forever with the Lord.[10] Oh, when I go there, how will God's dear Church on earth be upon my mind!"

Afterwards, the same morning, being asked how he did he answered: "I am almost in eternity. I long to be there. My work is done; I have done with all my friends; all the world is nothing to me. I long to be in heaven, praising and glorifying God with the holy angels. All my desire is to glorify God."

During the whole of these last two weeks of his life, he seemed to continue in this frame of heart; loose from all the world, as having finished his work and done with all things here below. He had now nothing to do but to die, and to abide in an earnest desire and expectation of the happy moment when his soul should take its flight to a state of perfect holiness, in which he should be found perfectly glorifying and enjoying God. He said that the consideration of the day of death, and the day of judgment, had a long time been peculiarly sweet to him. From time to time he spake of his being willing to leave the body and the world immediately, that day, that night, that moment, if it was the will of God.

He also was much engaged in expressing his longings that the Church of Christ on earth might flourish, and Christ's kingdom here might be advanced, notwithstanding he was

---

[10] He had, before this, expressed a desire, if it might be the will of God, to live till his brother returned from New Jersey; who, when he went away, intended, if possible, to perform his journey, and return in a fortnight; hoping once more to meet his brother in the land of the living. The fortnight was now near expired; it ended the next day.

about to leave the earth and should not with his eyes behold the desirable event, nor be instrumental in promoting it. He said to me one morning as I came into the room: "My thoughts have been employed on the old dear theme, the prosperity of God's Church on earth. As I waked out of sleep, I was led to cry for the pouring-out of God's Spirit and the advancement of Christ's kingdom, which the dear Redeemer did and suffered so much for. It is that especially which makes me long for it." He expressed much hope that a glorious advancement of Christ's kingdom was near at hand.

He once told me that he had formerly longed for the out-pouring of the Spirit of God and the glorious times of the Church, and hoped they were coming; and should have been willing to have lived to promote religion at that time, if that had been the will of God; but, says he, "I am willing it should be as it is; I would not have the choice to make for myself, for ten thousand worlds." He expressed on his deathbed a full persuasion that he should in heaven see the prosperity of the Church on earth, and should rejoice with Christ therein; and the consideration of it seemed to be highly pleasing and satisfying to his mind.

He also still dwelt much on the great importance of the work of gospel ministers, and expressed his longings that they might be filled with the Spirit of God. He manifested much desire to see some of the neighboring ministers with whom he had some acquaintance, and of whose sincere friendship he was confident, that he might converse freely with them on that subject before he died. And it so happened that he had opportunity with some of them according to his desire.

Another thing that lay much on his heart, from time to time in these near approaches of death, was the spiritual prosperity of his own congregation of Christian Indians in New Jersey. When he spake of them, it was with peculiar tenderness, so that his speech would be presently interrupted and drowned with tears.

He also expressed much satisfaction in the disposals of Providence with regard to the circumstances of his death; particularly that God had before his death given him an opportunity in Boston, with so many considerable persons, ministers, and others, to give in his testimony for God against false religion and many mistakes that lead to it and promote it. He was much pleased that he had an opportunity there to lay before pious and charitable gentlemen the state of the Indians, and their necessities, to so good effect; and that God had since enabled him to write to them further concerning these affairs; and to write other letters of importance that he hoped might be of good influence with regard to the state of religion among the Indians, and elsewhere, after his death. He expressed great thankfulness to God for His mercy in these things. He also mentioned it as what he accounted a merciful circumstance of his death that he should die here.[11] And speaking of these things, he said, "God had granted him all his desire"; and signified that now he could with the greater alacrity leave the world.

—J. E.

Monday, September 28. I was able to read and make some few corrections in my private writings; but found I could not write as I had done; I found myself sensibly declined in all respects. It has been only from a little while before noon till about one or two o'clock that I have been able to do anything for some time past; yet this refreshed my heart that I could do anything, either public or private, that I hoped was for God.

This evening, he was supposed to be dying; he thought so himself, and was thought so by those who were about him. He seemed glad at the appearance of the near approach of death. He was almost speechless, but his lips appeared to move; and one that sat very near him heard him utter such expressions as these, "Come, Lord Jesus, come quickly. Oh, why is His chariot so long in coming!" After he re-

---

[11] When Mr. Brainerd was at Boston, sick nigh unto death, it was with reluctance he thought of dying in a place where funerals are often attended with a pomp and show, which (especially on occasion of his own) he was very averse to any appearance of; and though it was with some difficulty he got his mind reconciled to the prospect then before him, yet at last he was brought to acquiesce in the divine will, with respect to this circumstance of his departure. However, it pleased God to order the event so as to gratify his desire, which he had expressed, of getting back to Northampton, with a view particularly to a more silent and private burial.

vived, he blamed himself for having been too eager to be gone. And in expressing what he found in the frame of his mind at that time, he said he then found an inexpressibly sweet love to those that he looked upon as belonging to Christ, beyond almost all that ever he felt before; so that it "seemed like a little piece of heaven to have one of them near him." And being asked whether he heard the prayer that was (at his desire) made with him, he said that he heard every word, and had an uncommon sense of the things that were uttered in that prayer, and that every word reached his heart.

On the evening of Tuesday, September 29, as he lay on his bed, he seemed to be in an extraordinary frame; his mind greatly engaged in sweet meditations concerning the prosperity of Zion. There being present here at that time two young gentlemen of his acquaintance that were candidates for the ministry, he desired us all to unite in singing a Psalm on that subject, even Zion's prosperity. And on his desire we sang a part of the One Hundred Second Psalm. This seemed much to refresh and revive him, and gave him new strength; so that, though before he could scarcely speak at all, now he proceeded, with some freedom of speech, to give his dying counsels to those two young gentlemen beforementioned, relating to their preparation for and prosecution of that great work of the ministry they were designed for. In particular, earnestly recommended to them frequent secret fasting and prayer; and enforced his counsel with regard to this, from his own experience of the great comfort and benefit of it; which (said he) I should not mention, were it not that I am a dying person.

After he had finished his counsel, he made a prayer in the audience of us all, wherein, besides praying for this family, for his brethern, and those candidates for the ministry, and for his own congregation, he earnestly prayed for the reviving and flourishing of religion in the world. Till now, he had every day sat up part of the day; but after this he never rose from his bed.—J. E.

Wednesday, September 30. I was obliged to keep my bed the whole day, through weakness. However, redeemed a little time, and with the help of my brother, read and corrected about a dozen pages in my manuscript giving an account of my conversion.

Thursday, October 1. I endeavored again to do something by way of writing, but soon found my powers of body and mind utterly fail. Felt not so sweetly as when I was able to do something that I hoped would do some good. In the evening, was discomposed and wholly delirious; but it was not long before God was pleased to give me some sleep, and fully composed my mind.[12] Oh, blessed be God for His great goodness to me, since I was so low at Mr. Bromfield's, on Thursday, June 18, last. He has, except those few minutes, given me the clear exercise of my reason and enabled me to labor much for Him, in things both of a public and private nature; and perhaps to do more good than I should have done if I had been well; besides the comfortable influences of His blessed Spirit, with which He has been pleased to refresh my soul. May His name have all the glory for ever and ever. Amen.

Friday, October 2. My soul was this day, at turns, sweetly set on God. I longed to be with Him that I might behold His glory. I felt sweetly disposed to commit all to Him, even my dearest friends, my dearest flock, my absent brother, and all my concerns for time and eternity. Oh, that His kingdom might come in the world; that they might all love and glorify Him, for what He is in Himself; and that the blessed Redeemer might "see of the travail of his soul, and be satisfied"! Oh, come, Lord Jesus, come quickly! Amen.[13]

The next evening, we very much expected his brother John from New Jersey; it being about a week after the time that he proposed for his return when he went away. And though our expectations were still disappointed, yet Mr. Brainerd seemed to continue unmoved in the same calm and peaceful frame that he had before manifested, as having

[12] From this time forward, he had the free use of his reason till the day before his death; excepting that at some times he appeared a little lost for a moment, at first waking out of sleep.

[13] Here ends his diary; these are the last words that are written in it, either by his own hand, or by any other from his mouth.

resigned all to God, and having done with his friends and with all things here below.

On the morning of the next day, being Lord's Day, October 4, as my daughter Jerusha (who chiefly attended him) came into the room, he looked on her very pleasantly, and said: "Dear Jerusha, are you willing to part with me? I am quite willing to part with you. I am willing to part with you; I am willing to part with all my friends; I am willing to part with my dear brother John, although I love him the best of any creature living. I have committed him and all my friends to God and can leave them with God. Though, if I had thought I should not see you and be happy with you in another world, I could not bear to part with you. But we shall spend an happy eternity together." [14] In the evening, as one came into the room with a Bible in her hand, he expressed himself thus: "Oh, that dear Book! that lovely Book! I shall soon see it opened! the mysteries that are in it, and the mysteries of God's providence, will be all unfolded!"

His distemper now very apparently preyed on his vitals in an extraordinary manner . . . [and] was attended with very inward pain and distress.

On Tuesday, October 6, he lay, for a considerable time, as if he were dying. At which time, he was heard to utter, in broken whispers, such expressions as these: "He will come, He will not tarry. I shall soon be in glory. I shall

---

[14] Since this, it has pleased a holy and sovereign God to take away this my dear child by death, on the fourteenth of February, next following; after a short illness of five days, in the eighteenth year of her age. She was a person of much the same spirit with Mr. Brainerd. She had constantly taken care of and attended him in his sickness for nineteen weeks before his death, devoting herself to it with great delight because she looked on him as an eminent servant of Jesus Christ.

In this time, he had much conversation with her on the things of religion; and in his dying state, often expressed to us, her parents, his great satisfaction concerning her true piety and his confidence that he should meet her in heaven; and his high opinion of her, not only as a true Christian, but a very eminent saint; one whose soul was uncommonly fed and entertained with things that appertain to the most spiritual, experimental, and distinguishing parts of religion; and one who, by the temper of her mind, was fitted to deny herself for God and to do good, beyond any young woman whatsoever that he knew of. She had manifested a heart uncommonly devoted to God in the course of her life, many years before her death; and said on her deathbed, that she had not seen one minute for several years, wherein she desired to live one minute longer, for the sake of any other good in life, but doing good, living to God, and doing what might be for His glory.

soon glorify God with the angels." But after some time he
revived.

The next day, Wednesday, October 7, his brother John
arrived from New Jersey; where he had been detained much
longer than he intended, by a mortal sickness prevailing
among the Christian Indians, and by some other circumstances that made his stay with them necessary. Mr. Brainerd was affected and refreshed with seeing him and appeared fully satisfied with the reasons of his delay; seeing
the interest of religion and of the souls of his people required it.

The next day, Thursday, October 8, he was in great distress and agonies of body; and for the greater part of the
day was much disordered as to the exercise of his reason. In
the evening, he was more composed and had the use of his
reason well; but the pain of his body continued and increased. He told me it was impossible for any to conceive of
the distress he felt in his breast. He manifested much concern lest he should dishonor God by impatience under his
extreme agony; which was such that he said the thought
of enduring it one minute longer was almost insupportable.
He desired that others would be much in lifting up their
hearts continually to God for him that God would support
him and give him patience. He signified that he expected
to die that night, but seemed to fear a longer delay; and the
disposition of his mind with regard to death appeared still
the same that it had been all along.

Notwithstanding his bodily agonies, the interest of Zion
lay still with great weight on his mind; as appeared by
some considerable discourse he had that evening with the
Reverend Mr. Billing, one of the neighboring ministers
(who was then present), concerning the great importance
of the work of the ministry. Afterwards, when it was very
late in the night, he had much very proper and profitable
discourse with his brother John concerning his congregation in New Jersey and the interest of religion among the
Indians.

In the latter part of the night, his bodily distress seemed
to rise to a greater height than ever; and he said to those
then about him that it was another thing to die than people

imagined; explaining himself to mean that they were not aware what bodily pain and anguish is undergone before death. Towards day, his eyes fixed; and he continued lying immovable till about six o'clock in the morning, and then expired on Friday, October 9, 1747, when his soul, as we may well conclude, was received by his dear Lord and Master as an eminently faithful servant, into that state of perfection of holiness and fruition of God, which he had so often and so ardently longed for; and was welcomed by the glorious assembly in the upper world, as one peculiarly fitted to join them in their blessed employ and enjoyment.

Much respect was shown to his memory at his funeral which was on the Monday following, after a sermon preached the same day, on that solemn occasion. His funeral was attended by eight of the neighboring ministers, and seventeen other gentlemen of liberal education, and a great concourse of people.—J. E.

# APPENDIX I

## Why Brainerd Was Expelled from College

### *Jonathan Edwards' Explanation*

THIS AWAKENING was at the beginning of that extraordinary religious commotion, through the land, which is fresh in everyone's memory. It was for a time very great and general at New Haven; and the college had no small share in it. That society was greatly reformed, the students in general became serious, many of them remarkably so, and much engaged in the concerns of their eternal salvation. And however undesirable the issue of the awakenings of that day have appeared in many others, there have been manifestly happy and abiding effects of the impressions then made on the minds of many of the members of that college. And by all that I can learn concerning Mr. Brainerd, there can be no reason to doubt but that he had much of God's gracious presence, and of the lively actings of true grace, at that time: but yet he was afterwards abundantly sensible that his religious experiences and affections at that time were not free from a corrupt mixture, nor his conduct to be acquitted from many things that were imprudent and blameable; which he greatly lamented himself and was desirous that others should not make an ill use of such an example.

And therefore, although at the time he kept a constant diary containing a very particular account of what passed from day to day for the next thirteen months, from the latter end of January, 1741, forementioned, in two small books which he called the two first volumes of his diary, next following the account before given of his convictions, conversion, and consequent comforts; yet, when he lay on his death-bed, he gave order (unknown to me till after his death) that these two volumes should be destroyed, and in the beginning of the third book of his diary, he wrote thus (by the hand of another, he not being able to write himself):

"The two preceding volumes, immediately following the account of the author's conversion, are lost. If any are desirous to know how the author lived, in general, during that space of time, let them read the first thirty pages of this volume; where they will find something of a specimen of his ordinary manner of living through that whole space of time, which was about thirteen months; excepting that here he was more refined from some imprudencies and indecent heats than there; but the spirit of devotion running through the whole was the same."

It could not be otherwise than that one whose heart had been so prepared and drawn to God, as Mr. Brainerd's had been, should be mightily enlarged, animated, and engaged at the sight of such an alteration made in the college, the town, and country; and so great an appearance of men reforming their lives, and turning from their profaneness and immorality to seriousness and concern for their salvation, and of religion reviving and flourishing almost everywhere. But as an intemperate imprudent zeal, and a degree of enthusiasm soon crept in and mingled itself with that revival of religion; and so great and general an awakening being quite a new thing in the land, at least as to all the living inhabitants of it; neither people nor ministers had learned thoroughly to distinguish between solid religion and its delusive counterfeits.

Even many ministers of the gospel of long standing and the best reputation were for a time overpowered with the glaring appearances of the latter; and therefore, surely it was not to be wondered at that young Brainerd, but a sophomore at college, should be so; who was not only young in years, but very young in religion and experience. He had enjoyed but little advantage for the study of divinity and still less for observing the circumstances and events of such an extraordinary state of things. To think it strange, a man must divest himself of all reason. In these disadvantageous circumstances, Brainerd had the unhappiness to have a tincture of that intemperate, indiscreet zeal which was at that time too prevalent; and was led, from his high opinion of others whom he looked upon as better than himself, into such errors as were really contrary to the habitual temper of his mind. One instance of his misconduct at that time gave great offense to the rulers of the college, even to that degree that they expelled him from the society; which it is necessary should here be particularly related, with its circumstances.

During the awakening at college, there were several religious students who associated together for mutual conversation and assistance in spiritual things. These were wont freely to open themselves one to another, as special and intimate friends. Brainerd was one of this company. And it once happened that he and two or three more of these intimate friends were in the hall together, after Mr. Whittelsey, one of the tutors, had been to prayer there with the scholars; no other person now remaining in the hall but Brainerd and his companions. Mr. Whittelsey having been unusually pathetical in his prayer, one of Brainerd's friends on this occasion asked him what he thought of Mr. Whittelsey; he made answer, "He has no more grace than this chair." One of the freshmen happening at that time to be near the hall (though not in the room) overheard those words.

This person, though he heard no name mentioned and knew not who was thus censured, informed a certain woman in the town, withal telling her his own suspicion, namely, that he believed Brainerd said this of someone or other of the rulers of the college. Whereupon she went and informed the rector, who sent for this freshman and examined him. He told the rector the words he heard Brainerd utter and informed him who were in the room with him at that time. Upon which the rector sent for them: they were very backward to inform against their friend what they looked upon as private conversation, and especially as none but they had heard or knew of whom he had uttered those words; yet the rector compelled them to declare what he said, and of whom he said it.

Brainerd looked on himself very ill used in the management of this affair; and thought that it was injuriously extorted from his friends, and then injuriously required of him, as if he had been guilty of some open, notorious crime, to make a public confession and to humble himself before the whole college in the hall, for what he had said only in private conversation. He not complying with this demand, and having gone once to the separate meeting at New Haven when forbidden by the rector; and also having been accused by one person of saying concerning the rector, that he wondered he did not expect to drop down dead for fining the scholars who followed Mr. Tennent to Milford, though there was no proof of it (and Mr. Brainerd ever professed that he did not remember his saying anything to that purpose); for these things he was expelled from the college.

Now, how far the circumstances and exigencies of that day might justify such great severity in the governors of the college, I will not undertake to determine; it being my aim not to bring reproach on the authority of the college, but only to do justice to the memory of a person, who was I think eminently one of those whose memory is blessed. The reader will see, in the sequel of the story of Mr. Brainerd's life,[1] what his own thoughts afterwards were of his behavior in these things, and in how Christian a manner he conducted himself with respect to this affair; though he ever, as long as he lived, supposed himself ill used in the management of it and in what he suffered. His expulsion was in the winter, 1742, while in his third year at college.

---

[1] Particularly under the date, September 14, 1743.

# APPENDIX II

*Jonathan Edwards*

(*page 159*)

BY THE INVITATIONS Mr. Brainerd had lately received, it appears, that it was not from necessity, or for want of opportunities to settle in the ministry amongst the English, notwithstanding the disgrace he had been laid under at college, that he was determined to forsake all the outward comforts to be enjoyed in the English settlements, to go and spend his life among the brutish savages, and endure the difficulties and self-denials of an Indian mission.

He had, just as he was leaving Kaunaumeek, had an earnest invitation to a settlement at East Hampton on Long Island, the fairest, pleasantest town on the whole island, and one of its largest and most wealthy parishes. The people there were unanimous in their desires to have him for their pastor, and for a long time continued in an earnest pursuit of what they desired, and were hardly brought to relinquish their endeavors and give up their hopes of obtaining him. Besides the invitation he had to Millington; which was near his native town, and in the midst of his friends.

Nor did Mr. Brainerd choose the business of a missionary to the Indians, rather than accept of those invitations, because he was unacquainted with the difficulties and sufferings which attended such a service; for he had had experience of these difficulties in summer and winter; having spent about a twelvemonth in a lonely desert among these savages, where he had gone through extreme hardships, and been the subject of a train of outward and inward sorrows, which were now fresh in his mind. Notwithstanding all these things, he chose still to go on with this business; and that although the place he was now going to, was at a still much greater distance from most of his friends, acquaintance, and native land.

# APPENDIX III

Inscription on the Tombstone of Jonathan Edwards at Princeton, N. J. Translated by Paul Coleman-Norton, Associate Professor of Classics at Princeton University

SACRED TO THE DEPARTED SPIRIT
OF THE VERY REVEREND MAN
JONATHAN EDWARDS, MASTER OF ARTS,
PRESIDENT OF THE COLLEGE OF NEW JERSEY.
BORN AT WINDSOR, CONNECTICUT,
5 OCTOBER,
A. D. 1703, OLD STYLE.
SPRUNG FROM (HIS) FATHER THE REVEREND TIMOTHY EDWARDS;
EDUCATED AT YALE COLLEGE;
AT NORTHAMPTON ORDAINED INTO THE MINISTRY, 15 FEBRUARY,
1726/7.
THENCE (HE WAS) DISMISSED 22 JUNE, 1750,
AND THE DUTY OF TEACHING SAVAGES HE ACCEPTED.
(HE WAS) MADE PRESIDENT OF NASSAU HALL 16 FEBRUARY,
1758.
(HE) DIED IN THIS VILLAGE 22 MARCH FOLLOWING, NEW STYLE.
(HE WAS) OF THE AGE OF 55, (AN AGE) ALAS TOO BRIEF!
HERE LIES (HIS) MORTAL PART.
WHAT SORT OF PERSON (WAS HE), DO YOU ASK, WAYFARER?
A MAN WITH A BODY TALL, BUT SLENDER, (AND WITH A BODY)
BY VERY INTENT STUDIES, BY ABSTINENCE, AND BY SEDULITY
ATTENUATED.
IN SHREWDNESS OF INTELLIGENCE, IN KEEN JUDGEMENT, AND IN PRUDENCE
SECOND TO NONE OF MORTALS.
FOR KNOWLEDGE OF LIBERAL ARTS AND SCIENCES NOTEWORTHY,
OF CRITICS OF SACRED THINGS THE BEST, A DISTINGUISHED THEOLOGIAN,
AS (WAS) SCARCELY ANOTHER CONTEMPORARY; AN HONEST DISPUTANT;
OF THE CHRISTIAN FAITH A DOUGHTY AND UNCONQUERED CHAMPION;
A WEIGHTY, EARNEST, DISCRIMINATING HARANGUER OF THE PEOPLE,
AND, GOD SPEEDING (HIM), IN (HIS) SUCCESS
MOST FORTUNATE.
IN PIETY REMARKABLE, IN HIS CHARACTER STRICT,
BUT TO OTHERS FAIR AND KIND.
HE LIVED BELOVED, RESPECTED—
BUT, ALAS! WORTHY OF BEING MOURNED
HE DIED.
HOW MANY GROANS DID HE DEPARTING CAUSE!
ALAS SO GREAT WISDOM! ALAS LEARNING AND RELIGION!
THE COLLEGE LAMENTS HIM LOST (TO IT), AND THE CHURCH LAMENTS
(HIM LOST TO HER):
BUT, AT HIS RECEPTION, REJOICES
HEAVEN.
DEPART, WAYFARER, AND FOLLOW (HIS) PIOUS FOOTSTEPS.

385